foozles & frauds

by harold f. russell

the institute of internal auditors, inc.

230885

Foozles & Frauds was written to help internal auditors and others understand these two subjects. It is not an interpretation of fraud law.

The Institute of Internal Auditors, Inc.

foreword

The Board of Directors of The Institute of Internal Auditors, Inc., adopted a *Code of Ethics* in 1968. Articles I, II, and III of the *Code* address the members' obligation regarding honesty and illegal or improper activity.

The *Statement of Responsibilities of the Internal Auditor* declares that the internal auditor should be concerned with any phase of business activity where he can be of service to management. Management has the responsibility to monitor the system of internal controls. One of this system's major objectives is to prevent fraud and other illegal acts which may result in misappropriation of organization funds. The internal auditor has an obligation to assist management in carrying out this responsibility.

Foozles and Frauds is the result of a project on this subject sponsored by IIA's International Research Committee. One of the major objectives of the project was to put fraud into the proper perspective for the internal auditor. Modern internal auditors play many roles in fulfilling their function of serving management. One of these roles is to assist management in caring for its responsibility to prevent and detect fraud. With the growing number of problems in the business community involving misappropriation of funds, this role becomes increasingly important.

The Institute of Internal Auditors is extremely grateful to Harold F. Russell for the months of voluntary effort he put into the compilation of material found in this book. Much of the work and many of the suggestions are the result of his many years of actual experience in internal auditing. Many IIA members participated in this project, and The Institute is indebted to them for their help. We also wish to thank Dr. Victor Z. Brink for preparing the introduction. Robert Symon, who acted as project manager for the International Research Committee, also deserves special recognition.

In publishing this book, The Institute recognizes that internal auditors have an obligation to work with management to help prevent and detect foozles and frauds.

Stanley C. Gross
International President, 1976-77
The Institute of Internal Auditors

acknowledgments

This study was undertaken with the assistance of more than 100 members of The Institute of Internal Auditors. They contributed their opinions and experiences to make this a truly cooperative effort.

References in this text are made to specific sources of information. Moreover, a great amount of background material is based on corporate annual reports, press releases, audit manuals, bulletins of public accounting firms, periodicals, and other news media from both the United States and other countries.

We are indebted to the Lawyer's Cooperative Publishing Company, Rochester, New York, for assistance in the preparation of the legal distinctions given in Part Four. Such cooperation was helpful in a most difficult area.

The Ivar Kreuger account is included through the courtesy of Random House Inc., publishers of Robert Shaplen's book *Kreuger*.

Among the individuals who contributed materially to the study are Don Booth, Alan Carey, Don Davies, George Estes, Thomas Falstad, R. Lynn Galloway, Richard Genin, Henry Hill, Chet Johnson, Ed Klingler, Richard Loechler, Winfield Major, Joseph Meehan, Ray Porter, Bob Richmond, Jeff Ridley, Lawrence Sawyer, William Stenken, and Leroy Tirrell. The assistance of the members of the International Research Committee is also deeply appreciated.

Visits with Douglas Carmichael of the American Institute of Certified Public Accounts, John C. Burton of the Securities and Exchange Commission, and Donald R. Cressey of the University of California at Santa Barbara were very helpful. Other organizations which supplied valuable material include the Surety Association of America and the Bank Administration Institute. Reviews of early drafts by Abraham Briloff of Bernard Baruch College, Lee Seidler of New York University, and Burton were appreciated.

My personal thanks go to William E. Perry, IIA's director of research and EDP, for his encouragement and assistance, and to Mary Jane Wylie for her patience in typing this manuscript from notes that, at times, were difficult to decipher.

H. F. R.

contents

introduction

In the modern world, it is almost inevitable that the impact of fraud will become increasingly significant. There are a number of reasons why this is so. Some of these are as follows:

- The scope of human interrelationships is continually expanding in both a national and international sense. The resulting complexities provide greater opportunities for all kinds of fraudulent actions, including many new types.

- The growth in population and the rising standard of living result in an increased volume of all types of transactions and activities, providing more opportunities for fraud.

- Increasing world resources are an increasingly attractive target for those who generate fraudulent activities.

- Advances in technology and other types of knowledge give us better means of dealing with fraud. But, at the same time, they provide new tools which can be used by the perpetrator of fraud.

- There have been major threats to the maintenance of high moral standards. The forces here include evidence of wrongdoing in government, excessive affluence in certain sectors of our society, and the depersonalization of human relationships through automation and electronic data processing. Under these conditions, we tend more to accept the existence and expansion of fraud.

In total, various forces have combined to induce more fraud, to extend its range, and to neutralize the forces which could otherwise oppose its expansion.

the expanding common interest

In an earlier day, there was a general tendency to define fraud in a narrow manner and to try to isolate it unrealistically from the mainstream of life. Indeed, we had some very precise ideas about fraud which were, in the main, overly simplistic. We thought of fraud as something very obvious or as not really existing. There were the "bad guys" and the "good guys." Sometimes, of course, the good guys got caught up in situations where they became bad guys. But our concept of what made up fraudulent actions was quite narrowly defined. A check was forged. Investors were swindled. Or funds were diverted. And, in most cases, the scope of fraud was restricted to the parties affected and not considered of major significance in terms of common interest. Thus, we tended to compartmentalize fraud and to isolate it.

An earlier related view was that rooting out and dealing with fraud was the job of particular individuals. We somehow left the problem to auditors, detectives, and other specialists. It was, for the most part, a problem we could adequately delegate. It was also a problem we found relatively distasteful. In short, it was something we did not really need or care to get involved in.

Now, however, we are beginning to realize more clearly that we cannot and should not set up such barriers. As consumers, we now know that there is an increasingly high price on fraud which must somehow be paid. As managers, we recognize that fraud is a threat to our productivity objectives. As citizens of a society, we more and more appreciate the fact that there is a responsibility to foster such conditions which do not provide undue temptations for the normal human being to commit fraud. All of these forces now combine to emphasize the truth—that controlling and minimizing fraud is *everybody's* business. In both economic and moral terms, we are all affected by fraud and must, therefore, accept a part of the total responsibility to deal with it effectively. Fraud is clearly a concern of the total society and one which deserves the attention of every member of that society.

the impact of fraud upon managers

In our world, managers have the role of administering available resources so that they are most productive in terms of promoting the welfare of their individual organizations and, in turn, of the total society. The responsibilities include both the protection of these resources and the manner of putting them to work. When protection becomes the dominant objective, we fail to exploit fully the benefits which come from new types of utilization, even though such utilization necessarily involves certain risks. On the other hand, a lack of consideration of the need for protection can generate waste and loss and, thus, unduly undermine productivity. In earlier days, the greater preoccupation with protection was expressed in part through an excessive concern with fraud. In later years, however, the excessive emphasis on entrepreneurial possibilities often resulted in a neglect for basic protective needs, including a disregard of activities pertaining to the detection and prevention of fraud.

The newer and more enlightened management approach is to accept risk taking as a necessary condition of adequate productivity but to endeavor at the same time to minimize risk wherever possible by reasonable protective actions. In such a blended approach, there is recognition of the importance of fraud and an inclusion of appropriate action pertaining to its total control. Thus, managers now endeavor more systematically to balance the efforts for the control of fraud with the need to accept the proper level of risk as a condition of either desired levels of profitability in a business or other measures of productivity in a nonprofit organization. The modern manager is, therefore, properly concerned with fraud and interested in knowing better how to cope with it in relation to his overall management objectives. These managerial concerns apply to all types of organizations, at all levels in every organization, and in every area of operational activity.

the impact of fraud upon internal auditors

In earlier days, the typical internal auditor was very actively engaged in organizational efforts dealing with fraud. A part of his direct responsibilities was usually to detect the existence of fraud, to determine the losses, to help make all possible recoveries, and to assist in punishing the wrongdoers. For the most part, he did this because it was exactly what top management wanted him to do.

During the next phase in the development of internal auditing, however, there was the realization by all parties that internal auditors could better serve organizational interests by extending the scope of their work to include the audit of operational activities. Now the objectives were directed more toward increasing the productivity of the various types of operations in the organization and helping management carry out its broader role more effectively. The internal auditor now saw his fraud-detection role as a hindrance to achieving his new objectives.

Fraud-detection activities both deprived him of time needed for other types of management service and prevented the development of a needed partnership relationship with auditees. Therefore, the internal auditor now drastically reduced his fraud role and, at best, concentrated on the more innocuous types of fraud prevention as opposed to needed fraud detection.

It would now appear that, in many organizational situations, the pendulum might have swung too far in the direction of ignoring fraud. Since it is increasingly clear that fraud is of real management concern, there must be someone to give that problem the needed attention to the maximum extent possible in a manner attuned to total management needs. Either the internal auditor must provide this service, or management will turn to others for help. It would seem, however, that the internal auditor should most properly have this responsibility, because he is uniquely fitted for the role and because there is always a danger in turning over a part of his job to another staff or line group.

the unique qualifications of the internal auditor

There are a number of compelling reasons why the internal auditor should cover fraud matters. The internal auditor, first of all, has the technical expertise to deal properly with all of the problems relating to fraud. Moreover, the prevention of fraud is always one basic element to be considered when effective controls are being appraised and improved. Also, the detached and independent vantage point of the internal auditor enables him to better assess all implications and interrelationships involved in total operations. And last but not least, internal auditors, because of their vital role in service to management, are in the best position to meet management's objectives with regard to fraud detection and prevention. They are able to meet these objectives and, at the same time, handle the many other important aspects of service to management.

the need for better balance

What this means is that the internal auditor has reached a point where he needs to come back to the fraud problem in a manner which is balanced in terms of his total responsibility for effective managerial service. This approach recognizes both the fallacy of abandoning the field and the truth that the internal auditor needs to serve management in all areas where there are important management concerns. It seems clear that the internal auditor can provide the total service most effectively and that management will greatly appreciate receiving it. For all of these reasons, the internal auditor needs to reexamine the various dimensions of the fraud problem and to demonstrate both his competence and interest in this area. This includes going beyond fraud prevention to assist in the follow-up of suspected fraud and the finalization of specific fraud cases. It means providing needed services pertaining to fraud but always within the framework of total service to management.

the special role of foozles and frauds

At a time when the increasing impact of fraud is being more clearly recognized, it is indeed opportune to have a book like *Foozles and Frauds* available. There is a general need for all persons—especially managers, accountants, and both external and internal auditors—to have a better understanding of the scope of fraud and how to deal with it. The range of interest pertaining to the problem covers a wide span: the nature of fraud, its interrelationship with other operational activities, the detection of fraud, the prevention of fraud, the handling of investigations pertaining to fraud, the legal aspects, obtaining maximum recoveries, finalization of claims, and the total range of human considerations, including those which involve the perpetrator. Fortunately, this book is helpful in all of these areas. It also combines needed technical knowledge with a great deal of valuable research into the experience and views of practitioners.

While the coverage of all of these dimensions of the fraud problem is fascinating, the subject is admittedly a complicated one. It follows that the reading and study of the material is demanding. First, the reader must fully accept the fact of the wider range of management service to include fraud and recognize the necessity of preparing adequately for that particular dimension of service. This provides the need, motivation, and patience to familiarize the reader with the subject. The understanding achieved through the study of this book and the base established for continuing reference should, then, provide major professional rewards.

It should also provide at the same time the basis for better serving the expanding needs of our society—a major objective of all good internal auditors.

Victor Z. Brink, PhD

part one
elements of fraud

chapter 1

interaction of foozles
and frauds

Many defrauders start their illegal careers by making one or more bad decisions—or *foozles*. They bungle their way into predicaments from which they see no escape except by fraudulent means.

A dictionary defines a *foozle* as "an awkward, unskillful act; a bungle." It defines *fraud* as "intentional deception to cause a person to give up property or some lawful right. The intention to deceive is the important phrase; and in some situations, it is not necessary that the fraud be successful."*

It is intended that these words in combination will be a term to describe a portion of the criminal activities described as white-collar or nonviolent crime. The phrase *foozles and frauds* excludes these practices that fall primarily within the province of security people or police. The concentration here will be on the illegal acts of forgers, embezzlers, and tricksters—the concern of auditors.

Defrauders cheat to protect their way of life—to maintain a facade of success or to nourish an ego.

They take from those who have and justify it as a fair redistribution of wealth. Some steal to give generously to less fortunate—a Robin Hood complex.

Some who find themselves in financial trouble welcome those who come to their assistance and seem grateful for the aid. They freely admit their past foozles. Possibly to ease the embarrassment of their own incompetence, they soon turn on their benefactors and defraud them without mercy.

People with fine reputations who have been highly regarded for

---

*See Part Four, Chapter 18 for more precise legal definitions in specific areas of law.

their many contributions to society will unexpectedly turn to an unlawful act when a sudden adversity strikes at the structures they have built. Ivar Kreuger, who built a worldwide, industrial empire, faced financial ruin and made a bad decision. His foozle concerned the forgery of millions of dollars worth of Italian government bonds, which he used for collateral on bank loans. It became a foozle when Kreuger misspelled the name of the Italian finance minister whose name he forged. The banks did not catch that foozle, and the fraud was consummated.

Frauds and foozles are usually so intermingled that it is difficult to separate them into cause and effect. Few frauds are designed from beginning to end. An error, or someone's bungle, can produce a monetary gain for a person who rationalizes that one such unlawful profit deserves another. He repeats the foozle. It now becomes an intentional fraud.

If it is difficult to understand the rationalization or motivation that permits a person to commit an illegal act, it is sometimes more difficult to understand the reactions of the victims. Those who fail to take precautions to protect themselves are embarrassed and want to cover their foozles by their silence. Whitney North Seymour, Jr., former U.S. attorney and author of *Why Justice Fails*, said: "The business sector cooperates the least with law enforcement."

Some years ago, an auditor discovered an intricate scheme to divert money from a company into the pockets of an employee and a coconspirator outside the company. It was a well-designed plan, cleverly executed. The architect of the project was a young man who had within a few years established himself as a creative, articulate individual with a promising future. When the auditor got to the bottom of the plot, he asked the employee to prepare a written explanation of his nefarious activities. He readily complied and in his written statement revealed his entire scheme. He was, quite naturally, under considerable tension; and the grammar and sentence structure were rather poor. He asked that the original copy be retained by the auditor until the following workday so that he would have time to prepare a more properly worded document. He kept his promise and delivered an extremely well-written expose of his embezzlement. It was obvious that he had taken a great deal of pride in what he had done and that he did not want to end his exploits with a manuscript that was a foozle.

After disposition of his case had been made, he made one last request of the auditor. He said that he knew some day the auditor would write a book of his audit experiences, so he asked that his case be included among those cases the auditor described. The auditor agreed, providing he ever got around to writing such a book. Somewhere among the pages that follow, that promise was kept.

Pride can be a foozle—and a fraud.

There are people who design clever frauds to gain riches. They equate wealth with superiority. They recognize that money is the one way to overcome the low opinions they have of themselves. But they make one basic mistake—a foozle—when they fail to understand that money will not turn an inferior person into a superior one.

chapter 2

project objectives

There has been an increase in all kinds of crime in recent years. Crimes that result in physical and property damage, crimes of stealth—shoplifting and pilferage—capture daily headlines. All levels of law enforcement are concerned and cooperate to try to reduce the hazards to life and property.

More sophisticated crimes—embezzlement, forgeries, bribery or payola, deceptive trade practices, securities offenses, and tax evasion—are also a growing problem. This is the area where the primary lines of defense are enlightened management and trained specialists. They have the skills to detect the usually well-concealed fraud and to build a well-documented case of evidence. In the past, auditors trained in complex accounting and investigative techniques have terminated many frauds in government, nonprofit institutions, and business.

But today, many auditors are concerned about their proper role in the struggle to control white-collar crime. They know that collusion in such crime is common, and defrauders working together are making traditional methods of control more difficult.

The purpose of this study is to:

■ stimulate auditors by making them aware of potential areas of fraud

■ provide methods for proper control of the elements that may lead to fraud

■ assist auditors by recommending steps to be taken from early suspicion through confrontation

■ discuss legal implications that the auditor should be aware of when fraud is encountered

- outline the extent and limitations of existing audit capabilities—including steps that directors and managers can take to assure that everyone in the organization understands his specific responsibilities for fraud control

Internal auditors, through The Institute of Internal Auditors, have adopted a *Code of Ethics* which states in part:

> A member, in holding the trust of his employer, shall exhibit loyalty in all matters pertaining to the affairs of the employer or to whomever he may be rendering a service. However, a member shall not knowingly be a party to any illegal or improper activity. A member shall refrain from entering into any activity which may be in conflict with the interest of his employer or which would prejudice his ability to carry out objectively his duties and responsibilities.

By initiating this study, The Institute seeks some of the answers as to how that *Code of Ethics* can be implemented.

One of the problems faced by all auditors—public and private—is the extent of their responsibility or legal liability for failure to detect well-concealed fraud not uncovered by techniques considered proper and adequate for normal examinations.

The law quite properly holds professional advisors liable when they knowingly give their clients a false opinion.

It is unwise to extend that principle by judicial dictum to include those people who *do not discover* that part of the information on which they base their opinions is false, misleading, or incomplete. The courts, to protect a segment of the public, should not impose a severe liability on advisors because facts were concealed from them. In any case, when the advisor is innocent of knowingly giving his client a false opinion, liability for damages should not exceed a remission of fees charged. To impose a harsher liability is to demand infallibility from those examined and certified or licensed by state or competent professional institutions as experts in their fields. No decree will guarantee that even the most diligent exploration or research will produce a hidden truth.

It is inevitable that professional advisors, challenged to meet unattainable standards, will increase their efforts to achieve an elusive perfection. This results in increased costs which will be passed on to all clients, some of whom may not be able to afford the added costs. It is very unlikely that the added effort will be productive in relation to the cost since the law of diminishing returns will tend to make the added effort an economic loss to the nation.

Already, the cost of malpractice liability insurance is a heavy burden. For some it is becoming difficult to buy at any price. Over a longer term, such cost could deter young people from entering professions where financial risks are too great.

Internal auditors are employees of the organization. They are also concerned with the steady increase in attempts to impose responsibility in the form of legal liability upon professional advisors. Many have expressed concern about their responsibilities to detect fraud within their own organizations. This study will have, as its last objective, a definition of that role.

part two
audit program

The cold vigilance of a sentry whose rounds are not without apprehension.

Djuna Barnes

chapter 3

background

The purpose of this section is to supply ancillary memorandums to audit programs which exist in every auditor's files. Only by vigilance and perception can an auditor recognize what should command his attention. The duties of an auditor are not unlike those of a sentry. Both are guardians, and, as they walk their rounds, they do not know the direction from which a crafty adversary may strike.

Fraud cannot be prevented by any system of internal controls, audit surveillance, or managerial alertness. But deterrents can be devised to make it more difficult for wrongdoers to accomplish their looting.

Some managements are lulled into a false sense of security because they do not consider their assets to be consumer-type merchandise that would attract thieves. Practically anything of value can be taken and is taken by larcenous individuals. For example:

■ A stock clerk stole small quantities of industrial dyes that he had removed from full drums. He found a ready industrial market for the dyes, which he repackaged in pound lots. Over a relatively short period of time, he took a substantial quantity of material. His operations were unique because he kept a very detailed list of his peculations by weight, type, and value.

■ Employees in a railroad computer center were reported to have altered computer system input data to show that 200 or more boxcars were scrapped. Actually, these cars were diverted to a little-used sidetrack, repainted, and sold to other railroads.

■ A group of factory employees arranged to gradually increase book figures showing the rate of a defective product. The plant continued to produce large quantities of saleable product, but a larger and larger percentage was diverted as scrap. The product, classified by the conspirators as *scrap*, was sold in competition with the company's regular product—toilet tissue. The plot was uncovered by company sales personnel when they lost sales to their fellow employees' sub-rosa operation.

- A foreman with authority to order truck movements called for a company truck, had one of his men load a portable overhead crane on it, and issued an order to have it delivered to a parking lot where he had parked his car. The truck driver, with a valid shipping order, had no difficulty passing through the company gates and making delivery to the foreman's car.

Well-designed, internal controls are, of course, effective as deterrents to fraud. Professional literature has provided guidelines for the design and implementation of such safeguards.

Possibly, one reason that fraud activity escapes the auditor's examination can be found in the attitude of the auditor. Too frequently, he has been told that the auditor does not and can not conduct his examination by presuming that fraud exists. The auditor should discipline his mind to approach an assignment as if there were a fraud buried somewhere in the records. He should develop the determination to find it if it is there. With that discipline under full control, the auditor must develop an empathy for the people whose work he reviews.

Many records are far from perfect because they are prepared by people who have little or no accounting training. These people often take a simple transaction and, by commission or omission, turn it into a tangled record. An auditor must evaluate his findings according to the facts. It is a grave mistake to become overly enthused about seemingly irrefutable evidence.

In one case, auditors felt they were on the trail of an embezzler. For three days, they made copious calculations and notes. As each approach appeared to lead to a blind end, they tossed their notes into the watebasket. Each day at 5 p.m., they bid the accountant good night and left. However, the accountant worked those nights, going through that wastebasket. By putting together the auditors' scrapped notes, he learned what they were trying to prove and where they had run into false leads.

Those auditors never did locate the source of the shortage. But a year later, another more careful team did because the accountant wasn't able to mislead them. The accountant boasted to the second team how he had been able to follow the course the first team had taken and had been able to divert them from the right direction.

Auditors should devote some attention to records and reports other than general and subsidiary ledgers. Some operating reports do not relate directly to nor agree with general ledger balances. However, they often tell a story that proves or disproves the financial condition that the general ledger shows.

An illustration of this is the record some automobile agencies keep of the multiple trades that follow the sale of each new car. The owner of one agency had produced financial statements which showed a healthy balance sheet and profitable operations. An auditor for a prospective purchaser of the agency found that the dealer had been giving unusually high trade-in allowances. Although sales were up, profit had been decreasing. The correct story was in the operating records—not in the general ledger. When the auditor learned this, he was able to spot where and how the figures in the general ledger had been "improved."

Auditors try to confirm the validity of asset values but often only to historical cost records. One company was turned down for a bank loan because the balance sheet prepared by an auditor showed a weak condition. The owner was unfamiliar with accounting techniques and had depended on his auditors to prepare his financial and tax reports. Overzealously, they had written down everything they could—inventories were priced on a LIFO basis; capital assets were heavily depreciated; and deferrals were forgotten. The owner negotiated the sale of the business on the basis of his *book value*. Actually, his realty had a minimum market value of four times the book value. Other assets were equally understated when current, realizable values became an important factor.

Because some auditors expect others to reevaluate their work, they tend to depend too much on conformance with generally accepted auditing standards. They do not judge whether their examination and the financial statements make sense to those who may use them.

Some auditors accept liabilities without as much verification as they would require for assets. There are countless ways of keeping liabilities and accruals off a balance sheet. And every dollar of proper liability omitted is a dollar of profit, unethically or fraudulently added to earnings.

Statements from vendors showing past-due balances can be disposed of with the explanation that a voucher system for each vendor's invoice is used, and that vendors' statements cannot be reconciled to invoices already processed somewhere in the system. That can very well be the truth.

Fees for professional services are, in some instances, rendered well after the work has been performed.

It takes a well-run Advertising Department to prepare reasonably correct accruals for preparatory work or actual insertion into publications.

Liabilities for taxes due at dates other than at the end of a company's fiscal year may present problems. Adequate provision for funding employee-benefit programs is often based on judgment or management policy and not on mathematical precision.

Frequent reclassification of cost and expense categories should alert auditors to possible fraud. It can cover up manipulation of expenditures.

- Technical representatives occasionally perform services for customers who are later billed for those services at flat rates. Total salaries and expenses appeared under cost of sales in one year and under selling expenses in another year.
- Freight out to customers was deducted from gross sales one year and added to selling expenses the next year.
- Convention expenses were charged to sales expense one year and then changed to advertising.

Another form of account manipulation is found in some of the reserves set up. Use of the same formula for a period of years may not be appropriate in a specific year when calculating a reserve for doubtful debts. The type of product sold or terms of sale might have changed. These could affect the collectibility of past-due accounts.

A customer who bought mostly consumable products now buys durable, capital equipment but still lets the account run six months before payment. The seller has a lien on the equipment, providing a substantial recovery in case of nonpayment. A smaller reserve would be in order for an equal dollar amount of debt.

Some auditors see a receivable on the books from a governmental body and incorrectly assume that it is a fully collectible item. Too often, that is not true. The proper procedure for processing an invoice might not have been followed; there is a lack of evidence of proper delivery; or the order might not have been validated by a proper purchasing agency. In these cases, the auditor should examine correspondence on the subject and, if significant, should try for independent confirmation of the debt.

Rigid schedules of audit visits are a boon for embezzlers. If visits to divisions, branches, or departments are made at fixed intervals, the perpetrator of a crime knows, after the last visit, how long the illegal act can be continued without possibility of detection through an audit examination. Thus, he can arrange to cover his deeds in an appropriate manner. More surprise visits at irregular intervals are desirable.

chapter four

assets

cash

Cash is obviously the most desirable asset to be acquired by criminals. Once it passes into the hands of the wrongdoer, it is usually impossible to prove from whom it was taken and is readily convertible into desirable goods or services. The protection of cash should be an auditor's prime concern.

There are countless ways that the white-collar criminal can come into possession of funds illegally. The following are merely a few illustrations of how it has been done.

■ *Use of Apparently Valid Authority* — A salesman was sent to a foreign territory to solicit orders. Before he left headquarters, he requested a letter to banks in the city to which he was going. As he was familiar with commercial practices in that country, he prepared the form of letter he needed. The letter was typed on company letterhead and signed by the treasurer of the corporation.

It contained a paragraph introducing him and another paragraph requesting the banks to accommodate him in every way—opening an account for him and, if the salesman found it necessary, loaning him funds to buy a home, and cashing company checks sent to him for reimbursement of his traveling expenses.

Armed with this letter, the salesman went to a bank and opened an account in the company's name with him as sole signatory. When he visited customers to take orders, he suggested that they give him payments on account, which they did. He used a rubber stamp with the company name to endorse those checks and deposited them in the company bank account that he had opened.

The customers had a valid receipt, and he had funds that he could withdraw as he wished. He started a lapping operation by sending the company remittances for earlier collections from later collections. This is an operation that can be successfully manipulated for only a relatively short time. Within a year, customer complaints about the failure to credit their payments caused an audit which uncovered the scheme.

■ *Collusion* — There is less likelihood of collusion when cash is the criminal's target than when another asset is the target. Surveys indicate that less than five percent of frauds involving cash are committed with collusion. However, when a computer controls the principal cash records, collusion probably occurs in about half the cases because more skills are required to conceal the fraud.

■ *Methods of Cash Frauds* — Banks are probably more susceptible to cash frauds than are most other organizations. A study by the Bank Administration Institute of about 900 cash funds showed the following methods were used:

Theft or mysterious disappearance	77%
Withholding or lapping	12%
Fictitious or forged entries	8%
Other irregular entries	3%
	100%

The disappearance of cash without some entry or alteration of records is usually a crime which falls outside an auditor's techniques to solve.

■ *Defensive Ploys* — A theft of cash may appear to be a rather simple operation perpetrated by a dull unimaginative character. This could be a naive assumption.

A cashier prepared a $175 check for reimbursement of petty-cash disbursements. He presented the check with paid petty-cash vouchers totaling $175 to the treasurer for his signature. The cashier took the signed check back to his office and changed the amount on the check to $475.

When the cashier presented the tampered check to the bank, the teller noted that it appeared to have been altered. She took it to an officer who called the treasurer and asked him for the correct amount of the check. When the treasurer was told that the check now read $475, he told the bank to pay the cashier that amount.

The cashier returned to his office. During the day he did not mention anything about the added $300 he had received. Late in the day, the treasurer called the cashier into his office and bluntly asked him where the extra $300 was. The cashier took him to the safe and showed him a sealed envelope containing the $300.

Asked why he had altered the check, the cashier replied that he was testing the internal control system. He added that he didn't think the internal auditors were alert enough to catch that type of fraud and that he meant it as an object lesson for them. The treasurer asked the auditors to make a special audit of the cashier's records. They uncovered no other shortage but recommended that he be discharged because of the poor and tardy condition of his records. He was fired.

■ *Check Kiting* — When properly executed, a fraudulent shift of funds may cover up an unrelated embezzlement. To illustrate, a company check dated as of the closing or cutoff date is drawn on Bank A and deposited in Bank B the same day. The check stub shows not the date on the check but a date subsequent to the closing. This scheme permits the embezzler to have his books show the amount of the checks in both banks as of the end of a financial period.

In England they have an expression for this type of cash manipulation which is very descriptive; they call it *cross-firing*.

Some of these schemes have involved large sums of money. In one case, it was reported that more than $5,000,000 was generated over a period of a few months by rapidly writing checks between accounts in two banks in one city.

It was alleged that 1,600 checks totalling more than $363,000,000 had passed between two Florida banks during 13 months. The individual who signed the checks was indicted, and his trial opened on March 5, 1975. The defense took the position that the state had to *establish the intent to defraud*. Under the *Bill of Rights* no person can be imprisoned for debt unless it is debt incurred by fraud. In order to gain a conviction, the state must prove that the defendant had no reason, on the basis of previous dealings, to believe that such a draft would be paid. The next day the defendant was acquitted and walked out of the courtroom a free man!

The judge commented: "I dislike the decision the law compels me to make. I am convinced beyond reasonable doubt that the defendant's conduct was reprehensible morally and ethically. But I must be convinced beyond reasonable doubt that the law against worthless checks has been violated."

The judge continued, by reading from the statute, ". . .when there is agreement or understanding ... between the check writer and the banks to honor insufficient-funds checks, ... the crime is not committed."

Witnesses testified that top bank officers had been advised of the check-kite operation during the early stages. They chose to take no action. A bank executive vice president testified that there were no limitations on payouts on uncollected funds.

The National Westminster Bank in England was alleged to have lost £450,000 when £4,000,000 was cross-fired with the aid of a compliant bank manager. A number of companies were involved. Payments were made into the account of one, and cash withdrawn before the checks were cleared.

The former bank manager was given 18 months in prison. Two directors of the companies were found guilty. One was sent to prison for a year, and the other was given a suspended sentence. A fourth man, the architect of the scheme, was reported in custody in Germany, awaiting extradition when the others were sentenced.

■ *It Can Be Stolen from the Most Unlikely Places* — Patrick Ennis, a 62-year-old accounting clerk in the Royal Courts of Justice, London, England, embezzled £2,928 from fees presented with writs to the lord chancellor. An audit team of 15 had to examine 129,000 writs to determine the loss. The auditors found the system so lax that it was open to any form of dishonesty. They also found that at least four other people had also stolen court funds. Ennis told Chief Inspector Peel: "I started doing this because I saw others doing it." The total loss was believed to have been at least £10,000.

some ways of detecting cash frauds

PETTY-CASH FUNDS ON IMPREST SYSTEM

Overages in cash may indicate that the fund is being manipulated and that a dishonest cashier might have failed to balance the funds with false vouchers.

Shortages may represent unauthorized borrowings. Investigation should include:

>   Frequent rechecks of fund
>   Reconstructing recent activity
>   Thorough examination of vouchers for authenticity over several past periods
>   Determining who might have access to the fund and who has been responsible for daily accountability for the fund over the past few months

Probe deeply into transactions that credit a customer's account with a remittance in the form of a third-party check.

Examine deposits for several days to determine if receipts include too many checks cashed for any one individual. In one case, an employee who daily cashed checks of ever-increasing amounts was kiting his personal checks with his employer.

Examine any available record of daily shortages and overages in these funds. Try to determine if the amounts are reasonable or if there has been a significant change in the pattern. The causes of large shortages should be traced.

Examine bank records to determine if there is a pattern of frequently bounced checks; identify the causes for repetitive instances.

Errant cashiers sometimes try to convince auditors to make their examination at some specific time on the premise that low volumes of funds will expedite the examination. Such suggestions should be looked at with skepticism. They may be the means by which the cashier can operate illegal schemes within a safe time sequence.

MANIPULATION OF CASH FUNDS

Some of the frauds described in Part Seven were complicated schemes which included manipulation of cash funds. For example:

Tino De Angelis, perpetrator of the Salad Oil Fraud, worked a check-kiting scheme with one of his customers.

Ivar Kreuger transferred funds between subsidiaries without reconciliation of intercompany accounts. Failure to tie down both sides of major cash transactions can be a weakness in audit techniques.

Penn Central serves as a good illustration of the potential risks taken when cash transactions are run through suspense accounts. The validity of all such entries should be verified.

The Equity Funding fraud was launched when it was decided to borrow money but record the receipt of the cash as a reduction of receivables. The receivable account had been artificially inflated by credits to income. An auditor should not be satisfied with his examination until he is sure that he fully understands the exact meaning of each major entry and determines that the accounting accurately reflects the facts.

It may seem redundant to emphasize that auditors should carefully examine underlying support data for disbursements. In the case described in The Embezzler's Ego, an employee attached evidence to his expense account that his bills were being paid by a credit card in the name of the supplier. His expense statements were approved by his supervisor and passed through the Accounting Department without question. Many defrauders leave a well-marked trail of their wrongdoing, but the evidence is missed by those who do not examine it with a *why* attitude.

marketable securities

The size of the market for stolen and counterfeit certificates is obviously impossible to determine accurately. But in 1975 there were some estimates that the total was as high as $50,000,000,000.

It is unlikely that many of these fraudulent securities are sold by thieves or counterfeiters to legitimate customers. Transfer agents can recognize counterfeits and can stop transfers of certificates that are reported to them.

It is likely that stolen and counterfeit securities have too often become collateral for loans. A ring of nine persons in Florida printed false stocks and bonds and put them up as collateral at seven banks in Jacksonville, two in Tallahassee, and one each in Orlando, Fort Lauderdale, and Miami.

In their examination of stocks and bonds in portfolios, auditors should be aware of the requirements of exchanges on which securities are traded. For example, all valid stock certificates traded on a major exchange should have certain characteristics.

- The text of the face of all certificates shall indicate ownership, number of shares, whether shares are full paid and nonassessable, their class, and par value where required by applicable law or where the dividend rate of a preferred share is stated as a percentage of par value.

- All certificates shall be signed by a transfer agent and by a registrar.

- All certificates should carry the authorized form of assignment.

- The name of the bank-note company must appear on all securities.

- A vignette, different for each company, is required on all listed securities except short-term or temporary securities. The design should include a human figure in a flowing robe. The figure should have plainly discernible features.

- Trade names, trademarks, and advertising are not permitted.

- The corporate title and the face text are engraved and have a raised (embossed) feeling. Printing must be sharp and clear.

- The paper used for securities must be an excellent grade of bond. It must have embedded, colored planchettes distributed in a random fashion.

- The exact denominations of certificates should be designated by engraved words and numbers, by perforation in punch-out panels at the extreme right-hand side of the face, or by maceration or perforation in the engraved border or in the denomination counter.

Photographic reproductions flatten lines and cause vignettes to have a muddy appearance.

Similar requirements are prescribed for corporate bonds.

Stolen treasury bills are much more difficult to identify. In May 1974, The Department of Justice said that it had recovered $30,000,000 in stolen securities in Chicago alone in the prior two years. Many of these stolen securities are marketed in Europe.

Auditors should verify that securities are purchased from reputable sources.

The Equity Funding case illustrates the necessity for great care by auditors in confirming securities in custodial accounts.

A city in a northern state required construction companies to post funds or negotiable bonds to guarantee performance of their contracts. The bonds were purchased with funds supplied by contractors through a municipal bond broker who was permitted by the city to retain the bonds.

On November 21, 1972, at a New York City bank, the broker showed a city auditor bonds valued at more than $2,200,000. A witness later testified that the broker had placed the bonds in the deposit box only two hours before the auditor had checked them.

On April 4, 1973, the brokerage company entered bankruptcy with few assets. The broker was charged with grand larceny of the money the city had turned over to him in order to purchase bonds.

At the trial, the district attorney's office contended that the bonds the broker showed the auditor did not belong to the city and that they were purchased just days previously so that the auditor would have something to count. The jury acquitted the broker because there wasn't proof that there was intent to steal the funds and grand larceny wasn't proved by the people.

To determine ownership, auditors should confirm not only the existence of securities but also the source and movement of funds.

An examination of securities should include substantiation that they represent real value. Some issues do not have an active market. Those should be checked carefully.

There are large quantities of tax-free bonds with no real, underlying value issued by small communities. Bonds issued by local or state industrial development authorities, health-care-facilities authorities, and similar groups often appear to have governmental backing. Yet frequently the full faith and credit of a responsible taxing authority is not pledged in support of such bonds.

Some bonds of this category are subject to the common practice of capitalized interest. Under this procedure, part of the funds raised from a bond offering is deposited in a bank. Interest payments are made from those deposits until the facility is operating and revenues flow to support interest payments. Investors receive their interest payments on schedule for the first year or two and are led to believe that everything is going well. This gives the promoter a couple of years' lead time before the investor knows he has a problem.

receivables

Receivables are believed to be the vehicle most used by defrauders to conceal thefts. The manipulations of receivables may be of a permanent or temporary nature. A *permanent* manipulation involves the introduction of false data to the system; for example, a false credit posted to an account in lieu of cash embezzled to balance a customer's account.

A *temporary* manipulation is one that entails switching entries from one customer's account to another in order to conceal a theft. But it requires a series of moves to continue the concealment. *Lapping* is the term used to describe the manipulation. Harvey Cardwell in his book *The Principles of Audit Surveillance* has a very well-written chapter on the manipulation of receivables by lapping.

Here are some illustrations of the use of receivables to conceal thefts of cash or to distort a financial position.

■ A furniture store was showing increasing operating deficits. Gross margins which theoretically should have been about 40% had dropped to less than 20%. The owner engaged a public accounting firm to prepare his tax returns and financial statements. The auditor, after his analysis of the accounts, told the owner that he was reducing his selling price too much and pointed to the declining margins as proof.

The owner knew that he was maintaining his prices and called in a business consultant. The latter discovered that the auditor had visited the store each quarter and had found that the detail list of customer balances was less than the general ledger control. To make the general ledger agree with the total of the supporting detail, the auditor had put an entry on the books debiting Sales and crediting Accounts Receivable.

Without realizing it, he had written off in a year a quarter of the receivables. And by charging Sales, he had reduced the gross profit to nearly half of what it should have been. When payments were made by a customer to complete a contract, the cash would be taken by an office employee who would destroy the ledger card. This reduced the total of the detailed receivables but did not reduce the general ledger total.

This illustrates the point that an auditor, by his adjustment of general ledgers and without inquiry into causes, should not make records balance and thereby bury potential fraud.

■ Stirling-Homex was incorporated in July 1968 to make modular housing units on an assembly line at a plant built for the purpose in Avon, New York. Many people thought that the economics of building homes in a factory and shipping them completely equipped to a site was an idea whose time had come.

In February 1970, the company went public when 1,175,000 shares were offered at $16.50 each. The next month, the shares were selling at a high of $51.50. The volume of business was reportedly growing rapidly. That year much publicity was given to a long train headed for Corinth, Mississippi, and carrying modules to provide shelter for victims of Hurricane Camille, which had hit the Gulf Coast in 1969.

In July 1971, an issue of 500,000 shares of convertible preferred shares was sold. The company reported the following results for fiscal years:

Fiscal Year	Sales	Net Earnings
7/31/1969	$ 4.2 million	$1.1 million
7/31/1970	22.6 million	2.0 million
7/31/1971	36.8 million	3.3 million

On July 12, 1972, the company entered bankruptcy. When the company collapsed, it had more than 9,000 modules valued at $35,000,000 stored in acres of open fields in several states.

As modules were produced, they were allotted to contracts. And entries were made to charge receivables and credit sales. Unfortunately, for Stirling-Homex shareholders, most of the contracts were not binding upon the purchasers. And financing for many projects had not been obtained. The modules had been produced and booked as sales before the company had obtained firm commitments. The receivables were actually overpriced and slow-moving inventory.

A hundred-million-dollar bubble had burst! Auditors should verify the validity of the sales of major items by confirmation of the order and contract status.

- The auditor should check the composition of receivables to make sure that they do not contain, without suitable reserves, unearned interest on contracts executed by customers. One company, in its interim reports, did not bother to adjust unearned interest and, thus, overstated earnings by a significant amount.

- In some companies, installment contracts are used as collateral for bank loans. The certified financial statements of one company showed $7,500,000 in contracts receivable. Notes to the financial statements showed that all of the contracts were pledged as collateral under a revolving credit arrangement. The notes further stated that the arrangement with the bank allowed the company to borrow up to $5 million with the restriction that the company not borrow more than 80% of the balance of contracts less than 60 days past due.

The report stated that the company had borrowed $1,500,000 under this arrangement. Presumably, either more contracts were hypothecated than necessary or about two-thirds of the contracts were past due. A loan of $1,500,000 would have required that no more than $1,875,000 of current contracts form the collateral. The maximum amount of current contracts required to cover the maximum loan under the credit arrangement would be only $6,250,000.

The auditor did not clarify the discrepancy in his comments. In this case, the unexplained difference was significant. It represented more than a third of the net equity in the business. Actually, the former bank credit arrangement had been terminated a year earlier, and the bank loan was not supported by the hypothecation of any contracts receivable. Auditors should understand the nature of large financial transactions, particularly substantial debt obligations.

- A medical center used a computer to process receivables. Incoming checks, totaling more than $60,000, were taken by office personnel. The computer records were fraudulently altered to show those receivables as uncollectible.

inventory

When profit margins on sales go down, the causes may be

many. Greater competitition could have lowered markups. Unit costs might have risen. Purchase discounts could have been lost. A closing inventory understatement may be a likely reason. The understatement may be the result of an omission in the physical count, pricing errors, or mistakes in footings or recapitulation.

A less obvious foozle or fraud may lie in the opening inventory. When management is changed during a year, it is not uncommon for the inventory at the end of that year to be more heavily depreciated, or written off, than under normal circumstances.

In this way, the previous manager's profit performance looks worse. And the new regime will be able to show a distinct but unearned improvement. Auditors should appraise such tactics. They should recognize that the magnitude of the abnormal change in profits had been made in order to clean house.

An unwarranted, heavy reduction in the value of the inventory at the end of one year may very well be an attempt to conceal a fraud in the subsequent year. We might call this *tunnel vision*.

In the illustration (page 26), the drop in the gross-profit percentage in the second year is ascribable to the added depreciation of inventory. Assuming this write-down was unwarranted by the condition of the stock and market conditions, it concealed the theft of 40% more than the inventory write-down through misappropriation of cash sales in the ensuing year when the gross profit remained at the "normal" 25%, even though $14,000 had been stolen from sales. After the theft in the third year, the culprit was apprehended. The 25% profit percentage in the fourth year was no larger than in the third year when the theft occurred. The alert auditor must develop the ability to recognize proper time horizons.

Inventory write-downs taken in the name of *conservative* accounting may become a snare for the unsuspecting auditor. An analysis of an inventory shrinkage in a bookstore was made when it was realized that the inventory showed a $250,000 loss. During the course of the examination, some employees made allegations that fraudulent activities had existed for at least five years. It was found that the cashier had voided cash receipts forms and had abstracted the money. The cashier was convicted and promised restitution, but the amount repaid was minimal.

It is important to receive information from employees who may be anxious to tell someone what they know of operating problems.

Stocks of slow-moving, obsolete, or unsalable accessory parts carried on the inventory at full cost without normal write-downs can mask shortages in fast-moving items. This can make the ratio

Concealing Theft Through Inventory Write-downs

	1st Year	2nd Year	3rd Year	4th Year
Sales, Actual	$100,000	$100,000	$110,000	$120,000
Less Employee Thefts	---	---	14,000	---
Sales as Booked	$100,000	$100,000	$ 96,000	$120,000
Cost of Sales:				
Opening Inventory	$ 50,000	$ 50,000	$ 40,000	$ 50,000
Purchases	75,000	75,000	82,000	90,000
Total	$125,000	$125,000	$122,000	$140,000
Closing Inventory Actual	$50,000	$50,000	$50,000	
Less Excessive Write-off	10,000	---	---	
Closing Inventory as Booked	$ 50,000	$ 40,000	$ 50,000	$ 50,000
Cost of Sales	$ 75,000	$ 85,000	$ 72,000	$ 90,000
Gross Profit	$ 25,000	$ 15,000	$ 24,000	$ 30,000
% of Gross Profit	25%	15%	25%	25%

of total inventory to sales appear reasonable. Such shortages can be either foozles or real losses through theft. The auditor must be prepared with a basic knowledge of product-stocking patterns in order to recognize deviations.

A stockman in an appliance-service area persuaded a supplier to deliver appliances to locations he specified and to bill the company for an equivalent dollar value of repair parts. Repair parts did not pass through regular Receiving. Instead they were received by the requesting department.

Since it was normal practice for this parts man to receive shipments directly, it was a routine matter for him to approve invoices for the bogus shipments and to pass them along for payment as legitimate invoices. Over a two-year period, he acquired $35,000 in appliances, which he sold to acquaintances.

He was caught because he tried to avoid calling attention to the number of illicit invoices he was trying to process by slowing down the flow to the Disbursements Department. Meanwhile, the supplier became dissatisfied with the delay in receiving his money and complained to the company that unpaid invoices, totaling $20,000, were overdue. The supplier claimed that he thought his arrangement with the parts man had company approval.

The parts man was discharged and prosecuted. He received a two-year, suspended sentence and made restitution of $19,000. The supplier agreed to cancel his claim for the delinquent invoices. He is no longer a supplier to this company.

This case illustrates a departure from good internal control practices. Many organizations, for alleged operating reasons, permit special circumstances to exist. Those exceptions must be carefully examined.

In a somewhat similar case, a college employee was responsible for several administrative functions such as the print shop, photo laboratory, and miscellaneous stores and services. He made an arrangement with a salesman to invoice the college for shop supplies but to ship readily salable merchandise. He sold this merchandise to students for cash, which he pocketed.

When making an inventory check, the dealer's auditor noted that invoice and shipping tickets did not agree with the merchandise sold. A sales analysis was made from copies of invoices, and a shortage in one sales classification became quite apparent.

The dealer went to the college, told the president what had happened, and offered to correct the deception. The college decided to handle the affair internally and promised to continue doing business with the dealer. This resolution of an embarrassing situation usually works out best for all concerned.

Auditors must be alert to transactions which not only cause losses to their own organizations but which may adversely affect customer relationships.

capital assets

Most people associate real property frauds with land promoters who dupe thousands of unsuspecting people by selling them land of little value at high prices. However, there are other schemes that are used by dishonest promoters to bilk the public.

One Southwest company allegedly swindled investors out of $5,000,000 in two years by selling securities as sales contracts, notes, or mortgages that had not been legally registered. A typical operation involved false sales contracts bearing the signatures of either nonexistent persons or persons who had been paid a small fee by land salesmen. There was no intention of ever making payments on the contract.

Managing real estate projects is often big business. One agent was found to have stolen nearly a half-million dollars in housing funds. An audit of the project's records uncovered falsification of accounts, misappropriation of rents and other income, and forged expenditure documents. Frequent occurrences of this type of loss indicate that too little auditing is being done on such projects.

One of the largest expenditures a corporation makes is for the acquisition or construction of additional buildings, equipment, fixtures, and furniture. The size of the expenditures makes them favorite targets of defrauders. Such expenditures may involve various categories which invite fraud. These difficulties fall into several categories.

Failure of the corporation to provide adequate sources of financing may eventually cause serious difficulties if the construction contract is on a cost-plus basis and if cost overruns are substantial.

Internal auditors examining cost-plus contracts should check change orders carefully for proper pricing and authorization. They should make certain that adequate controls exist for receiving materials and for protecting them on the construction site. They should also make sure that credit is received for materials and supplies not used. An adequate number of independent personnel should keep a time check on labor and verify that skill levels are properly utilized and identified.

Some lump-sum contracts may carry escalation clauses on labor and materials. In effect, these become cost contracts and should be checked as such. Contracts should specify who pays:

- sales taxes
- premium or overtime labor costs
- freight
- for small tools
- for repairs and maintenance of equipment
- rental for equipment and the competitive cost thereof
- field office expenses
- for insurance coverages and costs
- for subcontractors' contingent liability and contractual insurance

Internal auditors should also determine if all cost discounts are being taken by contractors and subcontractors. Even if the contractor does not earn these discounts, the owner should benefit from them.

Some contractors are solvent and completely credit worthy at the start of a project but become financially unable to complete that project due to difficulties on an unrelated job.

A contractor who had completed several projects satisfactorily was unable to collect money from clients who had run into financial problems. Lack of payments from customers prompted him to use tax-withheld money from employees' pay for operating expenses. When the government demanded the taxes, he couldn't pay and was arraigned on a fraud charge. With that charge against him, he could no longer secure performance bonds. Without them he was unable to obtain new contracts. And, without new contracts, he was unable to earn enough to pay his debts. Thus, far-removed circumstances caused difficulties on certain uncompleted contracts.

Capital assets often disappear without an explanation or sometimes with a false reason. Sales and leasebacks of real property are usually legitimate deals. But they are abused when insiders sell corporate property to a dummy corporation they control. They arrange for a long-term lease of that property at a rental that more than pays for the principal, interest, and upkeep of the property. A check of the principals of a corporation making a purchase of such property is often wise.

Many times management can use legal authority for illegal gains. A manager of a small unit of a large company transferred ownership of his company car to his own name. He did not notify the company of this transfer or make any arrangements for payment. The transfer was discovered when an auditor checked car registrations.

What the manager could accomplish by this was difficult to understand. However, further investigation revealed that he had also been stealing company inventory. An auditor cannot underestimate the extent of legal authority given to management to conduct proper company business and the extent to which such authority can be abused.

chapter five

liabilities

Frauds based on the manipulation of liabilities are probably the most elusive for an auditor to uncover. The omission of a debt improves reported net worth, earnings, and asset-to-liability ratios. The classification of a current liability as *long term* can improve the reported current ratio. The manipulation of a debt to give priority to favored creditors can, if successful, defraud others with equally valid claims.

Companies with serious financial difficulties have arranged to remove collateral from the support of a certain debt prior to the deadline preceding bankruptcy. Other companies facing similar circumstances have introduced additional debt into the balance sheet to secure a larger piece of the assets for insiders. Groups in control of a corporation have sweetened benefit plans that favor top personnel. Under generally accepted accounting principles, many of the costs of such unfair arrangements do not have to appear as current costs or as part of the present reported liabilities. But they are actually long-term obligations of the corporation. In the liquidation of those organizations, such obligations *do* become liabilities that *must* be dealt with. And the actuarial value of such obligations can be substantial.

Quite frequently, the business owner about to retire will sell to new owners at a fair price but with the added stipulation that he is to receive a stated salary for a specified number of years. If the business fails, the wage contract—along with other liabilities that have appeared on the balance sheet—must be honored.

In another variation, the owner sells the business but retains the real estate. He then rents—at a quite high figure—the real estate to the new owners. The excess of that rental over a fair rental does not appear as a liability until it is due or until the business is liquidated. And the excess cannot be passed on to a new tenant.

Actual liabilities for income taxes cannot be determined for certain until a government audit has been completed or the statute of limitations has expired. There are those who file income tax returns but pay an amount lower than that they eventually will pay. When that smaller amount goes onto the books, earnings temporarily improve.

To bolster poor earnings records, an unethical manager may deliberately conceal trade obligations or fail to make proper accruals of expenses. Such omissions are useful only for one accounting year and must be repeated or increased in subsequent years to continue the overstatement of profits.

A small railroad company owned about 20 miles of track, four locomotives, and 50 cars. The railroad was important to several industries in the community it served, since it connected to a major line. The entire stock of the railroad was owned by a score of people, but only four or five of them possessed a real insight into its financial affairs. Those few wanted to keep the railroad viable to serve their own interests.

Therefore, financial reports excluded a past-due $100,000 debt to one of their group for track maintenance performed by his construction crews. However, the group had taken the precaution of validating the debt so that in the event of the railroad's liquidation it would have a high priority. Although they had been made much earlier, payments on the debt were charged off as current maintenance costs. If that debt had been booked, the railroad would have been insolvent.

The payment by cash or check to fictitious persons for fictitious liabilities is a simple trick of an embezzler. But, if the payment is charged to an account on the books, the embezzler must have the opportunity and the skill to establish the liability on the books against which the charge can be made. Otherwise, an out-of-balance situation—one most embezzlers try to avoid—will exist.

It is necessary for many companies to delegate considerable authority to many people. In some cases, these people exercise more authority than might have been intended simply because it is difficult to interdict precisely that which they are not permitted to do.

Some years ago, a subsidiary manager decided that his unit needed a larger bank balance. Without obtaining the approval of the parent company treasurer, he borrowed $100,000 from a large New York bank on December 24 to meet bills due the first of the year. Because of the holidays, the loan did not come to the attention of corporate officers until after the first of the year.

It so happened that the parent corporation had accumulated a large cash position. In the annual report, it had planned to proudly announce that all bank loans had been paid. The manager of one subsidiary had incurred a liability to a bank and had—by his foozle—unwittingly thwarted a corporate plan.

He had never been told that he had a right to incur bank loans, nor had he been told that he did not have that right. If he had been dishonest, he might have very easily pocketed the loan and not have had it entered on the subsidiary's books as a liability.

sales

The account with the largest value in current operations sales is usually a tempting target for the manipulator or embezzler. The sales total might be improperly increased to impress a potential purchaser of a business or those from whom a loan is sought.

For example, a young man in a college town started a small retail business which became moderately successful. To make it appear even more successful, he added amounts in cash from his own pocket and from a personal bank loan to sales. These transactions did not appear as debts on his business records. The infusion of cash increased not only sales but also profit with the result that net worth increased as if he had paid in capital.

He then advertised the business for sale and soon found a buyer who not only paid cash for net assets but a sizable figure for goodwill. Too late, the buyer called in an auditor who spotted instances when extraordinarily large sales were recorded. He soon learned that *sales* consisted of a normal day's receipts *plus* the added cash investment. Bank deposit slips revealed that, on certain days, deposits included checks written by the owner.

Division or subsidiary managers have been known to artificially increase sales by shipping large quantities of goods on trial or consignment and by recording the shipments as sales, knowing there was little likelihood that bona fide sales would result. Some managers have postdated the original invoice or have marked it *field trial*. Office copies do not carry such notations. Those accounts, in some instances, are *rolled over* by credits and new charges monthly to divert attention to a past-due account.

Companies that promote managers showing exceptional sales increases are frequently the victims of supervisors seeking rewards through improper practices. Such people hope for transfers to better positions before the full effects of their improper activities appear on the records. In fact, a return to normal practice following their promotions can result in an apparent decline in sales and profit. This makes them look even better and makes their successors appear much worse than they actually are.

The appearance on the books of sales lower than they actually are may be the work of embezzlers appropriating funds from sales receipts or people trying to negate profitability. These people may range from the owner evading taxes to an employee bearing a grievance. They may remove actual cash or ship goods without charge to customers or conspirators. They may make excessive allowances for real or fancied reasons. They may delete proper delivery charges from invoices. They may apply improper pricing. Their methods are nearly infinite.

Under the guise of goodwill adjustments, improper allowances may be extended to real or fictitious customers for alleged defective, obsolete, or damaged goods. Allowances made for materials not returned to a central warehouse for inspection are probably subject to more improper treatment than allowances under some central control. One manufacturer was reportedly the victim of a plot by a major distributor who charged back to the manufacturer fictitious work done under manufacturer's warranties. It is believed that the false charge-backs totalled more than a half million dollars.

Many auditors find a careful review of credit memorandums and supporting documents and correspondence to be very productive.

During the first quarter of 1975, The Institute of Internal Auditors surveyed selected IIA leaders regarding the degree to which internal auditors should be concerned with the detection and prevention of fraud. One hundred and two internal auditors from North America, Latin America, Australia, Asia, and Europe replied.

The survey asked, " . . . assuming a sales level of $1 million, at what level of loss would you expect an auditor to detect the existence of fraud?"

Of the 81 auditors who replied to this question, 47, or 58%, answered $50,000. Sixty-eight, or 84%, said $100,000 (includes previous category).

Answers to a similar question showed that an auditor should detect fraud of the same relative magnitude in current assets.

In some businesses, an embezzler can manipulate cash discounts allowed customers to his own benefit. A change in the magnitude of the amount booked over a period of time should alert the auditor to the possibilities of improper activity.

royalties and license fees

Royalties and license fees receivable are other sources of income. An auditor may be able to rely on the record of patents owned and the contracts for their use by others to verify payments due—if those records are properly set up and maintained. If payments by users are delayed or overlooked, an understatement of earnings may result.

Some agreements permit the holders of patents to audit the user's production, sales quantities, or financial records. These audits are made when amounts are substantial or when there is some question of the accuracy of the user's reports because of other trade information.

dividends

Dividends from common stock investments may be less than they should be. A careful check of payment dates and dates of record for dividends should be made. This is especially true when securities are traded on or near the record dates for dividend purposes.

interest

Interest income may be omitted from financial statements for the same reasons. Securities placed on deposit with others for various purposes are usually interest bearing or have been purchased at a discount. The interest or appreciation should not be overlooked.

Interest on trade notes or accounts receivable deserves the attention of the auditor because, in some organizations, it may be among the easiest items for an embezzler to misappropriate.

combination figures

It is not uncommon for companies to combine other income and other charges into a net figure (plus or minus) and report no details of how the amount shown was determined. One company showed a sundry net charge—with no analysis—of an amount equal to 37% of the net profit. Another company reported—without any analysis—$12,000,000 of *other income net of other deductions*.

That figure represented more than 10% of net income. It was a substantial increase over prior years, and there was some indication that a major nonrecurring item had been included. The company did not report whether or not the *net of other deductions* consisted of applicable income taxes on that amount.

The custom for utility companies has been to charge interest on construction funds to capital assets and to credit the amount to other income. The fluctuations in that year-to-year amount are usually complementary to the balance of interest payable.

purchases

When it comes to an audit of the purchasing function, internal auditors are often guilty of criticizing minor, procedural rules violations rather than concentrating on detecting major failures.

Take, for example, the following excerpt from the report of a recent audit of the Purchasing Department of a local government.

> This is somewhat of an indictment. Purchasing personnel are violating their own procedures. Violating such procedures always opens the door to serious implications. It is the stated policy of the Purchasing Department that three vendors be contacted for price quotes before a purchase is made. Yet this was being done in only 20% of the purchases. This type of purchasing decreases competition and may result in higher costs. While there is a heavy work load on each buyer due to the volume of purchases to be made, the basic objective of purchasing should not become secondary to the expeditious processing of orders.
>
> The auditors examined several 1973 purchase orders to determine if purchases were being made at the best possible price and delivery time. In 30% of the items tested, purchases were made from a vendor suggested by the requesting department at a price also suggested by that department. In those cases, the buyer had not contacted any other vendors to determine if the suggested vendor and price were, in fact, the best possible. In another 20% of the items tested, purchases were made with only a single price quote being solicited from the suggested vendor.

The auditors who prepared that report accomplished little and reached some unsupportable conclusions. Consider the following:

■ Choice of words — They toss around such words as *indictment* and *violation. Indictment* is a legal term. It is an action by which a person is charged with an unlawful offense. *Violation* has the connotation of an offense.

- Broad and unsupportable statements — "Violating such procedures always opens the door to serious implications."

- Use of percentages without explaining their significance — What sort of purchases were made without three quotations? How many were too small to make such a policy practical?

- No evaluation was made to support the cliché ". . . the basic objective of purchasing should not become secondary to the expeditious processing of orders." In many instances, processing an order quickly could save much more than obtaining three quotes could save.

- Ambiguous terminology — "The auditors examined several 1973 purchase orders . . . In 30% of the items tested . . ." Thirty percent of *several* could be as low as three items.

The auditors did not present a single instance where the price was too high, the quality too low, or the delivery too late. They had reviewed controls and found what they regarded as a fault. The buyers were carrying heavy case loads. Yet they were getting the work done expeditiously. But the auditors could see nothing except the fetish of obtaining three quotations—a rule that was probably ridiculous when it was first adopted. Foozles or frauds might have existed, but the auditors saw nothing of either. Or they didn't recognize them if they did exist.

There are many variations of thefts involving the purchase functions. For example:

A routine audit of purchases at a branch disclosed extensive theft. The auditor asked an employee to explain the use of materials shown on invoices. The employee's reluctance to explain made the auditor curious. By persistent investigation, the auditor learned that the branch manager was a modern-day Robin Hood, who had been given many awards by community organizations for his contributions. He had purchased materials and charged them to the branch maintenance account but had delivered them to his pet projects.

His close associates in the company knew of his thefts but did not inform on him. The thefts covered many of the 28 years he had been employed. Admission of the theft was followed by his resignation and the forfeiture of his pension funds. He was not prosecuted.

The manager of a branch marketing unit prepared periodically a list of used equipment which he claimed he had purchased from a customer who had gone out of business. This was entirely fictitious. Yet he had the Disbursements Department draw checks to the order of individuals to whom he owed money. This practice continued on a regular basis without too much variation in amounts from year to year. After his death, he was succeeded by his former assistant. The new manager continued the fraud and became even more skillful at the deception than his predecessor. But he also became more greedy and kept increasing his illegal take. As branch profits fell, the fraud became apparent. Over the years, hundreds of thousands of dollars were taken.

A captain of an ocean research vessel submitted false vouchers to cover theft from official cash advances. When a disbursements audit disclosed the fictitious documents, the captain was dismissed. He made full restitution of $10,000.

A construction supervisor approved bills for payments to six fictitious companies. An auditor noted too many suppliers with post-office-box numbers but no listing in telephone or city directories. He, along with security personnel and police, contacted postal authorities, who reported that all boxes were rented to the employee's father. The fraud had been in existence for about ten months.

The finance manager at a division level defrauded his company of $60,000 over a five-year period in several ways. He approved invoices which represented personal charges. He prepared false invoices from bogus companies. He forged approvals on check requisitions. Internal auditors uncovered the fraud by a thorough review of voucher support. The manager pleaded guilty and received a one-to-ten-year sentence. At the end of nine months, he was paroled. He is to try to make restitution to the insurance company which paid the claim. As a result of this case, tighter disbursement audits will be made in the future; and internal controls will be strengthened.

An EDP employee was able to issue himself a check by inserting a fraudulent voucher and altering input control documents which were unsecured. The fraud was discovered when the bank questioned the large amount of the check for a relatively low-salaried employee. The employee was prosecuted. Input control documents are now under better control.

In another case, the principal was a junior officer in charge of purchasing $7,000,000 in supplies annually for a retailer. For a kickback, he arranged for payment to an outside organization for goods that were never delivered. The company also paid for goods which were received from a legitimate vendor but then transferred to the coconspirators without billing. In addition, a cleaning detergent was being purchased from a syndicated firm at twice the proper selling price. Criminal action was taken and convictions were obtained. The loss to the company was $535,000.

Inadequate segregation of duties resulted in the purchasing agent having authority to sign receiving reports. By preparing fictitious purchase orders, approving fraudulent invoices, and receiving reports, he was able to perpetrate the fraud for two years.

payroll

There have been countless instances of payroll frauds. In some cases, the amounts lost through payroll padding and other techniques have been very large.

- For example, collusion among a chief accountant, a payroll supervisor, and a work-site supervisor resulted in a $2,000,000 loss. This was one-eighth of a $16,000,000 payroll. Fictitious employees were carried on a facility project during a 12-week summer program. When police recovered an overdue rental car, they discovered that it was being used to store a bundle of unnegotiated checks. The individuals involved were prosecuted, proven guilty, and convicted.

- A salesman for a West Coast company worked on straight salary and was supplied with a company car. Unknown to his employer, he obtained another full-time position as a recreation director for a public playgrounds program. Meanwhile, he allowed a young girl to drive the car to add mileage to his expense report. Later, he asked the company for a vacation during December and took a temporary position for the holiday season. When supervisors of the playground program learned of his absence from work, they dismissed him and reported the incident to the other two employers. As a result, he lost all three jobs; and his first employer tightened control over the activities of salesmen.

- Late in 1974, a suspect in a major city was apprehended and charged with filing false instruments with state officials, forgery, and grand larceny. In applications for unemployment insurance, he allegedly used fictitious identities but gave bona fide companies as his employers. All of these companies had gone out of business. He had victimized the state employment fund for four years and more than $80,000 before he was caught by an investigator who recognized that the company addresses were incorrect.

- Some payroll frauds are uncovered by accident. One such foozle occurred when a man tried to cash a payroll check at a gasoline station. When the attendant would not cash it, the man left, forgetting a bag he was carrying. The bag contained more pay checks which the attendant turned over to the police. The checks were authentic payroll forms, properly signed, but drawn to the order of fictitious names. It was believed that former employees had submitted false information to the Payroll Department, which had processed the checks and returned them to the originating department. Eighteen months after the gas station discovery, no arrests had been made.

■ In an Eastern city, it was discovered that several people had been employed by the recreation bureau and the school system at the same time. They even submitted time slips showing indisputably that they were at work in two different locations at the same time. One of these employees filed for sick leave with pay from the bureau on the same day he was paid for working as a teacher. Another employee filed for overtime from the bureau on the same day he was paid for work with the school system.

■ Piecework operations, which are not machine paced, are subject to overloading pay tickets for production which is greater than gross output measured by deliveries to stock areas or other production areas. An analysis of both pay and production records will usually locate the source of the discrepancy.

■ An individual, widely known in his community because of his athletic ability, moved to another city to join a major league team. During the off-season, he had been working for another employer. When an auditor discovered suspicious-looking signatures on time cards, further investigation revealed that paychecks were being issued to the athlete, now living in another state. The paychecks had been cashed ... but not by him.

The time cards carried two signatures—the former employee's and his supervisor's. A blue ball-point pen was used for both signatures on most of the cards. A black felt-tipped pen was used once—also for both signatures. The employee's authentic signature had the capital letters of his name written with big, circular, sweeping motions. The more recent time cards bore a signature with straight, vertical capital letters. The paychecks were endorsed with the employee's name and that of his supervisor—evidence that the supervisor had cashed them. The case was turned over to the police, who were to arrange for grand jury action. Most forgeries of this sort are clumsy. Even an amateur graphologist can spot them.

advertising

It is quite common for foozles or frauds to occur in the advertising field because of the intangible nature of many projects. A summary of audit experiences in this area of business activity shows:

- Duplicate billings may occur if partial costs of an advertisement are billed before insertion in a publication, especially if the total cost is billed after publication. Duplicate billing of the first part as a part of the total is an easily overlooked error.

- Failure to receive credit for inadequate or erroneous insertions in publications is fairly common. A client should also receive credit for breakdowns in television and radio presentations.

- Credits for the best quantity rates are not obtained. A company working through several agencies neglected to coordinate efforts and, therefore, missed out on quantity rates.

- Agency records of artwork, merchandise, props, or films were inadequate.

- Kickbacks in advertising are difficult to trace, but several cases have been well publicized. There have been instances of officials accepting money for placing advertisements in certain publications. The practice of pressuring companies which supply services to organizations is sometimes abused. This is especially true in the political field or among fictitious charitable groups. Many allegations have been made in the travel industry of improper sales-promotion arrangements between carriers and agents. Some sources estimate that as much as $500,000,000 has changed hands.

Internal auditors can do management a real service by calling attention to untrue advertising, the result of overly aggressive advertising personnel. Such advertising can ultimately damage the corporate image.

Remember some advertising may be in violation of the fair advertising laws. One such type is *bait and switch*. This involves the unauthorized and undisclosed substitution of one article for another. In a recent case, the defendant advertised a certain brand of rebuilt home appliances at low prices—the bait—to invite inquiry by prospective customers. However, the defendant disparaged the advertised appliance in order to switch the customer to a more costly one.

The Federal Trade Commission is concerned not with technical truth but with truth as the consumer views it. To protect the public, advertising must be relevant, fair, and related to significant differences between competing products. Consumer groups, as well as the FTC, have been actively trying to control unfair advertising.

Internal Audit and Control of Advertising and Sales Promotion was published in 1963 by The Institute of Internal Auditors as *Research Committee Report No. 13.* It emphasizes the vital role an advertising agency plays and the need for the auditor to understand the written or verbal agreements the company has with an agency.

expenses

An embezzler can appropriate money for his own purposes in many ways. A simple way is by padding traveling expense vouchers. There are two types of fraud used to pad expenses.

The first is to report only normally acceptable amounts for transportation, meals, etc., but to spend less and pocket the difference. Some companies provide first-class air passage which, on certain flights, is considerably more than coach fares. A person who turns in that ticket and buys a coach ticket pockets the difference. Close examination of the duplicate ticket attached to the expense report will disclose that finagle.

The other type is to report excessive spending and to justify it by necessary customer entertaining, which probably never happened.

One individual reported, nearly every week, a large amount of entertaining for a group of people from one company. The volume of business secured from that firm did not justify the amount spent. When the individual was questioned about it, he claimed that he was working on a big deal that required many conferences. The deal was not consummated, and it is not known how much of that entertaining was fictitious.

A bank official in a small, country bank wrote cashier checks for some of his larger personal expenses and charged them to the bank's expense accounts. His take averaged more than $15,000 a year for several years. This was an improper use of cashier checks and should have triggered an inquiry earlier.

The president of a well-known company repaid more than $65,000 to his company because a court-ordered outside accounting of his corporation showed that he had submitted duplicate business expenses to the parent company and an affiliated company. He made the payment without any admission of liability.

The alleged double billing of expenses was called to the attention of the courts when a former executive was discharged and brought suit against the company. The outside auditors said that the previous five years' business expense accounts, totaling nearly $100,000, could not be found in the company's files. In defense of the case brought by the discharged executive, the company countercharged that the executive had been discharged for alleged kickbacks from other companies.

A careful comparison of actual expenses against budgeted amounts and prior years' expenditures will uncover expense accounts that are abnormally high. These may be the acounts used by an embezzler to accomplish a theft. However, a clever defrauder is likely to use several accounts to spread his illicit gains in order to avoid detection by the auditors' comparison of actual to budget. Adequate sampling is the only available method to combat that tactic.

chapter eight

other adjustments

foreign currency exchange

The mechanics of foreign exchange have become fairly well standardized. There have been, however, varying treatments of the net adjustments arising from the exchange of foreign currencies to US dollars. Based on annual reports for the years 1971 through 1974, it was found that:

- the net adjustment is deferred and amortized over the term of foreign currency long-term liabilities.

- the net adjustment is applied to the reserve for future foreign exchange fluctuations. The reserve is amortized to profit and loss for amounts in excess of a base amount deemed necessary for such fluctuations. Losses in excess of available reserves are charged to income.

- the net adjustment applicable to long-term borrowing is considered a part of the cost of that borrowing and is deferred and amortized over the remaining life of the borrowing. Generally, other gains and losses arising from foreign currency exchange are included in revenues, costs, and expenses.

- some companies explain the formula for conversion of foreign currencies but do not state the amount of the net adjustment. In other cases, when the amount is given, there is no indication of where the adjustment appears in the statements.

- the net adjustments are reflected in income for the period in which they arise. Changes in the market value of unperformed forward exchange contracts are accrued and included in the determination of net income for the period in which the market value changes.

■ gains on forward exchange contracts are recognized when such contracts are settled. Anticipated losses are recognized currently.

The many variations in the accounting treatment of foreign currency exchange contributed to misunderstanding of this part of the business activity.

The Financial Accounting Standards Board recognized the problem and issued *Opinion No. 8,* which became effective on January 1, 1976. Under these guidelines, all unrealized gains and losses from the translation of other currencies to US dollars on foreign balance sheets were to be reported as part of current earnings or losses each quarter.

The Bretton Woods, New Hampshire, conference in 1944 laid the foundation for post-World War II international monetary cooperation and created the International Monetary Fund. In the early 1970's, the Bretton Woods monetary stability began to collapse. After the devaluation of the US dollar, the value of other currencies fluctuated widely in relation to it. In the years immediately following the devaluation of the dollar, some American parent corporations with foreign subsidiaries or divisions recorded foreign exchange profits as described above.

During 1975, the US dollar increased in value against most other currencies, and many American corporations were faced with exchange losses. Those with sufficient reserves were able to charge the losses to reserves. Some companies elected to adopt FASB *Opinion No. 8* for 1975 year-end accounts.

Wide seasonal swings in the value of foreign currencies may have significant effects on the reported quarterly earnings of multinational corporations if balance sheets have not been designed to minimize those effects. It is possible that the potential effect of these adjustments may lead to abuses in the application of *Opinion No. 8.*

Auditors whose companies deal in the foreign exchange futures market may find it well worth their time to conduct a thorough audit of transactions rather than merely checking the accuracy and adequacy of accounting.

One company carried on its books hundreds of thousands of dollars in forward exchange transactions. An auditor found that the totals were not supported by actual contracts. Considerable dealing had transpired, and several transactions apparently had not been recorded. Since several banks had been used to handle these trades, it was difficult to determine to what extent the books were correct or how many futures contracts were missing.

Resolving the problem consumed considerable audit time. And, even then, the answers were not very satisfactory.

There have been several large embezzlements by employees who gambled company funds in unauthorized foreign exchange trading. These transactions deserve as many internal controls and as much audit attention as cash and securities.

commodity trading

Similar controls should be exercised over commodity trading. Many commodity future contracts are substantial, yet, because of their nature, are difficult to control.

One company reported a loss of more than $3,000,000 in fraudulent sugar futures contracts placed by an employee who sold sugar short during a time when sugar prices were soaring. The company claimed that the employee had no authority to execute the contracts. A federal grand jury subsequently indicted the employee on five counts of fraud.

chapter nine

financial interpretation

adequacy of footnotes in financial statements

The Securities and Exchange Commission advocates full disclosure of financial information by public companies. Most companies comply adequately. However, ambiguous language used in footnotes to explain the balance sheet and earning statement may be an attempt to mislead the reader. This is fraud. Or it may be that the company is insensitive to the need of investors to fully understand the important accounting principles the company applies.

For example, what is meant by the following?

Pensions — The company's policy is to fund pension costs based on recommendations of its consulting actuaries.

No further information is given, and the reader has no understanding of what was done about pensions.

The corporation deducted, for income tax purposes, all research and development expenditures, including those capitalized in the accounts.

Totals are not given, and there is no explanation of the divided policy. In 1975, companies following an FASB ruling charged off to income all R and D expenditures.

For the first time, the company deducted, for tax purposes, $ ___ of certain expenses which are capitalized for financial statement purposes.

The amount was a multimillion-dollar figure, and there was no further definition of *certain expenses*.

US government securities are carried at cost, which does not exceed market.

A negative-type statement which implies that the market is possibly higher than cost.

The company has provided appropriate income taxes on unremitted earnings of foreign subsidiary companies.

The word *appropriate* is ambiguous. Does it apply to foreign or US income taxes or both? Is it clear that the policy is in accordance with opinions 23 and 24 of the Accounting Principles Board?

escrow accounts

In the operation of businesses, escrow accounts and trust funds are important factors. Large sums of money pass through the hands of attorneys, real estate agencies, credit and collection bureaus, financial institutions, brokerage houses, and similar organizations. Some auditors tend to ignore such accounts on the books of an employer or client if the asset account agrees with the liability account on the general ledger.

It may be advisable, however, to examine such accounts more closely. There should be complete detail by creditor to support the total of the liability account on the general ledger. An analysis of all old balances should be made to determine if funds due a creditor were improperly withheld. Asset accounts should be checked to determine if they are in proper order.

In one audit of an escrow account, auditors found that the escrow bank account had not been reconciled for a year. In fact, envelopes containing bank statements had not even been opened. When the auditors reconciled the bank statements, they were not surprised to find that the balance did not agree with the balance due creditors on the general ledger.

An attorney resigned from his law firm and from positions with the city and county following the discovery that funds were missing from a trust he controlled. His letter to the mayor included the following:

"In a routine decision to close my old trust account, I quit making deposits to that account. When the bank called about an overdraft, we borrowed sufficient money to cover all outstanding checks. The reason for the shortage is unknown at the present time. I lead a simple and frugal life, primarily concerned with my clients, so I know that I did not take any money. An audit of the records has been started."

An audit under such circumstances is almost always difficult because information might have been mislaid, lost, or deliberately destroyed. If the cash was embezzled and if all traces of the creditor's identity are gone, the auditor can only hope that publicity will bring forth the creditors whose own records may in part, at least, help to restore missing details.

In New York State, premium payments must be kept in a trust fund. The New York State Insurance Department fined an insurance agency and two of its agents for operating for nine months with an expired broker's permit, allowing premium payments to be used as operating funds, and issuing six checks on an overdrawn bank account. Auditors should try to determine whether any transactions which are required by law to be kept in trust funds are comingled with operating funds.

The collection of income taxes and social security contributions withheld from the paychecks of employees represents the largest trust account of American corporations. As of June 30, 1974, it was estimated that more than $500,000,000 was overdue and unpaid to the federal government alone. Usually, the Internal Revenue Service assesses civil penalties for late payments, but employers with histories of late payments may be charged with criminal offenses.

The president of one company which had not paid more than $500,000 of collected taxes pleaded guilty to 16 counts of failure to deposit trust funds. He faced a maximum penalty of four years in prison and a $20,000 fine. In addition, the IRS filed a lien against the assets of the company.

unconsolidated funds

Many companies publish financial statements that are not fully consolidated. A financial analyst reviewing such statements may find it difficult to determine the approximate net book value if sizable foreign or domestic subsidiaries and affiliates are carried only at the amount invested.

One company carried on its books an investment in a wholly owned subsidiary at a value of $6,000,000 more than the subsidiary's net worth. The latter figure was shown in a separate tabulation. An additional $10,000,000 was invested in foreign subsidiaries. Another table showed the value of net assets, revenues, and net income of the fully consolidated foreign subsidiaries but nothing on the unconsolidated ones.

Another company, with an investment of more than $50,000,000 in associated companies, reported the increase in the equity of net earnings of those companies as a separate item.

Still another company reported the investment in unconsolidated affiliates at equity on the balance sheet and, accordingly, included the company's share of affiliate (20% or more ownership) earnings in the consolidated results of operations.

The size of many nonconsolidated enterprises has an important effect on the overall appraisal of a parent company's common stock valuation. Some accounting methods permit concealment or distortion of earnings, remission of earnings to the parent, loans and advances by the parent to the subsidiary or the reverse, guarantees of bank loans, liquidity of the associated company, degree of effective control, etc. Auditors responsible for reviewing financial statements should be concerned that investments of nonconsolidated, associated companies and wholly owned subsidiaries are presented fairly.

chapter ten

manipulative practices

international communications frauds

Banks throughout the world are concerned with the often successful attempts of international forgers to obtain funds through the fraudulent manipulation of payment orders, checks, wires, and letters of credit.

Banks suffer substantial losses as a result of fraudulent wire-payment instructions. Even though banks have done considerable work to develop effective test codes to authenticate wire transfers of funds, the controls are defeated too frequently.

Bank operations throughout the world are generally the same. This permits the international forger, knowledgeable of operational procedures and their weaknesses, to carry out worldwide activities.

A major New York bank received several tested cable transfers from a South American bank. The cables called for more than $400,000 to be transferred to numbered accounts in Swiss banks. Since a confidential cable-testing arrangement existed between the two banks, the transfers were made. Upon receiving the debit advices for the transfers, the South American bank questioned the New York bank. Soon the details were known.

A young officer in the South American bank had sent his wife to Switzerland, where she opened numbered accounts. Then he had sent the cables, and the funds had been collected by his wife. He had arranged to join her as soon as he had sent the cables.

Mail frauds usually depend on the cooperation of postal employees in the country where the fraud is set up. Here is an example of one such fraud.

A forger, living in South America, arranged with certain post office employees in his city to intercept mail from United States banks to local residents who maintained accounts with those banks. For a price, the post office employees turned over this mail to the forger. He steamed open the envelopes and made copies of bank statements and cancelled checks. He then resealed the envelopes and returned them to the post office for delivery.

The forger had learned the normal account balances and the makers' signatures. He also obtained letters sent from local banks to correspondent banks in the United States. This allowed him to print copies of local bank letterheads and to use authorized signatures appearing in the letters. When packages of blank checks arrived at his city, he intercepted them and removed the last checkbook from each package. The rest of the checks were then forwarded to the addressees.

Referring to the *Bankers Almanac*, the forger obtained the names of US banks which were correspondents of the banks in his city. He traveled to the United States and opened accounts in these correspondent banks using letters of introduction written on forged letterheads and bearing forged signatures with forged guarantees of his specimen signature. In several cases, he opened accounts with cash deposits. Officers who opened the accounts usually gave the forger counter checks and verified the signatures appearing on the letters of introduction.

The blank checks, stolen from the mail to South America, were filled in and the owners' names forged. These checks, made payable to the forger's assumed name, were deposited in the recently opened accounts. Since there were sufficient funds and the makers' signatures compared favorably with specimen signatures, the banks paid the checks. After depositing the checks, the forger waited the required number of days for the depositing banks to consider the checks paid. He then cashed some of the counter checks.

He also urged bank officers to put through a rush printing order for checks. As soon as he obtained the checks, he returned to South America. Then he mailed more stolen checks for deposit to his accounts in the United States. Several days later, he presented checks drawn against his US accounts to local banks on a collection basis and requested cable advice of payment. The banks in the United States had cleared all the deposited checks and, having allowed for the delay factor, cable advised the South American banks that the checks sent for collection were paid. The South American banks paid him in cash. The forger in South America was safe from prosecution.

Banks can avoid such losses by telling a stranger that le introduction from foreign banks cannot be honored confirmed by tested cable from the issuing bank and th account cannot be used until such confirmation is receiv

Any foreign account in a bank should be closely monitored for several months. All deposits and drawdowns should be reviewed. Computer printouts of substantial deposits or withdrawals could alert a bank to possible fraud.

There are many variations of fraudulent schemes employed in international transfer of funds, but most depend on intercepted mail and cleverly forged documents.

price-fixing schemes

The Federal Trade Commission provides guides for fair pricing. But those guidelines are not necessarily comprehensive, precise statements of law or detailed statements of the FTC's enforcement policies. Because of this situation, many practices that do not fall within the scope of the guides may be prosecuted under Section 5 of the FTC Act.

For example, in the Mary Carter Paint Company case, it was decided that, because the company had never sold single cans of paint, it could not be permitted to advertise every second can as *free*.

Warranties and guarantees are being considered as a part of the pricing structure. Representations do not need to be made directly by a seller to a buyer. A large automobile company distributed literature, saying that the glass in the windshield of its automobiles was shatterproof. A purchaser of a car was injured when a pebble struck the windshield and shattered the glass. The company was held liable without knowledge or negligence in its statement.

It is unlawful to conspire to restrain trade unreasonably. Although price fixing is unreasonable, *per se*, mere uniformity of price with competitors is not illegal. A company may meet competitive prices at any time. However, any agreement or understanding in any commercial field to change prices is unlawful. Auditors should be aware of the nuances of the laws governing price setting and be prepared to inform management and legal advisers of possible unwitting or deliberate violations.

There have been many violations of price fixing reported in the press. Fields in which violations were found include electrical equipment, steel, chemicals, retail trade, and many others. Many of these cases are settled by pleas of no contest and fines against participating companies up to $50,000. Individuals have been fined and imprisoned. The major economic consequences to a corporation found guilty of price fixing are possible civil suits for treble damages in accordance with antitrust laws.

It is in the corporation's best interests to avoid such involvement. An auditor should report any such illegal activity by company personnel to management and the legal counsel of the organization.

international pricing

Another area that may present future problems for international companies is the pricing of their products in world markets. Some countries are questioning the prices charged in their markets compared with others. Those companies which allocate profits fairly among subsidiaries probably will have few difficulties. Those which have flagrantly unfair transfer pricing may find themselves in trouble. There are, of course, myriad difficulties for outside investigators in detecting transfer-price manipulation. Internal auditors may find it worthwhile to check for glaring inequities.

special claims controls

Defrauders have many opportunities to file claims against an organization. Some of the fraudulent claims successfully perpetrated are primary; some are secondary. Claims filed with a third party under an experience-rated insurance coverage come under the latter category.

There are situations where part-time employees draw unemployment benefits against the employer's account while working for him. Depending upon the circumstances, state laws provide relief from such charges against experience-rated coverage. Careful checks of charges should be made.

A Personnel Department clerk submitted fictitious major medical claims using real last names of noneligible salaried people along with false first names. She used photocopies of modified medical reports of actual cases to substantiate the false claims and then forged the department head's approval. The clerk marked the claim *rush* and asked that it be returned to her. She had prepared one of these false claims—averaging $500—each month for more than a year. A review of cancelled checks showed the clerk's signature as a second endorsement on each false claim. She left a clue in each case.

An insurance company claim supervisor, investigating the reported thefts of cars, developed a profitable scheme. He paid off insureds promptly with insurance company checks and then arranged for the insureds to notify him if the cars were recovered. He made arrangements for an auto dealer to buy recovered cars and kept the proceeds. The scheme was uncovered when an assured noted that the theft claim experience report did not show any salvage recovery. Control over salvage needed improvements.

security over negotiable instruments

A clerical employee appropriated several checks from a local office. She forged some of them, making them payable to her and her friends. She passed the checks after she had resigned her position. When he reconciled his bank account, the office controller discovered this operation. The employee was identified by the writing on the checks. She had passed some of the checks through her uncle, who cashed them at the garage where he worked. Since he had to repay the garage owner, the uncle talked freely.

Prompt and careful reconciliation by the controller continues, but it is unlikely that a method will be found to prevent this type of fraud. Prosecution was considered but the local police said that they had too many other things to do.

A temporary employee was used to type drafts in a service office during vacation time. She typed drafts payable to fictitious persons—Jessie Jameson, for example—and signed fictitious names. These were cashed in various bars. Finally, a cashier recognized a fictitious signature and refused payment. However, this came to light only after several hundred dollars had been paid.

Temporary employees in sensitive jobs, such as those with access to blank drafts, should be checked through regular hiring practices. This employee had not been screened. Had she been checked, it would have been found she had a 30-year record and served time in federal, state, and local penal institutions. At the time of this fraud, she was on probation for forgery, so no trial was held. She was returned to prison for violation of probation.

A mail-room employee stole checks from outgoing mail. Some were payroll checks; others were regular disbursements. The thefts were discovered when the payroll checks failed to arrive at their destinations. After a local bank caught a person attempting to cash a check with a forged endorsement, the operation was found to be the work of a ring of professional check passers.

More careful scrutiny of mail-room employees was necessary. For a time, checks formerly mailed in window envelopes were sent in nonwindow envelopes. Then it was decided to use window envelopes again to eliminate typing costs.

Do not take printing security for granted. An employee of a printing firm intentionally caused an overrun of a check-printing order. He then stole the excess checks, and, after forging some of them, passed them in Connecticut and New York. Since the depository bank in New York had not been told that newly-numbered checks were to be used, it returned the forged checks to the paying banks.

To assist the depository bank in identifying additional forged checks, the company decided not to use any more checks from that printing run. Instead it printed new checks in a different color and with different numbers.

The printer subsequently learned that not only was the employee on federal probation when he was hired but that a warrant for his arrest on forgery charges had been in existence for a number of years. The printer agreed to improve employee selection and security methods.

Office security and inventory are important. When thieves broke into a branch office and looted a soft drink machine, branch officials assumed that cash from the machine was all that was taken.

However, during the normal course of operations, when paid items could not be matched to a processed voucher at the end of the month, officials determined that the thieves also stole a number of blank checks.

Meanwhile, the checks were forged for amounts ranging from $150 to $197, and, with the aid of a stolen credit card, were cashed in a two-day period at a number of banks. The total of the forged checks cashed came to $12,000. Officials also found that more blank drafts were stolen than those passed, but, after the two-day period, no further checks were passed.

The theft and forgery appeared to be the work of professionals. If reasonable office security measures had been taken—the blank checks locked up and a perpetual inventory of them maintained—it would have been apparent that the checks had been stolen and the check numbers would have been recorded.

kickbacks

A kickback is the return of a part of the money received as pay, commission, or profit as a result of a previous understanding or coercion. It is a form of bribery that is usually difficult for the auditors of the purchasing organization to detect. When kickback is discovered by those auditors, the discovery is usually the result of a tip from an informant.

When an auditor finds solid evidence of sales representatives bribing purchasing agents of prospective or present customers, it is unconscionable for him not to protest such action in the strongest terms. Such a protest is not merely altruistic. The organization that permits such payments may be too naive for its own best interests.

A small supplier employed three salesmen. One salesman was more productive than the others mainly because he had demanded and received several prime accounts. Later he told his employer that it would be necessary to pay off a certain purchasing agent of a large manufacturer, his best customer, or lose the account. The supplier, consequently, began to make regular payments of $500 by check to his salesman and charged them to travel expenses. After cashing the checks, the salesman reported that he was turning over the money to the purchasing agent.

A friend of the supplier knew the manufacturer's auditor and mentioned to him that it didn't seem right to have to buy business that way.

The auditor made a thorough investigation of all purchasing activities. He found that the purchasing agent under suspicion had been on sick leave when the payments reportedly had been made and that another agent was in charge during that period. The auditor finally concluded that the salesman was lying and was pocketing the money.

Kenneth J. Bryza annually controlled about $40,000,000 in International Harvester Company purchase contracts. In June 1974, he was indicted for accepting more than $30,000 in kickbacks from representatives of companies making assembly-line parts for International Harvester. Bryza subsequently was discharged by International Harvester but soon became sales manager for another company.

Two of the six companies Bryza had victimized disclosed the kickback schemes. The other four companies remained silent. William Elsbury, an assistant US attorney on the case, said the kickbacks were a percentage of sales and were paid directly to either Bryza or to a fictitious Charles W. Morgan, supposedly the head of Searsport Company, a dummy corporation.

Bryza was found guilty on 39 counts of mail fraud. On February 26, 1975, he was sentenced to 177 days in federal prison and fined $5,000. In addition, he was placed on probation for two-and-one-half years. Following his sentencing, Bryza made a significant statement. He said he knew what he had done violated International Harvester policy but he did not realize he had violated federal law.

Trade associations have established standards of conduct and, in some cases, have the power to discipline members. In 1974, the International Air Transport Association fined 17 major airlines a total of $296,000 for alleged misdealings, including kickbacks to travel agents.

In April 1974, government investigators reported that they uncovered firm evidence that as much as $500,000 in illegal payments had been made to employees of Grumman Corporation from 1970 to 1973. They reported that companies in the technical writing field had kicked back substantial sums of money— averaging from 5% to 10% of a contract's face value—for inside information and the influence of Grumman program managers. The president of one such company was given a jail sentence, a fine of $10,000, and two years on probation.

Kickbacks are found in almost all types of business; and the payments are not only in cash but in cars, trips, real estate, etc.

A 1975 survey of a selected sample of 91 members of The Institute of Internal Auditors showed that 85 thought that an internal auditor should participate in the investigation of kickbacks. Two disagreed that this was a function of internal auditors, and four expressed no opinion.

relationships between sellers and customers' employees

In some industries, sales managers offer bonuses, prizes, trips, etc., to employees of their customers or dealers. These are not kickbacks paid under the table but well-publicized sales contests. Properly designed and operated, they are beneficial to seller, dealer, and sales people.

Some sellers, however, offer gifts to customer employees. They base the size of the reward on the increase in the volume of sales recorded by the seller to the dealer and not on the sales by the dealer to his customers. Several kinds of abuse may follow.

In one instance where trips abroad were offered for the attainment of a set goal of purchases from sellers, dealer employees purchased heavily. They increased the dealer's inventory, but made little effort to move the goods.

In another case, dealer branch managers worked together to consolidate purchases so that a different manager collected the reward each year. Of course, the dealer had to pay the freight to redistribute the purchases to a normal pattern. The rewards announced as a sales contest among salesmen were accepted by supervisory personnel who could influence purchases by dealers.

This did not disturb the seller since those who can influence purchasing tend to favor products offering the greatest personal reward. In effect, the supplier and supervisors, working in tandem to create overstocks and additional freight costs for inventory redistribution, defrauded the dealers.

conflicts of interest

It is difficult for many people to properly divide their allegiance between their employer and their personal interests. Some rationalize that what is good for one can be equally good for the other.

■ After a purchasing agent tried unsuccessfully to find a supplier of a particular article needed by his company, he decided to design it himself in accordance with company specifications. Since his idea was original, he was able to patent it. He had another company manufacture the article under a license arrangement giving him a profit and then purchased the needed quantities for his employer. Within three months tho background of this deal came to light.

Was this a foozle or a fraud? Did he perform a service for his employer by acquiring a needed article which could not otherwise be obtained? Did his job responsibilities include product design of a patentable nature?

■ In a similar case, an internal auditor, reviewing a deal involving the purchase of technical know-how, sensed some irregularities and investigated further. An employee with authority to make certain contracts for the company had arranged the purchase. The company paid $50,000 for part ownership of a patent. The auditor learned that the payment went to an uncle of the employee, and further discovered that the uncle did not own the patent. The endorsement on the check led the auditor to the employee, who turned out to be the true owner of the patent.

■ An insurance company clerk, noting that 30 to 40 checks were being sent to an investigative agency each month, suggested that one check, covering all payments, be sent monthly. The suggestion prompted an investigation which revealed that the agency had been incorporated by the insurance company claims manager, his wife, and a front man. Although the agency did some productive investigation on three fraudulent claims, resulting in significant recoveries, most cases assigned to the agency by the claims manager were trivial. Some even involved closed claims.

■ Some companies ask supervisors and other key employees to complete a questionnaire regarding possible conflicts of interest.

A survey of 102 internal auditors asking whether their organizations have such a program showed that 60% do. Approximately 30% do not. The rest of the auditors did not respond to this question. Only 18% said that internal auditors review the completed questionnaires. Most of the respondents (52) said they felt such questionnaires are not a good source of information for detecting potential fraud. Nearly one third (33) said that a review of the completed questionnaires is worthwhile. The remaining 17 did not give an opinion on this question.

computer frauds

■ Joseph A. Barry, a mess steward in the British Army, was discovered misapplying funds entrusted to him. He was court-martialed and discharged from the service.

In 1967 he obtained a position with Barclays Unicorn Ltd., a subsidiary of Barclays Bank. Unicorn manages a large number of unit trusts. In 1969, Barry began to enter bogus transactions into computer records. In 1972 there were indications that some staff members were backdating their own investments to obtain the benefit of share-price changes. The department conducted a limited investigation but did not report its findings to corporate inspectors. At that time, Barry's immediate supervisor reprimanded him for alleged improper actions. Yet, within a few weeks, Barry was promoted, on someone's recommendation, to computer liaison officer, a position of even greater trust.

Barry was a compulsive gambler. He had lost nearly £80,000 to the turf accountants in the betting shops of England. To support his addiction, he stole from the Savings Department at the Forest Gate office through his system of bogus computer entries. He confessed to the theft of £65,930 (about $160,000 US) when Scotland Yard's fraud squad caught him in 1974.

When Judge Corcoran sentenced Barry to five years in jail, he said in his courtroom at the Old Bailey: "I am drawn to the irresistible conclusion . . . that the company's administrative and supervisory staff, together with the procedure adopted for selecting suitable and responsible staff, was lamentable."

He could have added that the company did not investigate thoroughly indications in 1972 that employees were back-dating their own investments for personal profit at company expense.

■ One of the most widely publicized computer frauds occurred at a bank in a major city. An individual, still unknown, substituted his own electronically coded forms for the regular deposit slips at the customer writing desks in the bank. Since the bank computer credited deposits according to the precoded forms, every customer using a deposit slip from the supply at the desks deposited his funds in the culprit's account. After only three days, the thief withdrew $100,000 and disappeared.

■ A large manufacturer installed a computer system for purchasing and receiving activities. The computer was programmed to generate priced purchase orders when the quantities wanted from specific suppliers were entered. Then, after invoices and receiving tickets were received, the computer would match the quantities and dollar value. If the figures agreed, the invoices were approved for payment.

The company purchased large quantities of certain parts from one supplier. An auditor, checking that supplier's invoice prices against prices in his latest catalog, found prices had fallen an average of 20%. The company, however, was still paying the higher prices.

Further investigation revealed that a Purchasing Department clerk had failed to reduce unit prices in the computer program. This oversight caused purchase orders to go out at the higher prices. Over an 18-month period, it also meant that the company had been paying tens of thousands of dollars too much for those parts.

The supplier was asked why he had billed the company at the higher purchase order prices rather than at his own lower catalog prices. He said his billing clerk thought that since the purchase order had been prepared by a computer, the prices must be correct. Therefore, the billing was prepared from the purchase orders.

As a result of the investigation, the supplier gave the company a credit for the overbilling. Still, it was impossible to determine whether the entire situation was merely a *foozle*—the result of too much dependence on a computer—or a long-time deception.

■ There have been instances where a computer system printer was triggered to create false documents. It was reported that a West German computer operator running a payroll caused his own check to be printed out 200 times. All checks, of course, had the same number. When the operator tried to cash a bundle of the checks at one time, a bank teller recognized the implausibility of so many checks for the same amount and with the same number. The computer operator was arrested.

■ Another printer foozle: A manufacturer sells product *A* with 120 units to a package. There are 10 packages or 1,200 units to a carton. A dealer, anticipating he would receive 1,200 units, ordered 10 packages. In error, an operator in the manufacturer's computer-billing area entered the order for 10 cartons (12,000 units). When the shipping notice was received in the stock and shipping area, the shipper knew that 12,000 units would be far too many for the customer to use within a reasonable time. The quantity also exceeded his own stock, so he changed the notice and shipped 10 packages (1,200 units). When the dealer's Receiving Department checked in the 1,200 units, the shipment agreed with the purchase order, so the shipping ticket that accompanied the goods was approved. However, the invoice was processed for 12,000 units. The dealer paid it since his Receiving Department had approved the receipt of the goods. Subsequently, an auditor discovered the error and recovered more than $10,000 from the manufacturer.

■ Donn B. Parker, senior information processing analyst at Stanford Research Institute's Information Science Laboratory, wrote an interesting report on computer misuse. The report, *Computer Abuse*, was issued by SRI and lists many computer frauds. The National Technical Information Service of the US Department of Commerce later assumed publication of the report.

credit-card frauds

Most credit-card frauds amount to only a few hundred dollars, but occasionally one will involve a spectacular loss.

One of the most unusual of these classic cases is that of Michael Henson. Henson was 18 years old in 1973, when he *borrowed* a friend's credit card to finance a trip from New York to Orlando, Florida. He was a soft-spoken, meek young man from unpretentious surroundings in New York City—the exact opposite of the debonair, suave, cosmopolitan-type normally cast as the master swindler.

Using the *borrowed* credit card, he flew to London on October 5 and back to New York soon after. A short time later he flew to Paris via London. He returned soon to New York and left again on the same day for Madrid. From Madrid he visited two African countries and Lisbon. Then he returned to New York and continued on to Los Angeles, Hawaii, and Hong Kong.

During his visit to Hong Kong, he stayed in a $135-a-day room. He attempted to purchase two diamond rings for $21,000, but the jeweler refused to deliver them until Henson's checks cleared. Michael never picked up the rings. Instead, he flew to Singapore and then on to Greece. There he passed three more checks for $25,000 each by converting them into valid traveler's checks.

His less-than-a-month-long excursion ended in Orlando, his original destination. There, a motel clerk became suspicious of Henson's credit card. He called representatives of the credit-card company and learned that the card had been reported stolen. Police staked out Henson's motel room and arrested him on October 23. Evidence found in his room indicated he had used stolen and forged businesslike checks and a check-writing machine.

An interesting insight into the operations of such a fraud is that most of the victims parted with money, services, air transportation, and hotel facilities on a major scale without checking the validity of Henson's documents. The jeweler would not relinquish the rings until the checks cleared, yet that amount in cash was obtained three times without apparent difficulty.

Following his guilty plea to a mail fraud charge, Henson was sentenced to three years in federal prison. Although authorities estimate that he cashed $200,000-worth of bad checks, his global caper might have cost his victims as much as $500,000. When arrested, Henson had only a small amount of money. No one has ever learned what happened to the rest.

arson

It is a well known fact that arson is the cause of one-third of all fires reported. What is not so well known is that arson is often used to perpetrate or to cover up fraud.

The simplest type of *arson accounting* was practiced in an eastern United States community. Basically, it went like this:

> Two men bought inexpensive buildings, insured them for four times their net worth, and then burned them. Within two years, they destroyed 11 houses and two barns—a property loss exceeding $150,000. When they staged an auto accident and claimed personal injuries, an investigation led to their connection with the fires.

While it is certainly not the function of auditors to make a decision on the cause of a fire, they may well become involved in claims for business losses—inventories, receivables, payables, etc.

If fire destroys business records, the auditor may have to reconstruct statements from outside sources such as customers and vendors. Even if the records are available, the auditor should be cautious when establishing inventory values by a gross profit method. Consider these possibilities:

- Goods may have been moved to a safe place prior to a fire without a record of the move being made.

- Deliveries from suppliers may have been diverted by direct shipment to customers without being reflected in the accounts. Such sales may have been recorded in another set of books.

- Slow-moving, obsolete, or unsalable merchandise in a previous inventory may have been priced too high. This has the double effect of creating (1.) an abnormally high gross profit margin which could be the basis of a low cost-of-sales deduction from purchases and (2.) an overstatement of values allegedly lost through fire or water damage.

Don't overlook the fact that arson is sometimes used to cover up embezzlement. As a result, substantial losses may be incurred.

A corporate president and nine other people were indicted on federal charges of dynamiting his corporation's manufacturing plant. Not only did insurance claims from the destruction of the plant reach a reported $18,000,000 but 900 plant employees lost their jobs.

credit frauds

Most Sales Department and Credit Department personnel can recognize ploys that customers use to obtain credit or to extend credit limits.

Occasionally, someone who has been a good customer for years will run into financial difficulties. Often, the person will try to cover the difficulties by misleading the supplier's credit manager with tall tales of impending success. Meanwhile, the past-due account continues to grow.

One credit fraud case involved a sales representative working with a manufacturer on a five percent commission. Under normal operating procedure, the sales representative sold merchandise which was then delivered by the manufacturer directly to customers.

The rep convinced the sales manager to supply him with a small stock of merchandise on an open account. He pointed out that he could make rush deliveries which would increase sales. The two agreed that the rep would make payments on the account only when he needed to replenish his stock. The sales manager assured the Credit Department that everything was all right. And since he and the rep were close friends, no questions were asked.

When the rep found that he could make a 20% profit on sales from the stock, he increased his inventory rapidly, hired some employees, and set up his own operation. The initial stock ran his open account to about $20,000 on which he paid nothing. Within a couple of years, he owed nearly $500,000.

The sales manager's assurances that everything was all right did not satisfy the manufacturer's internal auditor. He decided to look into the rep's operation.

A letter from the credit manager advised the sales rep of the auditor's visit. By the time the auditor arrived, the rep had sold fixtures, equipment, and automobiles and had left the country. The auditor found three different sets of books and less than $75,000 in tangible assets, including inventory and receivables. After salvaging everything possible, the auditor recommended that slightly more than $400,000 be written off.

It is always vital to know with whom you are dealing. Credit fraud rings have purchased reputable firms with high credit ratings. They then order large quantities of goods on credit and never pay for them. After selling the merchandise, the rings disappear, leaving the corporation as an empty shell. One such ring cost several suppliers $1,000,000 for goods purchased on credit.

Similar schemes are worked by diverting assets and then allowing the corporation to become bankrupt.

Such experiences point out the need for internal auditors to review credit worthiness, circumstances behind an extension of credit when there are large past-due balances, and any departure from standard operating procedures.

bribery

The most publicized examples of bribery concern people in the public eye.

Politics — Courts have convicted state governors of accepting bribes to influence the investing of state funds in certain financial institutions. Bribers have reached municipal officers who have, in turn, changed zoning laws or assigned profitable concessions to them. Legislators have accepted bribes in exchange for their votes for or against certain bills.

Athletics — Sports figures have taken bribes to throw games or matches or to "shave" points.

Finance — People in the financial world have accepted bribes to tout certain securities or to influence the purchase of certain securities by their employers.

Government — A banker seeking government mortgage money for bank-owned property pleaded guilty to bribing government employees in exchange for high appraisals of that property. In order to land a multimillion dollar construction job, contractors bribed a government employee to guarantee a surety bond.

Banking — A speculator was charged with bribing a bank officer to approve a loan.

One of the largest bribes on record was made by a company president to a head of state in exchange for favorable tax treatment for his company.

The executive officer of any company has a most difficult decision to make when it comes to paying extortion demands or suffering the consequences if he does not pay.

What is the internal auditor's role? If internal auditors uncover the fact that their company is paying a bribe, they should attempt to learn the circumstances involved in the bribe and to whom it is being paid. Above all, they should make sure that top management is aware of the situation.

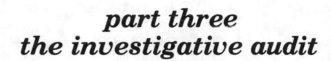

part three
the investigative audit

chapter eleven

activation of the audit

Signals of improper or illegal activity within an organization may come to anyone at anytime. Such signals may be received by management, by security people, or by auditors. It is not vitally important just who receives the signals. The important thing is that whoever receives them recognizes them for what they are and investigates them immediately and judiciously.

When, for example, management or the Audit Committee of the Board of Directors hears about frauds perpetrated in other companies, they may ask their auditors to look into their company operations to see if the potential exists for similar breaches of control.

People write to presidents of organizations with complaints about the product, service, charges, credit pressures, etc. Employees write, often anonymously, about things they think are not right within their group. Other persons will seek out someone in the organization in whom they feel they can confide and relate irregular activities that they have witnessed in the expectation that the information will be passed to someone in a position to act on the matter.

Those who have the perception to recognize the signal of a grave irregularity can perform a useful service by relaying the information to a person skilled in account analysis: the auditor. One divisional manager who was informed by an outsider that there was incontrovertible evidence that one of his purchasing agents was accepting kickbacks replied: "Who cares; everybody has a racket." The communication ended there. How grave was this irregularity? Why did the divisional manager respond in this way? Did his reply constitute a signal in itself? One can only speculate.

A more likely response to a bit of information about a probable fraud sent to a top officer is for him to confer with the chief auditor who is supplied with all known facts. Because top management can never be certain how far up in the organization the irregularity goes, it is best to keep the details confidential until an audit is made.

It is usually best for the auditors to announce a routine audit at an unexpected time. Under the guise of a routine audit, the auditor can concentrate on the suspected area.

In one instance, it was necessary for the corporate auditors to initiate a special investigation of a division just a few months after the regular annual audit was completed. The divisional auditor wasn't told why a certain department was being given extra attention, and he complained to his controller that the corporate auditors were wasting their time. He was a long-time, close friend of the head of the department under investigation. He claimed that he had recently given that department a very thorough audit and that everything was in excellent order. Two days later, both the department head and the assistant department head confessed to a complicated embezzlement. The importance of revealing solid information about fraudulent activities in a specific area to only a few involved people cannot be overemphasized.

The auditor should activate an investigation of a specific situation under any one of the following circumstances:

- He may receive complete information or just a hint. Many people are torn between their moral standards and their reluctance to get involved. Some try to ease their conscience by making vague references to something wrong, while holding back the vital details. The auditor knows that the would-be informer wants to talk, but he also knows that it won't take much to scare him away since he may be under a severe emotional strain. A casual approach with a few open-ended questions is often the best way to obtain specific information.

- In the course of a regular audit that includes all the aspects of a financial or operational audit, the auditor may find vouchers that appear altered or which lack proper support: abnormal changes in accounts; shortages in cash, inventories, or other assets; mathematical errors; omitted entries; unusual write-offs; or other deviations. Poor housekeeping, laxity in handling customers' orders, and many back orders are proof of poor management and provide opportunities for employee theft. In one instance, a manager in charge of a branch operation was an alcoholic. Housekeeping had deteriorated badly, and it was found that three of the 15 employees were stealing from the company.

- An auditor should take advantage of any opportunity to learn from customers if there is an indication of any irregularities. Attendance at trade shows, customer meetings, and visits with sales people when they call on customers are good ways to learn of improprieties. Sometimes accompanying credit personnel when they visit customers whose accounts are past due will uncover improper transactions that remain unresolved. In these circumstances, the auditor should maintain a low profile with customers and not aggressively interrogate clients.

■ Those who volunteer information may do so only with the understanding that they not be identified as the source of the facts they give the auditor. In a desire to get information, a pledge to keep the source of the "facts" may be given too readily. If the auditor is not in a position to guarantee the anonymity of his source of information, he should not pledge to do so. It may be unwise to extend a pledge to respect the informant's identity before the nature of his accusations are known. If the facts supplied by the informant can be buttressed with solid evidence, the identity of the informant may not be needed. However, a situation may arise wherein the auditor becomes aware of a criminal act; yet because proof is lacking, he cannot proceed to uncover it. In effect, he may tie his hands with a pledge of secrecy.

chapter twelve

the soft query

Once the auditor suspects that something is wrong, he must find out if the irregularity is a foozle or a fraud. For this he needs solid evidence.

At this point, cautious questioning of all suspects is necessary. This is best done by the auditor as part of a "routine" audit. One person may pursue a logical line of inquiry, but two or more may get their lines tangled. There must be a definite objective: an admission of guilt or a credible explanation of why they are not guilty.

The auditor should keep the following rules in mind:

■ Every normal person wants to be regarded in a favorable light. People want their accomplishments to be recognized. Many who steal are really craving appreciation and recognition. Their aberrant behavior may be a result of that lack. A sincere compliment on a positive accomplishment may be the best opener.

■ Frame questions in a way that permits the respondent to explain his reasons for doing specific things the way he does. To justify their actions, people will often tell more than they intend. A good listener will get the information he needs.

■ Know your suspect. Personnel and payroll records will provide background on length of service, number of dependents, former positions held, education, anniversary dates, absenteeism, sicknesses, etc. Be quick to extend congratulations or sympathy on various aspects of his life. Remarks like *Next month you are celebrating your 24th year with the company. That is a record to be proud of* or *Sorry to learn that you have had a lot of sickness in your family lately* will accomplish two objectives. First, the suspect will appreciate your interest. Second, he realizes that the auditor knows a lot about him and that there must be some reason for his having so much knowledge. In more than one case, this simple step has caused the offender to confess to deeds the auditor did not even suspect, because the suspect thought that the auditor already knew the whole truth.

■ Direct the conversation to the area of the indicated irregularities. Keep probing until resistance sets in. Then quickly change to subjects which will keep the suspect talking. People tend to talk about the things in which they are interested: their ambitions, desires, hopes, family, friends, obligations, problems, hobbies, personal responsibilities, or achievements. Keep them talking. When the opportune moment arrives, return to the probe of the irregularities.

■ Be considerate of your suspect's reputation and do not impugn his character, integrity, ability, or morals.

■ An auditor's pleasant, confident, and considerate manner will influence the other person favorably. But the auditor has a job to do, so he must be firm and proceed at a deliberate pace so that the suspect will feel the importance of the questioning.

■ Accounting records carry much, but not all, of the pertinent information about a company. The questioning should include those areas not covered by book records. For example:

1. Unbooked sales, expenses, assets, and liabilities
2. Returns to suppliers not recorded
3. Uncollected old accounts and bad debts written off
4. Rebates due but not booked
5. Status of deposits on bids, utility services, containers, etc.
6. Scrap sales not booked or underbooked
7. Quantity discounts lost
8. Unauthorized access to premises after hours
9. Loose loading-dock controls
10. Lost cash discounts

At some point in these discussions, it may be appropriate to show the suspect *a part, but not all,* of any documents that appear to have been altered or false and ask for an explanation.

In one case, false vouchers were prepared for about four years in order to support a salesman's request for reimbursement of traveling expenses. He had purchased a pad of blank receipts. Each week he would prepare a receipt for motel expenses on the same form but make them out for different motels in different cities. The receipts purported to be signed by different motels, but each was signed "per CB." The use of the same form and the same cashier at all of the motels at which he claimed to have stayed was not noticed for over 200 weeks. When four of them were laid out before him and when he was told that a few phone calls had disclosed that there were no motels by those names in the locations he gave, he admitted that he had falsified his vouchers for the entire four years.

In a good percentage of the cases where the auditor pursues a determined line of questioning, the suspect will choose to go to his superior and admit his guilt rather than to the auditor.

In one such case, an auditor showed a suspect a piece of evidence that could not be readily explained. As it was late in the day, the auditor said that he wanted a valid explanation the first thing the next morning. The suspect left the room, went to his employer, and said that the auditor had to have an explanation of irregularities by the next morning and that he couldn't give an answer that would satisfy the auditor as he had been embezzling for several years. The suspect had worked for his employer for over 30 years. He found it easier to admit his crime to his victim that he knew well than to a stranger who had uncovered his crime.

Although there is always the possibility of repercussions, an ultimatum sometimes works. In one instance, it was necessary to obtain the personal checks a suspect had written to prove a bribe had been made. The individual repeatedly claimed that he could not find his cancelled checks for the month in question. Finally, the auditor told the suspect to discontinue the search and that the next day they would go to the bank together and ask the bank to furnish photocopies of the missing checks. The next morning the culprit came in with the missing checks, including the crucial one that proved the case.

When an auditor obtains an admission of guilt by these techniques, it is generally best to have the guilty party write out his role in the affair in a letter to his supervisor. Some investigators prefer to have the culprit address his letter: "To whom it may concern." They claim that a cold statement of the facts addressed to no one seems more comfortable to the writer.

In some instances, letters addressed to the supervisor have produced more information, as the culprit tries to explain or to justify his actions and tends to be uncomfortable until it is all down on paper. The auditor can help get the entire story down on paper by suggesting that he or she include why the fraudulent act started, how much was taken, any falsification of records that could affect relations with customers or suppliers, any accomplices, and exactly how it was done. An offer of restitution and the means by which it could be paid should be included. The letter should be voluntarily written, but no conditions of forgiveness or freedom from prosecution should be included.

It has been found that, in most cases, those who respond to the soft-query technique are not habitual criminals and merit better treatment than those who stonewall against solid evidence.

Of course, there are exceptions to every rule. This case is exceptional: One individual, guilty of several offenses, took an entire month to write a 50-page letter explaining his nefarious actions. His family made full restitution, and he was discharged without prosecution. Within a year, he obtained another position and repeated his crimes in much the same way. Again, he was discharged; and, again, his family reimbursed his employer.

The fact remains that those who respond to the soft query are not likely to repeat their crimes.

chapter thirteen

the interrogation

There are times when a soft-query approach will not work, and a different approach must be used. The auditor who interrogates persons suspected of criminal acts should be aware of the legal liability which may result from participation in a fraud investigation. Liabilities may include actions against him and his employer for libel, slander, false arrest, false imprisonment, malicious prosecution, and compounding a felony. Wrongs to the person or property of another are called "torts," and the person committing a tort is a "tortfeasor."

defamation

Libel is written or printed defamation of another, whereas slander is spoken defamation. Three elements are necessary to provide a cause for action. One is that statements must be defamatory or "words injurious to the person's character or reputation or to hold him up to ridicule." The second is "publication" by uttering or showing those words to someone other than the injured person by, or on behalf of, the person accused of being libelous or slanderous. The third element of libel and slander is that the person claiming injury must actually suffer damage as a proximate result of the defamatory statement. Certain words or phrases are inherently defamatory, and damages are presumed to have occurred. No further evidence is required. To say that a person *committed a crime* is one such phrase.

A person who was libeled or slandered maliciously or willfully may recover not only the actual damage that he might have suffered but punitive damages which may be as much as 100 times the actual damages.

The internal auditor may report his findings or suspicions verbally or in writing, whether proven or not, to appropriate officials of his company as a necessary and justified communication. His report is privileged as a legitimate duty of notification to management. Discussion of the case with others who have no need to know may well subject the auditor to libel or slander as the case may be.

false arrest and imprisonment

The auditor should avoid any possibility of causing the false arrest or imprisonment of a suspect or any restraint of free movement. An employer may not use force or threats to restrain an employee from leaving.

Even a momentary restraint in unlocked premises may be construed as false imprisonment. Any interference with the right of another person to move about freely may, unless justified, be considered false imprisonment. Any inconvenience to another, such as preventing him from driving away in his car, may also be ruled as false imprisonment.

malicious prosecution and abuse of process

Malicious prosecution may be claimed by a person tried for a crime but not convicted if he can prove that the person who instituted the criminal proceedings had no reasonable grounds for making the charge. It should be understood that malice need not be ill will. It may be implied from a lack of justification. Abuse of process is "proceeding to prosecute but halting it before actual criminal action is taken in order to force an individual to repay money." The criminal process cannot be used for settlement of private grievances.

restitution risks

Everyone is interested in obtaining restitution. When a perpetrator is willing to admit his guilt and offers restitution on the basis that no action be taken against him, he places those who accuse him in a difficult and dangerous position. The money he took may be gone, and he may be able to pay back what he has stolen over only a fairly long period of time. If he cannot earn enough to make the agreed-upon payments, his promises are worthless. The acceptance of restitution as compensation for not prosecuting may constitute the compounding of a felony by the accuser; and the *accuser* may be charged with a criminal offense, particularly where criminal proceedings have already been instituted.

If the accuser demands restitution with the threat or implied threat of arrest, the accuser might have committed extortion. If the accused or his attorney recognizes either a threat or implied threat of arrest, he has little fear of punishment.

It is tantamount to the admission of guilt to offer restitution to an accuser; therefore, it is an advantage to secure an offer of restitution if it can be done without making any agreements to withhold prosecution or threatening arrest.

surreptitious recordings

Generally, the use of tape recordings is of questionable value. In some states, the recording of conversations without the consent of any party thereto makes the "eavesdropper" guilty of a statutory crime. It is preferable to have a written statement signed by witnesses as to its authenticity.

criminal prosecution

It is the employer's prerogative to prosecute or not, as he has no legal obligation to do so. He may supply information to the police and cooperate fully with them in their investigation but refuse to file a complaint which the police could use to make the arrest. It frequently happens that the police, in their investigation of another illegal operation, will inform an employer of probable irregularities by certain employees before the employer realizes he was defrauded. It may seem unnecessary to say that, in these instances, a prompt and thorough audit of all transactions in which such individuals are involved should be made; yet it is not unusual to find such warnings ignored.

contractual consideration

Some union contracts require either that a representative of the union be present when an employee is being interviewed on suspicion of fraud or that the employee has the right to request a union representative to be present. There have been some instances where management denied an employee these rights and later found that the National Labor Relations Board sustained the employee's request. All employees are entitled to pay while under interrogation and nonexempt employees must be paid at overtime rates if the interrogation takes place after working hours.

the confession

A typical form of confession appears in Exhibit A. Some states have statutory provisions for the admissibility of confessions, and these should be consulted. Confessions are not indisputable evidence. A confession once made can be disavowed if the maker can prove he made it by mistake or that he was frightened, confused, or suffering some mental defect. Another effective defense is a claim that the confession was obtained by coercion. A confession is a complete acknowledgment of guilt, whereas an admission is any relevant statement made by the guilty party which may be introduced in a trial as evidence. To be valid evidence, the confession must have an authenticated signature, proof of execution, and evidence that it is the original or a copy.

Exhibit A

The following format of a confession was devised for our use by a Law Department, and it is suggested that this format be followed in obtaining confessions. Any deviations from this format should be cleared with the manager of internal auditing prior to its use. Our experience has also proven that a confession is of extreme importance when filing a claim with our bonding insurer for the amount of the loss.

STATE OF _____

                : SS:

COUNTY OF_____

BEFORE ME, the undersigned, a notary public, in and for the state and county aforesaid, personally appeared _____ , who being duly sworn according to law, did depose and say as follows:

1. My name is _____ , and I reside at _____

_____

2. I have been employed by the ABC Company, Inc. since

_____ , most recently as _____ at

_____

3. Before making any statement I was advised by _____ , a representative of the ABC Company, Inc. that:

   a. I am not obligated to make any statement whatsoever with respect to matters hereinafter set forth.

   b. I am entitled to consult with and be represented by an attorney before and during the making of any statement by me.

   c. Any statement I make may be used in evidence in any civil or criminal proceeding which may be commenced against me.

4. I am making this statement of my own free will without threat or coercion made or offered directly or indirectly and with a full understanding of my rights as aforesaid, and I hereby expressly waive my right to remain silent and to consult with or be represented by counsel in connection herewith. I have not been offered or promised, directly or indirectly, anything of value in connection with the making of this statement, including, without limiting the generality of the foregoing, any promise on the part of the ABC Company from instituting any criminal information or proceeding under applicable state or federal law.

5. The facts relating to this matter are as follows:

_____

_____

_____

6. This statement was given by me orally in the presence of
_____ , representative of the ABC Company,
Inc., and was reduced to writing by _____ .

7. I have read the foregoing; and the same is true, correct, and
complete and is adopted and affirmed by me. I have further
initialled each page for identification.

SWORN TO and subscribed before me this _____ day of _____ ,

19 _____ .

_____
Notary Public
My Commission Expires:

preparation for the interview

The ideal place to hold an interview of a suspect is an unlocked
room without windows or other means by which others can observe
the discussion. It is desirable that it be sparsely furnished with only
a table and chairs to avoid distractions. It should be as soundproof
as possible. Some psychologists claim that certain color schemes in
the room create an atmosphere which encourages the suspect to
talk. They recommend light shades of green, gray, tan, or blue as
most effective. The best lighting is the recessed-ceiling fluorescent
light with a plain cover. It is well to arrange for no telephone
interruptions. Remove any heavy objects that could be used as a
weapon in case the suspect suddenly turns on his questioners or tries
to harm himself. When interviewing a member of the opposite sex, it
is advisable to have present a person of the same sex as the suspect.
This is protection against possible allegations of improper conduct
by the interviewer.

There are times when such an ideal setup is not possible nor
tactically advisable. In some cases, it is necessary to interview the
suspect at the scene of the crime. There are a few advantages to this
approach. It carries the interview to the spot where the crime
happened, and that very fact may persuade the suspect to admit his
role in it more readily. It has the disadvantages of lack of privacy,
distractions, and possible third-party interference.

Some interviews must, because of circumstances, be held in a
neutral or negative place. A neutral place might be at some

prearranged spot in a public or private area. The most inadvisable place may be the suspect's home with his family or even a clergyman present, the office of the suspect's attorney, or a hospital. The latter possibility of meeting in a hospital is not too far-fetched as many suspects, aware of their imminent detection, become physically ill. In one instance, an auditor conducted the interview by himself in the office of two nonemployee coconspirators of a suspected employee. All three admitted their guilt.

Nevertheless, the auditor should select the most favorable location possible in which to conduct the interview.

The auditor should get all the information he needs in the first interview. In subsequent discussions, the suspect will be prepared to refute the questions or to say: "I told you everything last time." The auditor should plan in advance what he wants to accomplish. His purpose may be to gain information, confirm unknown evidence, tie evidence to the suspects, identify accomplices or eliminate other suspects, determine if there have been other crimes committed of which he was unaware, recover loot, or find out what became of it.

He must be prepared to meet a person who may be hostile, overemotional, reluctant, or even suicidal. The interrogator should have as many facts about the suspect as possible before the interview starts.

the interview

The interview is best conducted by the person who makes the investigation and who is in possession of not only a summary of the facts that were uncovered but all the nuances of the situation. That person should possess an inquisitive mind and be able to follow a logical line of reasoning without being distracted by the suspect's contentiousness or emotionalism. In this type of interview, it is desirable that two or three others be on hand for the interview but that one person be designated to conduct it. These individuals, depending upon the company's organization, may be from the Internal Auditing, Security, or Personnel departments. Line supervisors and legal staff should not be present. Supervisors should be told that a fraud appears to have been committed by one of their people and that the suspect is going to be interviewed.

The purpose of the interview is to learn more about the fraudulent activities. It is possible that some element of management is directly or indirectly involved. Many people steal when they see the boss getting away with something or to offset a real or fancied wrong done to them by their supervisor. In one case, an employee informed management that his supervisor was stealing from the company. An audit proved he was right, but it also proved that the informer was stealing.

At this stage of the investigation, it is better that the suspect not have his attorney present. An attorney would likely advise his client to refuse to answer questions, and the interview would come to naught. If the client does not have his attorney present, the employer should not have his there either.

In one instance, an employee who had joined with others to embezzle a considerable sum refused to discuss his role in the affair with the internal auditor and the division controller until he saw his attorney. The suspect was told that he had that right and that the interview was over. The auditor said that the matter would be referred to the company's attorneys and that the suspect's attorney could get in touch with them. The suspect was told that, if he wished to reconsider, the interview would be reopened. He thought for a moment and said he had decided to discuss the case further without talking to his attorney as he had decided to throw himself on the mercy of his employer.

Something that often gives an insight into the suspect's motivation is his relationship with his family. Probably, in a majority of cases, spouses do not know or realize that their mates are stealing from their employers. But in the case above, the man said he and his wife had planned the illegal operations together. There are many other cases where the wife embezzles to support the gambling habits of the husband. In such cases the husband may be charged with receiving stolen money. As an example, a wife stole nearly $100,000. She was sentenced to a maximum of ten years in prison and was given a $5,000 fine. Her husband was sentenced to ten years in prison and paid a $10,000 fine on a conspiracy charge. The husband was also made responsible for restitution.

Another thing to remember is that the perpetrator of a crime has a natural desire to "tell someone" about it. The interrogator should develop a climate which will help the suspect to talk about it.

In most companies and organizations, the decisions of any action to be taken on possible discharge of the employee, prosecution, claims against the bonding company, etc., are made by top management with the advice of the Legal Department or outside counsel. Therefore, the interrogator must firmly avoid any commitment to the suspect on the disposition of the case. There is usually an attempt by the suspect to "make a deal" with the interrogator in exchange for a bit of information the interrogator wants.

The interrogator must sell the suspect on the idea that the best possible course for him is to give the interrogator complete and honest answers. The benefits that the suspect will gain are peace of mind, relief from fear of detection in the future, and restoration of a clean conscience.

chapter fourteen

evidence

The preparation of evidence for a court trial is often a complex and arduous task which can only be performed by or under the direction of attorneys. Admissible evidence depends upon the nature of the offense and the statutes involved.

It may be that the attorneys will use the auditor's knowledge of a case, final written report, working papers, and exhibits to help them build their case.

For this reason, it is important that the auditor collect as much solid evidence as he can. He should avoid hearsay and rumors. He should collect original documents that are evidence of wrongdoing and carefully authenticate them with times, dates, signatures, descriptions, etc. Photocopies or photographs are so easily faked by temporary or permanent alterations in the original or an intermediate copy that the admissibility of such evidence is usually based on authentication by a witness.

In a case of alleged fraud, the importance of well-prepared audit working papers cannot be overemphasized.

In one instance, an auditor completed his examination and prepared a comprehensive but brief report on his findings. The report was a bland statement of conditions without any strong comments or recommendations. Normally, such a report would be read and filed without much notice. However, in this case a matter related to the audit came up and the working papers were pulled and sent to top management without a second review.

During the audit, the auditor had become suspicious of a foozle and pursued the matter as if it were a potential fraud. On several pages of his working papers, the auditor made incriminating notes that appeared to involve a fairly high level of supervision.

However, as the auditor advanced in his investigation, he found that his original premise was wrong and decided that nothing was improper. To account for the considerable amount of time he had devoted to that phase, he did not remove those pages from his working papers. He felt confident that, by not including the matter in his report, the matter was closed. However, when top management saw those pages, they were disturbed. At first, they couldn't decide if the auditor had found a fraud and not a foozle and wondered if the auditor had lost his courage to report a damaging situation which involved supervisors. They were eventually convinced that there was nothing wrong, but it took a long time to erase the memory of the overexplicit and misleading audit working papers.

In another instance, an auditor discovered shortages in the cash fund and spent several days writing up his notes and schedules in meticulous detail. While the auditor was busy on his working papers, the guilty individual confessed to a supervisor and was terminated. When he turned in his well-written report, the auditor was surprised when he was told that he had everything on the case but the conclusion.

chapter fifteen

attitudes of the profession

In a recent article, Walter E. Hanson[1] said: "The containment of fraud is founded on three closely related functions: (1) a strong, involved, investigative Board of Directors; (2) a sound, comprehensive system of internal controls; and (3) alert, capable independent auditors .... In all my years in the accounting profession, I have not seen any case of sizable management fraud where all three functions were pursued with full diligence and professionalism." He added: "Working hand in hand with the Audit Committee (of the Board of Directors) are the financial officers of the company and the entire internal audit team. Needless to say, this team must be competent and conscientious. But it also must be dedicated, aggressive, and creative."

In the 1975 survey on fraud described earlier, about 70% of those who expressed an opinion on the question "Should internal auditors have the responsibility for uncovering material fraud in the records of his employer?" said "yes." The questionnaire asked that the dictionary definition of the word "responsibility" be used in the reply but also asked for the respondent's definition.

Those voting yes made the following comments:

While the auditor should not be completely responsible, he should certainly be doing a significant part.

He should not have responsibility for fraud prevention but should be capable of detecting fraud.

---

[1]Senior partner of Peat, Marwick, Mitchell & Co. in the *Financial Executive,* March 1975.

Fraud discoveries may come from many sources. The auditors, of course, should be ever alert and promote preventive measures also.

Those which have such impacts as to create signals which a reasonable person should detect in the course of his assigned tasks.

In actual practice, the Internal Audit Department uncovers nine out of ten defalcations.

Uncovering pilferage or fraud is not the key; having the opportunity and the freedom to report it is.

Auditors should have the responsibility of looking for internal fraud but not necessarily of detecting it.

Our Security Department is also involved in uncovering fraud.

In banking, fraud work by the auditor is pretty much routine.

If the internal auditor isn't the principal one responsible, who should it be?

Collusion frauds make the term 'responsibility' a bit strong.

The auditor uses tests to determine adequacy of records. The tests performed should be sufficient in scope to uncover material fraud.

Those voting no made the following comments:

They should have this responsibility as a part of their job, but it should not be the responsibility of this group alone.

I feel that internal auditors should be responsible for investigating fraud, whether discovered by the auditor or operations people, but not the responsibility for uncovering various types of frauds.

Controls should indicate fraud. An auditor should follow through when discovered.

I had a hard time answering this. He should get most material frauds; but it is conceivable that, on a testing basis, no evidence of fraud would show up.

The auditor should be on the alert for such things but cannot be held responsible.

Reliance on the auditor to detect fraud or error is not a reliable feature of control either in practice or law.

The questionnaire included the following question: "In your opinion, should an internal auditor's responsibility include

participation in the investigation of the conditions listed below?"
The answers are rearranged to show the largest number of yes
answers first and the rest in declining order. The last five questions
received a minority negative response.

	Yes	No	No Answer
Kickbacks	95	1	6
Conflicts of interest	90	7	5
Slow receivables and bad debt charge-offs	89	6	7
Excessive entertainment charged to company	87	7	8
Bad or insufficient-fund checks	85	7	10
Gifts or bribes to secure business	83	5	14
Inaccurate financial statements to be used to improve apparent profitability of a subsidiary or a division and, thus, deceive top management	82	2	18
Payoffs to government regulatory personnel	70	13	19
Inaccurate financial statements to be used to obtain bank credit	70	7	25
Consistent shortages in weights of product	69	2	31
Very extravagant living habits of management people	69	22	11
Unfair credit practices	67	6	29
Inaccurate financial statements to be used to influence price of company stocks	65	7	30
Underbidding on contracts with the intention of supplying inferior products or other shortcuts	59	5	38
Illegal contributions to political parties	58	20	24
Unfair treatment or discrimination of employees	57	38	7
Marketing defective merchandise	50	19	33
Illegal price fixing	47	16	39
Excessive alcoholism of supervision	47	48	7
Antitrust activity	40	30	32
False advertising claims	38	29	35

Leonard M. Savoie, a CPA with Price Waterhouse & Co., in an
article on business ethics in the *NAA Bulletin* (April 1965),
included this thought in his paper:

*Moral suasion. For an idealist who is not directly in charge of an
organization, moral suasion can perhaps accomplish much in the
way of elevating and maintaining high moral and ethical
standards among his peers and superiors. As one who is really
dedicated to the cause of high ethics and not just giving it lip
service, he has the opportunity to serve as the moral conscience of
business.*

chapter sixteen

honesty insurance

coverage

The functions of auditors and surety companies are complementary. Honesty insurance is of no value if the loss is not detected and the extent of the theft determined. The auditor can, through his investigation, disclose the fraudulent act and calculate the loss. Those who claim that investigative audits are unnecessary if adequate fidelity insurance is carried are akin to those who buy a flashlight but do not buy batteries. Both in the blackness say: "You see, we have no problems." An audit does not insure against losses from dishonesty, but it can be the means by which fidelity insurance can replace that which was taken.

One retail business was on the verge of bankruptcy when, too late, an auditor was called in to analyze the condition of the business. He found that the business had been plundered by a few employees for tens of thousands of dollars. There was no fidelity insurance nor any hope of restitution. The business was liquidated with sizable losses to creditors and no proceeds to the owner.

Blanket fidelity bonds constitute about three-quarters of all coverage. To carry an inadequate amount of coverage or to bond only a few, rather than all, employees is equally unsatisfactory.

Forms of bonds available for commercial concerns include:

- Individual bond
- Name schedule
- Position schedule

- Commercial blanket

- Blanket position

The purpose of fidelity bonds is to indemnify the employer for loss of money and other property through the dishonest acts of his bonded employee. This insurance covers larceny, theft, embezzlement, forgery, misappropriation, wrongful abstraction, willful misapplication, or other dishonest acts of the employee alone or in collusion. The fidelity bond is not an all-risk form. There are other forms which provide fidelity coverage as part of other coverages. Examples of multiple protection are the Comprehensive Dishonesty, Disappearance, and Destruction Policy and the Blanket Crime Policy.

The Individual Bond was the most common form in the early part of the 20th Century. It is still used where only a few employees are involved. It is for a stated amount on a named employee. It had many advantages. It was a status symbol to have it known that one held an important position that had to be bonded. The larger the bond, the higher the status. It also had the advantage that prospective employees, when told that the position to be filled depended upon the applicant's being able to qualify for a bond, would not seek the position if their past record showed any evidence of dishonesty.

The two types of schedule bonds are somewhat similar. The Name Schedule Bond covers the employees by name for stated amounts, regardless of the position they may hold. In effect, it is like the Individual Bond but gathers them into one policy. The Position Schedule Bond supplies protection against the dishonest acts of employees occupying certain specified positions such as cashiers, bookkeepers, etc., at stipulated amounts for each position; but the employees in those positions are not identified by name.

Under the schedule form of bond, salvage may be applied ratably; or the employer may be completely indemnified first, depending upon the terms of the bond.

Under schedule bonds, the period of time in which the employer may discover a loss after termination of the employment of the guilty employee or termination or cancellation of the bond varies, depending upon the terms of the bond.

The Commercial Blanket Bond covers all employees and officers. It may be issued to any employer other than a financial institution or a public official. Payment of loss for any one employee does not reduce the amount of coverage available for other losses. The premium rate for additional coverage is reduced as the penalty of the bond is increased. Coverage starts from a stated minimum and is somewhat broader than in schedule bonds. For example, it provides indemnification by the surety for losses of property or money for which the insured may be liable legally or otherwise. Under the Commercial Blanket Bond, the insured is reimbursed for any excess loss he may sustain before the surety may participate in salvage.

Under this form of bond, the discovery period is uniformly 12 months after cancellation of the entire bond.

Specific excess indemnity may be purchased for additional protection on selected individuals in key positions.

The Blanket Position Bond has a collusive-loss feature. For example, under a $10,000 Blanket Position Bond, if five employees acting in collusion stole $50,000, the full loss would be recoverable if all five were identified. Under a Commercial Blanket Bond for $10,000, liability would be limited to that amount, regardless of whether the five were identified. Of course, a $50,000 Commercial Blanket Bond would cover that loss. The Blanket Position Bond is as broad in coverage as the Commercial Blanket Bond; but, after termination, it allows the employer two years instead of one to discover the loss.

A comprehensive Dishonesty, Disappearance, and Destruction Policy covers employee dishonesty as well as other risks. It is available to any assured except public officials or organizations eligible for a banker's or broker's bond. This policy covers employee dishonesty on either a commercial-blanket-bond type or a blanket-position-bond type of coverage. It also covers inside robbery, safe burglary, or losses of money or securities within the premises by destruction, disappearance, or wrongful abstraction. Losses of money or securities while being conveyed by messenger are covered. In addition, losses are covered if incurred in good faith due to accepting money orders or counterfeit paper currency in exchange for merchandise, money, or services. It covers losses through forgery or alteration of checks, drafts, and other specified instruments issued by or purporting to have been issued by the assured. The basic policy may include or exclude any of these five insuring agreements independent of each other in specific protection and amount.

A Blanket Crime Policy is similar to the above except that none of the five insuring agreements can be eliminated and that a single dollar limit applies to all its coverages.

Surveys indicate that 90% of all fidelity losses are not covered by insurance. The cause for the high percentage of uninsured fidelity losses is probably due to the large numbers of small business which do not have adequate insurance programs.

Studies by the Surety Association of America show that, in smaller exposures, 85% of the reported losses were underinsured, whereas over 77% were underinsured in the larger brackets. These are, of course, based only on losses reported by assureds.

The SAA recommends the following formula for determining the exposure risk: Five percent of inventory plus 20% of all other current assets plus 10% of annual sales equal the total exposure index. The amount of the bond for each level of the exposure index is given in Exhibit B.

Exhibit B

SUGGESTED MINIMUM AMOUNTS OF HONESTY INSURANCE

Exposure Index		Bracket No.	Amount of Bond	
$ 1,000 - $	25,000	1	$ 15,000 - $	25,000
25,000 -	125,000	2	25,000 -	50,000
125,000 -	250,000	3	50,000 -	75,000
250,000 -	500,000	4	75,000 -	100,000
500,000 -	750,000	5	100,000 -	125,000
750,000 -	1,000,000	6	125,000 -	150,000
1,000,000 -	1,375,000	7	150,000 -	175,000
1,375,000 -	1,750,000	8	175,000 -	200,000
1,750,000 -	2,125,000	9	200,000 -	225,000
2,125,000 -	2,500,000	10	225,000 -	250,000
2,500,000 -	3,325,000	11	250,000 -	300,000
3,325,000 -	4,175,000	12	300,000 -	350,000
4,175,000 -	5,000,000	13	350,000 -	400,000
5,000,000 -	6,075,000	14	400,000 -	450,000
6,075,000 -	7,150,000	15	450,000 -	500,000
7,150,000 -	9,275,000	16	500,000 -	600,000
9,275,000 -	11,425,000	17	600,000 -	700,000
11,425,000 -	15,000,000	18	700,000 -	800,000
15,000,000 -	20,000,000	19	800,000 -	900,000
20,000,000 -	25,000,000	20	900,000 -	1,000,000
25,000,000 -	50,000,000	21	1,000,000 -	1,250,000
50,000,000 -	87,500,000	22	1,250,000 -	1,500,000
87,500,000 -	125,000,000	23	1,500,000 -	1,750,000
125,000,000 -	187,500,000	24	1,750,000 -	2,000,000
187,500,000 -	250,000,000	25	2,000,000 -	2,250,000
250,000,000 -	333,325,000	26	2,250,000 -	2,500,000
333,325,000 -	500,000,000	27	2,500,000 -	3,000,000
500,000,000 -	750,000,000	28	3,000,000 -	3,500,000
750,000,000 -	1,000,000,000	29	3,500,000 -	4,000,000
1,000,000,000 -	1,250,000,000	30	4,000,000 -	4,500,000
1,250,000,000 -	1,500,000,000	31	4,500,000 -	5,000,000

preparation of claims

It is important for the person preparing a claim under an honesty policy to understand the losses which the insurance policy covers. Much misunderstanding, expense, and even lawsuits can be avoided if the claims are prepared properly. The responsibility for the preparation of the claim and the burden of proof lie with the insured and not the insurer.

A confession by the culprit is usually accepted as evidence of dishonesty but not as evidence of extent of loss. Only rarely does an embezzler keep a record of what was stolen; and, once caught, the usual tendency is to minimize the size of the theft. Problems sometimes arise when the confession is confined too narrowly — to one specific act and to one specific amount.

In one instance, an employee who was a minor confessed to taking a small amount which was punishable as a petty crime. A subsequent audit investigation indicated a crime of substantial size, and a claim for the larger amount was placed with the bonding company. Armed with the youth's confession of the theft of a small sum and the auditor's calculations of a large loss, the bonding company demanded that the youth's father make restitution of the larger amount. The father hired an attorney who threatened to bring a countersuit on the basis of defamation of character of the youth who, while admitting a minor misdeed, had not admitted a serious wrongdoing. This threat was effective, and the bonding company dropped the attempt to secure restitution from the father. The youth was discharged but not prosecuted. The bonding company paid the larger sum.

The most useful confession is the one that details all of the areas and kinds of illegal operations in which the culprit was involved. If a comprehensive confession is obtained, it may be used as a basis for a searching examination of all the records within that individual's sphere of activity. There is always the possibility that a claim may be litigated; therefore, it is important that a complete report be made with all supporting evidence and proof of loss.

The report should include:

- A complete description of all of the alleged dishonest transactions, dates, and amounts of losses

- The methods employed by the embezzler and steps taken to conceal the crime

- How, when, and by whom the dishonesty was discovered

- A listing of any offsets that may be applied to reduce the loss such as unpaid wages, bonuses, etc.

- A list of any debts owed the organization which may not be recovered such as traveling advances

- Any sources of restitution which may be known to be available

It is advisable to avoid the inclusion of large, unsupportable items in a claim as this action may cause the adjuster to delay the settlement of the entire claim. In many cases, it will be impossible to document every instance of theft. In these cases, it is possible to make reasonable projections based on past experience.

In the preparation of a dishonesty claim, it should be recognized that the insurance coverage may include a deductible of a stated amount. Such deductibles may apply either to each instance of loss or to the complete theft or embezzlement by that individual.

It may be important to list the dishonesty losses by time sequence if coverage was transferred from one insurance company or policy to another during the time the losses were incurred as two or more claims may be required.

chapter seventeen

polygraph systems

characteristics of the systems

Polygraph machines are manufactured in a variety of models from relatively simple to very complex. The standard machine records the subject's physical reactions to questions posed by the tester. Ink-filled needles trace a pattern on a moving strip of graph paper as the questions are answered. It is believed, by those who have faith in the effectiveness of the polygraph, that discomfort over a false reply will activate the needles by means of rubber tubes around the chest, a blood pressure cuff on an arm, and electrodes on the fingers. Usually the tester establishes a "norm" by asking questions known to be true. There are sophisticated accessories that record muscle movement, involuntary throat movements, elements in the blood stream, volume of blood flow through the veins, and inaudible voice tremors. The skill of the tester in asking the questions is undoubtedly important, but the tester is limited by the background material which he is given by the client.

There are other testing techniques available which utilize a series of questions which, when answered, allegedly give clues to a person's personality and possibly to the moral standards of the subject.

for and against

Some companies use polygraph systems extensively and believe that their use reduces employee thefts. Roswell Steffen, who embezzled $1,500,000 from Union Dime Savings Bank in New York, stated: "I was not polygraphed when I was first employed. The bank did not have a policy of periodic polygraphing. If they had, it would have stopped me cold."

A survey of a selected group of leaders in The Institute of Internal Auditors showed that about one-half of the respondents had experiences with polygraphs but, for the most part, only occasionally. About a third of those who said that polygraphs were sometimes used reported that the results were good. Another third said the results were fair. The remaining third said the results were poor, inconclusive, or that the testers were unable to evaluate the results. Many reported that their managements or legal departments would not permit their use.

There is opposition to the use of polygraphs by unions and civil liberty groups. Some states have banned their use under certain circumstances but allow the machines to be used when an individual volunteers to take the test.

Two studies recently concluded by the New York State Bar Association Committee on Federal Legislation recommended passage of a bill which would prohibit polygraph testing of any presently employed person or of any individual applying for employment. Arguments against its use are that it violates the principle that one is innocent until proven guilty, that it forces the subject into a position of self-incrimination, and that it represents an illegal search and seizure of the subject's thoughts, attitudes, and beliefs.

a case history

On a visit to a branch office, an auditor found that the cashier had prepared daily reports of receipts and disbursements properly. The entire excess of cash received over payments as shown by his books should have been deposited each day. The amount sent to the bank, however, was $50-$100 less than it should have been every day for the past ten months. When the auditor asked him where the missing funds were, the cashier said he didn't know. Asked why he had not reported the fact that money was disappearing daily, he claimed that he had not been properly trained for his job and didn't know that he should report such things. His explanations were so implausible that it appeared that he must be the guilty party. His assistant was a young girl who gave straightforward answers. While she had as much access to the funds as the cashier, he was the one who balanced the funds each day. He knew about the shortages yet had not reported them. Both agreed to take a polygraph test to prove the innocence they both claimed. A well-known firm gave the tests.

The assistant took the test first and was cleared completely of any implication in the case of the missing funds.

The cashier took the test with inconclusive results and agreed to return the next day for retesting. The second test was as inconclusive as the first.

It was decided to transfer the cashier to a less sensitive position but to leave the girl as assistant cashier. Four months later, the girl was caught in a provable theft of funds. She was discharged without prosecution. The full story will never be known, but it is easy to theorize that a clever girl had convinced a naive, confused, and incompetent man to cover up shortages; and he did not comprehend the probable cause of the problem. Management bore part of the responsibility for the missing funds because it had placed an individual in a position where his competence was far below the requirements and responsibilities of the job. He was appointed to the position despite poor performance in other jobs because of long tenure with the company.

The polygraph gave a true reading on the cashier and a wrong one on the assistant, although the opposite seemed true at the time of the tests.

part four
fraud and the criminal law

chapter eighteen

introduction to the law

It is necessary for the auditor who may be confronted unexpectedly with evidence of a fraudulent activity to be prepared with at least a fundamental knowledge of the many laws that have come down to us from common law and the U.S. state and federal statutes on fraud.

Criminal offenses consist of treason, felonies, and misdemeanors. The statutes classify violations under one of these categories. Felonies are more serious crimes which are punished more severely than misdemeanors. A crime is a wrong against the public, even though only one individual actually suffers, because the effect is felt by society as a whole. A crime may be punished by the government under a criminal law, but the injured party may have recourse to a civil right of action as well. An act may be both a tort and a crime. A tort is a wrong to the person or property of another, other than a breach of contract.

Larceny is defined as the "unlawful taking and carrying away by trespass of personal property which the trespasser knows to belong to another with a felonious intent to deprive the owner thereof." It is a common law offense and is divided into grand larceny or petty larceny, depending upon the value of what is stolen. There are a number of related crimes: possession of stolen property, criminal facilitation, helping others commit a crime, etc.

Pilferage is a term widely used to describe the taking of small amounts or articles of little value. Shoplifting is the theft of goods from a shop by stealth. It is not intended that this study be concerned with those crimes, robbery, or burglary. These are usually the concern of internal security departments or public police.

The list of significant fraud crimes that follows is by no means complete, but definitions of some of the major offenses and a brief description of some of the significant statutes are provided.

the legal heritage

The laws of many countries are based on customs and usages together with statutory laws. When the English colonists settled in America, they brought with them the common laws of England. After the colonies won their freedom from British rule, most of the states retained the common laws of England as their own. The criminal law in the United States is derived from early English common law and laws passed as statutes by legislative actions.

The legislatures of the American states, after the separation from England, passed statutes based on British models. For example, an English statute passed in 1799 during the reign of George III, against whom the Americans fought a long war of independence, became a model for the first state laws on embezzlement.

embezzlement

Embezzlement is a criminal breach of trust. Usually, it is committed by an individual who acts in a fiduciary or similar capacity. It may be an offense of breach of trust with only fraudulent intention. An embezzler deprives another of his property by felonious or fraudulent conversion of the property entrusted to him. The statutes of some jurisdictions list the acts which constitute embezzlement as, for example, fraudulently to conceal — convert to one's own use, make away with — or to secrete with intent to embezzle or to convert to one's own use. In some jurisdictions, the law has been simplified by declaring embezzlers guilty of larceny, whereas other jurisdictions have consolidated the offenses of larceny, embezzlement, and false pretenses.

Embezzlement is a statutory offense not founded in common law. Statutes on embezzlement were designed to remedy defects in the criminal law of larceny. These defects made it difficult to punish the fraudulent appropriation of property by persons in certain occupations because they had a relationship of trust with their employers or principals and gained possession of the property through that relationship. The statute of the state in which the crime is prosecuted determines both the specific offense and the grade of the offense. Embezzlement is not confined to the relationship between employer and employee.

The *U.S. Federal Government Code* provides for punishment of "whoever embezzles, steals, purloins, or knowingly converts to his use or the use of another, or without authority, sells, conveys or disposes of any record, voucher, money, or thing of value of the United States or of any department or agency thereof or any property made or being made under contract from the United States or any department or agency thereof."

In most jurisdictions, it is very important to distinguish between custody and possession of property. Mere custody exists where an accused has not been given sufficient control over the property wrongfully appropriated. An employee who receives money from a third person is usually a custodian when he places the money in a till. His subsequent theft of that money most likely constitutes larceny.

Defendants who could not be guilty of embezzling funds because these were not entrusted to their care may, nevertheless, be guilty as accomplices of those who were entrusted and may be punishable as principals. It is also a crime to solicit another to commit embezzlement.

As a rule, if an individual intended to convert another's property to his own use at the time he received possession of it, his subsequent conversion is larceny, not embezzlement. If he received the property honestly and did not form the intent until some time later, his conversion is embezzlement.

Some courts hold that a stockholder who owns all of the shares in a corporation may be guilty of embezzlement from that corporation on the principle that a corporation has an existence separate and distinct from the shareholders who own it. This rule has been applied regardless of the fact that there has been no proof of injury to corporate creditors and despite the fact that the appropriation of corporate funds was agreed to by all the stockholders and officers of the company.

A general partner cannot be convicted of embezzling partnership property which comes into his possession or under his control by reason of his being a partner.

A cotenant may be found guilty of embezzlement of money owned under cotenancy; but as a general rule, one cannot be convicted of embezzlement of property of which he is a joint owner or in which he has a legal interest.

Although the value of the property appropriated is not an element of the crime of embezzlement, that which is void or has no value is not subject to embezzlement. Credit cards, for example, have a value to their owners and may be the subject of embezzlement, although the value is nominal.

Promoters of new corporations may be guilty of embezzlement by wrongfully converting money received from a subscriber for its capital stock.

As a general rule, property delivered by mistake cannot be embezzled because there is no condition of trust or confidence. The moral turpitude in cases of mistaken delivery is not as great as in the cases usually included within the offense of embezzlement.

Generally, when dealings between two persons create a relation of debtor and creditor, a failure of one of the parties to pay does not constitute embezzlement. The facts of the particular case will govern.

When one wrongfully and intentionally misappropriates to his own use the property of another lawfully in his possession, the offense of embezzlement is complete. The fact that he intends to return the property later does not make his offense any the less embezzlement.

An embezzlement of property is punishable even if the owner obtained it illegally. It is possible for the money of a thief to be embezzled.

An attorney may, under certain circumstances, be guilty of embezzling money coming into his possession if, after making the collection, he appropriates the client's money to his own use with intent to deprive the owner of it. An attorney may properly be convicted of embezzling funds held by him as trustee. Others acting as executors, administrators, trustees, and brokers may commit embezzlement.

Under the statutes in some jurisdictions, officers of corporations may be guilty of embezzling property in their possession. For example, an officer of a corporation who takes corporate money under the guise of salary with the intention of embezzling it is guilty of embezzlement.

To constitute the crime of embezzlement, there must be a fraudulent conversion of property which means some physical dealing with the property of another by the accused. Some embezzlement statutes, especially those proscribing embezzlement from a bank, provide for punishment for something less than conversion; for example, a fraudulent taking and secreting with intent to convert. Making false entries in books of accounts is not sufficient evidence of an act of conversion; but when such false entries are made, when funds are deposited in one's own account, and when there is a failure to turn them over when obligated to do so, there is evidence of conversion.

Some courts have ruled that the basic facts in the prosecution for embezzlements must be proved independently by evidence other than the defendant's admission or confession. In some jurisdictions, a conviction may not be had on the uncorroborated testimony of an accomplice.

Where the criminal design originates with the accused embezzler, it is well established that he can not claim the defense of entrapment, provided the owner does not actively urge the accused on to the commission of the embezzlement. For example, a shopkeeper gives money to a third party to spend in his shop so as to detect the illegal actions of a clerk who has aroused the owner's suspicions. If the clerk appropriates the money and is caught in the trap, he is guilty of embezzlement and may be properly convicted. Similarly, decoy letters may be used to detect tampering with the mails.

Usually, evidence of the honest character of one accused of embezzlement is admissible in his defense as well as proof of his financial condition at or immediately prior to the time of alleged embezzlement. Evidence is held admissible that, during the time in which the embezzlement occurred, the defendant spent money considerably in excess of his known income or made large bank deposits. Evidence of restitution is generally immaterial and inadmissible.

It is generally held that the defendant's giving a note or other contractual obligation which is accepted by the owner of the property is no defense to a charge of its embezzlement if the essential elements of the crime are present.

Defalcation is a term used at times to describe an embezzlement. While dictionaries give this word as a synonym for the act of embezzlement and for the sum abstracted, the word "embezzlement" is the word used in legal distinctions and is preferable for that reason.

forgery

Common law defined forgery as the "fraudulent making or alteration of a writing to the prejudice of another's rights." The offense of forgery is now defined by statute which confirms common law and extends its scope.

There are three elements to forgery:

- There must be a false writing or alteration of an instrument.
- The instrument must be apparently capable of defrauding.
- There must be an intent to defraud.

It is not necessary that the accused sign the instrument in person. It is sufficient to be guilty of forgery if he procures its commission or is present, aids, and abets another in procuring it.

A person may be guilty of making a false instrument, although he signs it with his own name, if it is false in any material part and calculated to induce another to give credit to it.

A person may be guilty of forgery if he intentionally and fraudulently signs his own name when it is identical with the name of a person who should have signed it. However, if a bank in error informs a person that it holds money to his credit and if the addressee requests a draft for the amount, endorses it, and .receives the money, his endorsement does not constitute forgery.

A false entry in one's own books is not forgery. In some jurisdictions, false entries by employees in their employers' books in order to cover up frauds are punishable as forgery.

Altering a receipt with fraudulent intent is forgery, but altering an endorsement of money received on the back of a note which is unsigned by the payee is not forgery unless it was intended as a receipt by the parties. A check given in payment, endorsed by the payee, and paid by the bank is a receipt. Any alteration with intent to defraud after it was cancelled by the bank is forgery.

A concomitant of the act of forgery is the uttering of an offer of a forged instrument with knowledge of the falsity of the writing and with intent to defraud. Under most statutes, the forging of an instrument and its uttering are separate offenses. An acquittal of a charge of forgery is no bar to a prosecution for uttering and passing the forged instrument under those statutes.

insufficient-funds checks

Issuing a worthless check with false representation may be the basis of a prosecution for obtaining money by false pretenses under general statutes. However, most jurisdictions have separate statutes for this offense. Most worthless-check statutes make fraudulent intent an essential element of the crime, and the passer of the check must have present knowledge of the insufficiency of the funds.

A conviction may not be had where the drawer shows he had reasonable expectation of covering the check. For example, it would be paid if:

- He had a previous arrangement with the bank.

- He expected to make a deposit sufficient to cover the check before it was presented for payment.

- The bank, without his knowledge, applied his funds on some indebtedness owed it.
- His account had been sequestered by legal proceedings.
- The checks he had deposited had been unpaid and charged back.

A worthless-check statute is not violated if the payee knowingly accepts a postdated check.

Usually, the giving of a worthless check in payment of preexisting debt does not come within the statute. Moreover, it can be defended by the fact that the maker did not deprive the payee of a right or procure anything of value; therefore, he did not commit an offense.

Some worthless-check statutes punish the passing, with intent to defraud, of a check drawn by a payer who, to the knowledge of the passer, does not exist. Other statutes make the passing of fictitious checks forgery.

conspiracy

A conspiracy is an agreement between two or more persons to commit a criminal act or to achieve by unlawful means an act not in itself unlawful. The legal consequences of a conspiracy to commit a crime are separate and distinct from the commission of the crime itself. Conspiracy is an act prohibited by statute in those jurisdictions having enacted it. To commit conspiracy, the following elements must be present: agreement, unlawful object, intent, knowledge, and overt act.

A corporation may be guilty of participating in a criminal conspiracy if it conspires with its officers or agents. In most courts, a husband and wife can be held guilty of conspiracy if they agree between themselves to conspire.

In conspiracy cases, an accused person may claim the defense of entrapment and be sustained if the conspiracy involved only one other person.

Usually, circumstantial evidence is admissible in conspiracy cases and is often sufficient to prove guilt.

bribery

Early common law defined bribery as "corruption in the administration of justice." By statute, most states now define bribery to include offerees or receivers of criminal bribes to all persons whose official conduct is in any way connected with the government. The *U.S. Code* makes it a punishable offense for anyone to give, to offer, or to promise anything of value to any public official with the intent to influence any official act so as to cause him to violate his duty or to commit fraud against the United States. The offer of money to a government employee for the performance of his duty is not a bribery. It is an offense to bribe a juror or witness in court cases.

Under federal statutes, a bribe in connection with the procurement of materials under a federal defense program is considered graft and is punishable under that section of the law. A distinction between graft and bribery is that the intent to improperly influence or be influenced does not have to be alleged or proved in a case of graft.

A conviction of bribery under a statute penalizing any public official who should solicit any valuable thing for his official vote was sustained where the funds solicited were not to go to the defendants themselves but were to be paid into a campaign fund.

Some jurisdictions have statutes which penalize nonofficials for bribery. Some of these are representatives of labor organizations, employees of trust funds, and participants in sports activities who solicit or agree to accept a bribe to influence their decisions or performance of their duties.

Commercial bribery is the offense of bribing an agent or an employee to influence his relationship with his principal or employer. Several jurisdictions have statutes punishing such offenders.

Two or more persons who conspire to receive or to solicit a bribe, although one could not for some reason accept the bribe, are nonetheless guilty of bribery. There may be a conspiracy of two or more persons to offer a bribe. In such situations, a defendant may be both guilty of the crime of bribery and of conspiracy to commit bribery.

It is legitimate to adopt measures which are reasonably necessary to detect crime. If the act and the criminal intent originated in the mind of the accused, the fact that an officer appeared to cooperate in order to consummate the act will not constitute entrapment. Cases in which illegal entrapment has been found are those where government officials, for the purpose of arresting and prosecuting the accused, took the first step.

extortion

Common law defines this crime to be the "unlawful taking by an officer, by color of his office, of anything that is not due him, or the taking of more than is due, or the taking of something before it is due." In some jurisdictions, the statutes have enlarged upon that definition to include the obtaining of the property of another with his consent through a wrongful use of force or fear under circumstances not amounting to robbery by either an officer or a private person. Fear may include threats or attempted threats of physical injury, to impute to him any crime, or to expose him to disgrace.

The difference between extortion and robbery is that property taken against the will and consent of its possessor is robbery, whereas it is extortion if consent is obtained.

The distinction between extortion and bribery is that a bribe is a present offered and received, whereas extortion is the demand of an illegal fee or present by color of office or other position of power.

Some statutes have enlarged the common law definition to include what is ordinarily called "blackmail." They contain provisions that a person is guilty who accuses or threatens to accuse any person of any crime punishable by law or of any immoral conduct which, if true, would tend to degrade and to disgrace such person. Guilt also includes threats to injure the person or property of anyone with intent to extort or to gain from such person a pecuniary advantage or with intent to compel the person threatened to do any act against his will. It is a federal offense to send a threatening extortion communication across state lines.

Threats to injure a debtor if payment is not made on a valid, enforceable debt is extortion. However, accusing or threatening to accuse the debtor of a crime connected to the debt is not blackmail. Therefore, it is not illegal to threaten to refer the matter to a collection agency or to commence a civil action.

The federal antiracketeering act (Hobbs Act) provides that whoever affects interstate commerce in some degree, moves any article by robbery or extortion or attempts or conspires to do so, or commits or threatens physical violence or economic loss to any person or property in furtherance of a plan or purpose is subject to a fine or imprisonment or both.

fraud and deceit

The term *fraud* is generic and is used in various ways. Fraud assumes so many different degrees and forms that courts are compelled to content themselves with only a few general rules for its discovery and defeat. It is said that "It is better not to define the term lest men should find ways of committing fraud which might evade such a definition."

However, fraud is generally considered to be anything calculated to deceive. This includes all acts, omissions, and concealments involving a breach of legal or equitable duty, trust, or confidence justly reposed which result in damage to another or by which undue and conscienceless advantage is taken of another.

Bad faith is the antithesis of an honest intention to abstain from taking any conscienceless advantage of another. It may seem that there is little difference between bad faith and fraud. Yet fraud is an action of a more affirmative, evil nature such as intentionally and deliberately proceeding or acting dishonestly with a wicked motive to cheat or to deceive another.

Deceit is a kind of fraud. It consists of any false representation or contrivance whereby one person overreaches and misleads another to his hurt. While the word *fraud* is in common use in courts, an action for damages at common law based upon fraud is called *an action of deceit*.

Collusion is an agreement between two or more persons to defraud another of his rights by the forms of law or to secure an object forbidden by law. It is also a kind of fraud.

Most fraud cases are based on false representations or concealment of material facts. False representations are those made directly by an interested party to induce action on the part of another, those made with reference to the subject matter, those made by a third party touching some fact which is not the subject of the contract, and those made under such circumstances as to cause unknown persons to act on them.

According to most of the courts which have attempted to define it, a fact is material when it influences a person to enter into a contract, when it deceives him and induces him to act, or when the contract would not have been made without it and the transaction would not have occurred.

A sale of property induced by fraud is not void but only voidable. A sale of property induced by fraud entitles the buyer to rescind the contract of sale and recover the consideration he has paid. He may claim the fraud as grounds for the recovery of damages in an action for deceit.

It is a general rule that fraud cannot be predicated upon statements which are promissory at the time they are made and which relate to future actions or conduct. However, where the promise is the device to accomplish the fraud, it will be considered a fraudulent act in most jurisdictions.

Usually, representations of property value are to be regarded only as expressions of opinion or commendatory trade statements and as such do not constitute fraud.

In most cases, a vendor should know the value of his own property. If he is so indiscreet as to place reliance upon the statement of a prospective purchaser, he should be left to make the best of a bad bargain. However, if the purchaser has special information that enhances the ordinary value of land, it places him under a legal obligation to make no act or representation to mislead the owner into the belief that there was no special condition affecting the value.

False representations of facts concerning one's financial position or ability constitute the basis for a charge of fraud. For example, false representations by borrowers in financial statements submitted as the basis for loans or extensions of credit are held to be actionable fraud. This rule applies also to false representations made about a third party such as a corporation for which the accused worked as an officer, director, shareholder, or employee.

One of the fundamental tenets of the law of fraud is that fraud may be committed by a suppression of the truth as well as by the suggestion of falsehood. Failure to disclose a material fact for the purpose of inducing a false belief is fraudulent, but the law distinguishes between passive and active concealment. Mere failure to volunteer information does not constitute fraud. In other words, either party may be innocently silent regarding matters upon which each may openly exercise his judgment. However, when either has a duty to speak, the disclosure must be full and complete. As an illustration, one who sells an article knowing it is dangerous due to concealed defects is guilty of a wrong and is liable for damages to anyone suffering an injury. This is willful deceit and concealment.

False representations in a report required by statute to be filed with certain public officials are actionable by a party sustaining damages as a result of relying upon the report if it disseminates information to the public.

Under the ordinary law of agency, a principal is responsible for injuries resulting from his agent's fraud committed during and within the scope of the agent's authority, even though the principal is not aware of the fraud.

A corporation may be held liable for the fraud and deceit of its officers and agents acting within the scope of their corporate authority or employment, even though the corporation did not authorize, concur in or know of the fraud. A corporation is not relieved from liability for the fraudulent acts of its officer within the apparent scope of his authority by the fact that the officer, in committing the fraud, acted for his own benefit and that the corporation did not profit from the fraud.

The applicable statute of limitations in most jurisdictions commences with the discovery of the fraud or when, with reasonable diligence, there ought to have been a discovery of the facts constituting the fraud. A defrauded person must be diligent and prudent in his efforts to detect the fraud. He cannot excuse his delay in instituting a suit if his failure to discover the fraud was due to his own neglect. The law does not require positive knowledge of a fraud but only that which would lead a prudent man to inquiry or action.

The law recognizes that the individual has the right to dispose of his property as he desires. However, he may not dispose of his land or goods in any way which would infringe on the rights of another person. Under the Uniform Fraudulent Conveyance Act and similar statutes, a conveyance is fraudulent if it is made without a fair consideration to creditors and if it results in insolvency.

A debtor may not devote his capital, industry, or credit to the accumulation of property held by a third person for use by the debtor or the debtor's family to the exclusion of creditors. Nor may he, to the prejudice of creditors, transfer property to another to be held in trust for him.

A classic type of fraud is the sale in bulk. This occurs when a merchant suddenly disposes of his entire stock in trade to one buyer. Then the merchant disappears with the proceeds of the sale without paying off his creditors. To prevent such defrauding of creditors, most states adopted bulk sales acts. These prevent a sale of goods in bulk until creditors are paid in full. They also put all creditors on an equal footing rather than favoring certain creditors.

The *Uniform Commercial Code* provides that a sale at an auction is a bulk transfer and subject to certain rules. The transferor must furnish a list of his creditors and assist in the preparation of the property to be sold. The auctioneer must retain the list of creditors, prepare the list of property to be sold, and then notify the creditors ten days prior to the action. After the auction, he must apply the receipts as provided in the code. If the auctioneer does not perform these duties, he may be liable to the transferor's creditors. Violations of some bulk sales acts are not punishable as criminal offenses.

A professional advisor, such as an accountant or a physician, may be liable in tort for fraud if he expresses an opinion within the scope of his professional capacity which he knows is not true. Court decisions in several jurisdictions have expanded on this principle. It has been held that knowledge of the falsity of his opinion is not required to hold him liable for damages for it is his duty to present correct statements and to give sound advice. Therefore, because of his professional employment, some courts have held that it is futile to say that he is not liable. His advice cannot be regarded as mere opinion. For a recent development on this subject, see the First Securities Co. of Chicago case.

obtaining property by false pretenses

Caveat emptor — "let the buyer beware." This was the basis of common law that held that obtaining money or property by false representation of fact was *not* a crime. Today, in any particular jurisdiction, statutes and their judicial construction determine the crime of obtaining property by false pretenses.

Some statutes combine the common law offense of cheat with the statutory offense of false pretenses. The law of cheat was effected by some device having the semblance of public authenticity such as spurious money, false weights or measures, or false impersonation.

The crime of false pretenses may be committed by presenting and attempting to establish a claim known to be false against a governmental agency, even though the officer approving the claim knew it was false or had the means of learning it was false. Most false-pretense statutes deem it a crime to obtain money or property by means of a worthless check.

Larceny by trick or fraud is taking property when the owner voluntarily parts with it after being influenced by fraudulent representations. The owner does not, however, part with his title. If he parts with both title and property, relying on the taker's fraudulent representations, the crime is obtaining property by false pretenses — not larceny.

Obtaining money for goods with no intent to deliver them or purchasing goods with no intent to pay for them does *not* constitute the crime of obtaining property by false pretenses.

Ordinarily, expressing an opinion does not make a person liable to prosecution for obtaining money or property under false pretenses. In most cases puffery and trade talk cannot be the basis for criminality.

In some jurisdictions, unless a false statement of a financial condition for the purpose of securing goods on credit is not in writing, it is not considered a criminal offense.

false advertising

Both competitors and consumers are injured by false and misleading advertising.

Many states have adopted a model, false-advertising statute. It states that if anyone selling a product or service to the public publishes and disseminates an advertisement containing any untrue, deceptive, or misleading statement, he is guilty of a misdemeanor. Some statutes have been amended to include radio and television advertising.

The U.S. Supreme Court ruled that advertisements which are false in fact constitute an unfair method of competition, even though it is commonly practiced and not intended to mislead the trade.

State laws dealing with false advertising are usually applied to local or *intrastate* advertising activities. The Federal Trade Commission has prime jurisdiction on *interstate* advertising.

food, drug, and cosmetic offenses

The Federal Food, Drug, and Cosmetic Act was passed to protect public health and safety. It excludes deleterious, adulterated, and misbranded articles of specified types from interstate commerce.

Section 301 of this act includes prohibitions in interstate commerce involving:

- introducing adulterated or misbranded food, drugs, devices, or cosmetics

- adulteration or misbranding of food, drugs, devices, or cosmetics

- the delivery or receipt of adulterated or misbranded food, drugs, devices, or cosmetics

It also prohibits:

- refusal of access to records which must be maintained on new drugs

- giving a false guarantee

- improper use of identification marks, labels, etc.

- misbranding

- failure to carry proper warnings on dangerous or habit-forming drugs.

To protect consumers, the U.S. government imposes criminal sanctions on activities which could endanger public health and safety. It makes no exception for good faith or ignorance. Therefore, the government does not have to prove the alleged violator's guilty knowledge or intent. This differs from the usual fraud statute.

deceptive trade practices

By the end of the 19th Century, legislators recognized that the common law remedies for deceptive trade practices were inadequate. In 1914, U.S. President Wilson signed the Federal Trade Commission Act into law. It contained in Section 5 the simple prohibition: *Unfair methods of competition in commerce are hereby declared unlawful.*

In 1938, the Wheeler-Lea Act amended the FTC Act. Section 5 now reads: *Unfair methods of competition in commerce and unfair or deceptive acts or practices in commerce are hereby declared unlawful.* Many other acts have enlarged the scope of regulation. They cover such products as wool labeling (1939), margarine advertising (1950), fur products labeling (1951), flammable fabrics (1953), and textile fiber products (1958). Recent acts have dealt with such subjects as fair packaging and truth in lending.

The FTC has broad, investigative powers. It has the power of access to documentary evidence, the authority to require annual and special reports from any firm, and power of subpoena.

Justice Brandeis interpreted the act which created the FTC as follows:

> *Instead of undertaking to define what practices should be deemed unfair as had been done in earlier legislations, the act left the determination to the commission. Experience with existing laws had taught that definition, being necessarily rigid, would prove embarassing, and if rigorously applied, might involve great hardship. Methods of competition which would be unfair in one industry, under certain circumstances, might, when adopted in another industry, or even in the same industry under different circumstances, be entirely unobjectionable.*

The act was designed to protect the consumer. And since, as it has been said, some consumers are ignorant, unthinking, and credulous, nothing less than the most literal truthfulness is tolerated.

In the case of FTC vs Standard Education Society, FTC was overruled by the Court of Appeals. The U.S. Supreme Court reversed the Court of Appeals and held:

The fact that a false statement may be obviously false to those who are trained and experienced does not change its character, nor take away its power to deceive others less experienced.

The Supreme Court added the following significant statement:

There is no duty resting on a citizen to suspect the honesty of those with whom he transacts business. Laws are made to protect the trusting as well as the suspicious. The best element of business has long since decided that honesty should govern competitive enterprises and that the rule of caveat emptor should not be relied upon to reward and deceit.

The FTC has defined many descriptive and designative words. For example:

automatic — Completely automatic is erroneous. The term is properly used only in reference to such operations as actually are performed without manual effort.

glass — Essential ingredient is silica.

leather — Unqualified, means top-grain leather.

eight-cup coffeemaker — Each cup must be at least five ounces.

Virginia ham — Virginia misdescribes the origin of hams that are not the product of hogs raised in that state. The name comes from the fact that they are cured by the old Virginian process.

The FTC has issued a number of publications including *Guides Against Deceptive Pricing, Guides Against Bait Advertising,* and hundreds of advisory opinions on specific products and subjects.

Many industry groups have undertaken the task of applying high ethical standards in marketing and advertising. But constant attention by both government and private groups is necessary to eliminate trickery in the marketplace and to ensure that reputable businesses do not slip into shoddy practices due to some individual's lack of sensitivity to the public good.

mail fraud

To commit mail fraud, a person must devise a scheme to defraud. He then must place a letter, postal card, package, writing, circular, pamphlet, or advertisement in the mail for the purpose of executing that scheme. It is not necessary for a scheme to be unlawful, nor need it be a fraud at common law or by statute. The essence of the offense is the use of the mail in executing the scheme — not the scheme itself. It is not necessary that the scheme defraud so long as it is reasonably adapted to do so.

corporation criminal liability

Under common law, a corporation was not indictable, although its members were. Now the general rule is that a corporation may be criminally liable for the acts of its agents or officers while they are exercising authorized powers.

A corporation cannot claim as a defense that it had a prohibition against violation of the law. A corporation is not liable if its agents deliberately violate instructions and if the act is not ratified by the corporation. Corporations may be indicted for criminal negligence in the discharge of a duty imposed by law. In some cases, a corporation may be held criminally liable for homocides, larceny, and obtaining money by false pretenses. The punishments that can be applied to a corporation are fines or seizure of its property and, in some instances, the forfeiture of its charter. The exact wording of the statute of the specific jurisdiction provides guidelines for the punishment which can be applied to corporations.

monopoly and antitrust offenses

The Sherman Antitrust Act, passed by Congress in 1890 to regulate interstate commerce, declared every contract, combination, or conspiracy in restraint of trade illegal. For several years adverse Supreme Court decisions reduced its effectiveness. However, in 1911 the government used it to dissolve the Standard Oil Company and American Tobacco Company. In 1914, the Clayton Antitrust Act supplemented it.

While the Sherman Act deals with restraints, monopoly, or attempts already accomplished, the Clayton Act goes further. It is concerned with probable future effects that could arise from a lessening of competition or a tendency toward monopoly.

In 1936, Congress passed the Robinson-Patman Act as an amendment to the Clayton Act. The Robinson-Patman Act was designed to protect the independent retailer from chain store competition. It not only prohibits price discrimination but also prohibits payment for services or facilities for processing, handling, or sale of products unless the payment is proportionally but equally available to all other customers.

Restraint of trade must be unreasonable in order to be unlawful. Price fixing and excluding a competitor from a market are deemed unreasonable *per se*. A company may meet the price of another company or may change its price simultaneously. Such actions are legal. It is also lawful to advise a competitor of a decision to raise prices prior to the price increase.

securities offenses

In 1909, Congress declared that the use of the mail to defraud is illegal and a criminal offense. It was an attempt to cover all types of schemes and frauds, including securities sold through the mail. In 1920, the Interstate Commerce Commission was given the authority to regulate the issuance of securities by interstate railroads. A series of test cases upheld this power and set the stage for later laws.

Nearly all of the states have enacted *blue-sky laws* to regulate the issue and sale of securities. Twenty-two years after the first of these state laws was enacted, the federal government passed the Securities Act of 1933. This was followed by the Securities Act of 1934 and then the Investment Advisers Act of 1940. These are the principal federal statutes that have shaped the law against fraud in securities, but there have been additional acts and judicial decisions.

State blue-sky laws — Some statutes prescribe license requirements and name an official to check fraudulent practices. Some states attempt to control financing of corporations. Others try to regulate securities dealers and salesmen. In many jurisdictions, the statute requires state approval after an investigation and before securities can be issued and sold. Most state securities laws impose criminal liability for false statements on a registration, the sale of unlicensed stock, and other violations.

Securities Act of 1933 — This act was passed to protect investors by requiring full disclosure of material information at the time stock was issued. Misrepresentation, fraud, and deceit are prohibited. Willful violation of the act or rules issued by the Securities and Exchange Commission under the act are punishable as criminal offenses and/or by civil penalties.

An antifraud provision states that it is unlawful (1) to employ any device, scheme, or artifice to defraud; (2) to obtain property or money by means of an untrue statement or an omission of a material fact; (3) to engage in any activity which would be a fraud or deceit upon a purchaser in the offer or sale of a security by mail or in interstate or foreign commerce.

Securities Act of 1934 — This act extended disclosure to securities listed on the national securities exchanges and provided for the registration and supervision of exchanges. Listed companies must file reports required by the commission. This statute gives the SEC authority to protect the public by maintaining fair markets for listed securities and to punish misrepresentations, deceit, market manipulation, and other fraudulent practices. The provisions of the act are applicable to all securities handled by registered exchanges and brokers. Both listed and unlisted items are covered. The over-the-counter markets are controlled through the registration of brokers and dealers.

When it finds possible violations, the SEC may seek a civil injunction. It may rely on an administrative remedy or may refer the case to the Department of Justice for criminal prosecution.

Under *Rule 10b-5*, insiders are precluded from trading for personal benefit on information not available to those with whom they deal. *Insiders include not only directors or management officers but those whose positions make them privy to the information.* An insider with material information must divulge it to the public or must abstain from trading or recommending the securities concerned.

The courts have defined *material* to include not only earnings information but facts which affect the probable future of the company and those which may affect decisions of the investor.

Other important features of this act are the rules governing the solicitation of proxies. These rules prohibit false or misleading statements in proxy material.

The Investment Advisers Act of 1940 — The object of this act is to protect investors from malpractices by those who are paid for advising others about securities. Investment advisers are required to register with the SEC, which is empowered to deny, suspend, or revoke registration in certain cases. The commission has the authority to inspect the books of advisers, to prescribe the records to be kept, and to require reports.

Antifraud provisions are not limited to common law fraud but include a fiduciary obligation of full disclosure of conflicting ties. *Scalping* is the practice by which an adviser makes a profit on the market reaction to his advice. It is a fraud or deceit upon his clients.

The Investment Advisors Act is Title II of the Investment Company Act. It was passed to assure proper management of investment trusts. All investment trusts intending to use the mail or to operate in interstate commerce must register with SEC and supply information as required.

evasion of taxes

All crimes against the United States result from violating acts of Congress. Common law offenses are not punishable by the federal government. The *Internal Revenue Code* lists a number of specific tax crimes and offenses. In addition to the crimes of willfully attempting to evade or to defeat a tax and willfully failing to collect, to account for, and to pay over another's tax, there are several other offenses. These include:

- interference with tax collection or administration
- offenses by revenue officers and agents
- offenses relating to stamp taxes
- making false statements to purchasers or lessees so as to lead them to believe that part of the price consists of a federal tax
- representations that a retailer's excise tax is excluded from the price of an article
- failure to obtain a license for collection of foreign payments of interest or dividends
- violations of the laws relating to narcotics

Section 7201 of the *Internal Revenue Code* of 1954 states: "Any person who willfully attempts in any manner to evade or to defeat any tax imposed by this title or the payment thereof shall, in addition to other penalties provided by law, be guilty of a felony."

In revenue enforcement, the crime of willful attempted evasion of taxes is the principal offense. This is an independent, complete crime. Nothing is added to its criminality by its success, as would be true in the case of attempted murder. Even though an attempt may actually succeed in evading taxes, there is no such criminal offense. The prosecution may be only for the attempt. A willful attempt to evade income taxes is a separate offense for each year it is attempted.

In Section 7201 of the *Internal Revenue Code*, the term *in any manner* is an all-inclusive concept. It is intended to cover not only filing a false return but also:

- keeping a double set of books
- making false entries or alterations
- falsifying invoices or documents
- destroying books or records
- concealing of assets
- covering up sources of income
- placing property in the names of others
- using fictitious names on bank accounts

- filing false tentative returns
- filing false amended returns
- making false statements during negotiation

Other sections of the code include penalties for the following willful acts:

- failure to pay the estimated tax on tax
- failure to make a return or declaration
- failure to keep records
- failure to supply information
- failure of an employee to furnish tax information to an employer
- failure of an employer to furnish payroll-withholding information on employees
- filing income tax refund claims for fictitious persons and endorsing the subsequent refund checks

There is nothing morally or legally wrong in attempting to avoid taxation and in taking proper and legal steps to do so. One of the judicial doctrines developed is that tax-free transactions must have some legitimate business purpose and not be a mere tax-dodging device. Separate trusts are recognized for income tax purposes, even if they were separated only for reducing taxes.

Tax evasion, as opposed to tax avoidance, is synonymous with fraud because it has the ultimate objective of paying less tax than the amount known by the tax payer to be legally due. It is done deliberately, willfully, and in bad faith.

chapter nineteen

condemn or condone

the sociometry of guilt

The auditor who completes an extensive investigation of a suspected fraud case is frequently consulted by management as to how to deal with the suspect. Some managements have firm policies that state all guilty individuals must be discharged and prosecuted. Auditors of organizations with such inflexible rules must make only one decision—Is the evidence strong enough to present to public authorities or a surety company?

If procedures are written out in detail, he knows how to proceed. In response to a survey made in conjunction with this study, about half of the respondents said that their organizations treated all transgressors alike. Some of the comments were:

From a theoretical viewpoint, 'yes'; from a practical viewpoint, job level and status are influencing factors.

More lenient with long-service employees than for short-timers.

Leniency shown toward a first offender; consideration of length of service and magnitude of transgression.

Try to treat all transgressors alike by having a fraud committee determine the disposition of the employee.

They are not treated alike in courts. It depends on one's past record and contributory factors such as system weakness, location, effect on staff, etc.

Auditing attempts to assure uniform treatment by reviewing coordination between employee relations and security.

Departmental supervision generally takes appropriate action. This will vary from department to department.

Prosecution occurs only in selected cases.

It depends on the rank of the employee and how severe the case is.

It depends on circumstances which mitigate: family, etc.

Minorities receive special consideration.

Some personnel are sacred cows and can do no wrong.

They are basically treated the same. All are asked to make restitution. Very few are prosecuted.

There are different procedures for students, faculty, and staff.

In small amounts, the usual penalty is discharge after a union hearing. In larger amounts, there are probably prosecutions.

Depending on the seriousness, preferential treatment is given to minorities, higher levels of management, and those with seniority.

Lower level hourly or clerical personnel are dealt with more severely than management personnel. Also, the length of employment is a consideration.

All transgressors are treated alike. They are terminated, not prosecuted, and asked to make restitution.

It depends on whether the act was premeditated, repetitive, or opportunistic.

Of 102 respondents, 50 said definitely that proven defrauders were prosecuted; 36 said they were not; and 16 did not answer this question.

Another survey question was: "Are some suspects, against whom a case cannot be proven without a doubt, discharged?" Nearly half (46) said "yes," whereas 49 said "no." There were seven abstentions.

By almost two to one (58 to 30), the respondents said they believed an offer of restitution (in certain cases) would save transgressors from prosecution.

In most cases, legal counsel and management decide whether to prosecute.

Employee fraud can cause executives severe emotional stress. Many will be concerned not only about the defection of a trusted employee but about that employee's family and reactions of coworkers. Some fear that they may be criticized for inept supervision. In fact, some supervisors and managers, normally logical and unemotional, will react in an unexpected manner. Here are four reactions that have been observed.

- A general manager of a large organization criticized an industrial relations manager for discharging a young lady cashier who, over a period of months, had stolen funds entrusted to her and falsified records to cover the stealing. The industrial relations manager was told that he should have shown more compassion and should have given the employee another chance. Because of the general manager's attitude, no claim was filed under surety insurance and there was no prosecution. The young lady shortly thereafter obtained a position with a bank as an experienced cashier with a clean record. This policy of *compassion* made the surety coverage a needless expense. It also prevented a second employer from learning the character of a new employee who was placed in a cash-sensitive area. If compassion is the policy, it should be the responsibility of the organization adopting that policy to transfer employees to less sensitive positions and not to discharge them with unspotted records thus allowing them to go elsewhere and repeat their acts.

- A mid-level executive recommended a substantial increase in salary for one of his favorites, an innovative, energetic, and creative fellow who had been given increasingly important assignments. One day the auditors discovered that this *creative* young man had applied his talents to sizeable bribery, forgery, and embezzlement. The culprit readily admitted it and wrote a full statement of his operations. When the executive read it, he said he was going to fight the auditors "all the way to the top" because, in spite of the admitted dishonesty, the young man's great talents justified keeping him. The executive carried the battle all the way to the top but lost both his protégé and his own credibility with top-level management.

- Auditors concerned about continuing losses in a certain division decided to make a surprise visit without telling the group vice president. Within a few days, the assistant manager confessed privately to the manager of the division that he was the guilty party. The assistant manager had become convinced from the auditors' questioning that they knew of his wrongdoing. The manager phoned his group vice president to tell him the auditors unknowingly had persuaded his assistant to confess. The group vice president, piqued because he had not been informed of the audit in advance, ordered the manager not to inform the auditors that his assistant had confessed and to forget the whole matter. The manager, caught between his superior and the auditors, resisted further discussion. Upon continued pressure, however, he admitted only that, if he had to suspect anyone, it would be his assistant. His manner led the auditors to report what they had learned and the strange reactions of the manager. When the group vice president was confronted with that report, he admitted his role in the cover-up. The manager and the vice president were reprimanded by the president of the company for the cover-up. The auditors' position was strengthened, and their future independence was made more sure.

■ A janitor was caught stealing small change from the aprons of production workers while he was doing his work after the plant closed. A group of supervisors discussed the case at lunch the next day. One, an industrial relations director, argued strongly that the company should "throw the book at him." A week later, auditors, following up on an informer's tip, discovered that the industrial relations director was embezzling employees' recreational funds in a complicated scheme. The conversation of the previous week was recalled, and management decided to follow the industrial relations director's own advice.

a concept of exculpation

Internal controls often break down when management introduces new systems or organizational alignments. Some changes disturb employee work patterns. Innovations introduce uncertainties in established authority and frequently result in new lines of responsibility.

In one company, a powerful treasurer was shorn of much of his responsibility with little explanation of what responsibilities he was to retain. Prior to that change, he had the responsibility for financial supervision of a major capital construction program. The controller, who might have inherited that responsibility, became seriously ill about this time. The architect, a nonaggressive, placid type, considered himself a designer and not a supervisor.

Recognizing that no one appeared to be in control of expenditures, the general contractor proceeded to increase expenditures to unreasonable levels by installing more equipment than was budgeted: fixtures, furniture, etc. He also charged the company for work and material not delivered to the job.

When an auditor began to investigate because of the cost overruns, the contractor tried to minimize the problem by offering the auditor a bribe. This led to the discharge of the architect, a downward revision in his fee, and a rebate by the contractor for the overcharges. The member of management who had stripped the treasurer of his authority attempted to blame him for "dropping the ball."

Top management wisely decided that the cause was a lack of proper communication and control from the top through several levels of supervision and that no one individual should shoulder the blame.

Too often, the primary causes of losses are overlooked and a scapegoat is sought. If the right lessons are learned, a *white wash* may be the right solution to a foozle and even to a fraud.

criminal justice

The judicial system is based on laws that denote the category of the crime and prescribe minimum and maximum penalties. A judge may impose penalties ranging from a suspended sentence or probation to the maximum allowed by law. Attempts by legislative bodies to impose mandatory sentences have been met by judicial reversals on the grounds that they are unconstitutional. Plea bargaining and assistance to prosecutors often result in an equally guilty party's being indicted on lesser charges when he has actually added to the original crime by betraying an associate to gain an advantage for himself.

A former president of the American Bar Association, Chesterfield Smith, said: "Crowded court dockets, case backlogs, overworked and harassed judges, and slow-motion justice are the rule. Long delays in trial contribute largely to the burgeoning of crime."

One survey showed that 98% of felony arrests were reduced to lesser charges. Another showed that only one felony conviction out of six resulted in a prison sentence. Four men were found guilty of stealing more than a quarter of a million dollars in merchandise from their employer. Even though two of them had criminal records, they all received a sentence of five years on probation.

Recidivism is the pattern in probably 50% of street crimes, but those who commit white-collar crime are less likely to be repeaters. The main reason for this may be that, once apprehended, the white-collar criminal finds it more difficult to reestablish himself in a position of trust where the opportunities for crime are equal to those in the original position.

Criminal justice is seldom satisfactory, especially for those who defraud others. For most, there is only pity that trusted, well-respected people barter away their good reputations too often for but small gain. For predators who, without consideration of their victims, steal for self-aggrandizement, stern punishment should be imposed. The real loss to society is when punishment fit for the latter is meted out to the former or vice versa.

The obvious purposes of prosecution are to:

■ punish the transgressor by a fine or prison term

■ rehabilitate the guilty

■ deter others from emulation

The present U.S. legal system does not appear to be reaching any of these goals. It costs between $5,000 and $10,000 a year to keep a person in prison in a nonproductive capacity. And society probably is unwilling to pay taxes for the cost of imprisonment for significantly longer terms for all those who could be given prison sentences. Present prison terms are short when we consider the size of the loss.

Fines are usually quite low in comparison with amounts embezzled or otherwise stolen. It is more equitable for any funds in possession of the defrauder to be applied to restitution than to be diverted to society through fines paid to the government. The stigma of a conviction is often minimized when the culprit moves to another community for a new start.

It is doubtful whether short prison terms rehabilitate culprits or whether the present judicial decisions deter those whose greed is so great that it cancels out their moral sense.

A national crime file on all convicted persons, readily accessible to the public, might be a more effective deterrent than the present penal system.

controls on employment practices

The survey of 102 internal auditors early in 1975 included eight questions on hiring practices. A slight majority replied that their employers obtained police checks on some employees.

To the question "Does your company have any restrictions on hiring certain types of individuals?" the replies were:

Restrictions on Hiring	Yes	No	N.A.
Ex-convicts	44	36	22
Individuals on probation	47	34	21
Individuals whose salaries are garnisheed	25	58	19

One respondent stated that such restrictions were illegal, but a search of U.S. statutes on the subject disclosed no law requiring an employer to disregard such backgrounds on prospective employees when considering them for positions in sensitive areas.

The replies to the question "Does your company obtain credit bureau checks on employees and prospective employees?" were as follows:

	Some	All	None	N.A.
Employees	51	7	34	10
Prospective employees	47	12	34	9

Forty-two respondents said that such information was given to the employees' supervisors as a guard against placement in sensitive areas.

The internal auditors surveyed were asked whether employees, under any circumstances, should be required to give the company personal financial statements. Thirty-four said "yes"; fifty-nine said "no"; and nine did not reply. Some of the comments added to these replies were:

Middle management and above—yearly

If liabilities could embarrass the employer (a college)

All management-level employees and those in security work

As proof of innocence

On questions of conflict of interest or suspected fraud

When a fraud is discovered, to decide the extent of the employee's involvement

Positions which are financially sensitive—payroll, cash

Critical areas of employment such as data processing

In circumstances such as garnishments and bankruptcies in an effort to help the employee manage affairs better

If they have broad responsibility for negotiating or disbursing

Officers submit a statement of indebtedness and the source of outside income on an annual basis

Where the suspected employee's known income does not support his standard of living

Conflict of interest and kickback investigations

Deferred compensation programs

If he had declared bankruptcy

On request for loans

part five
suggested
audit recommendations

chapter twenty

discussion

The increase in fraudulent activity in the economic life of most industrial countries has caused some top managements to adopt measures informing all managerial personnel in divisions and subsidiaries of the approved procedures to be followed when a suspected fraudulent act is discovered. These provide an orderly method of assigning responsibility for the investigation, assuring that proper officials are notified, and providing guidelines so that all managerial staff will treat suspected offenders fairly and consistently.

Exhibit A-1 is from a procedure manual of a major company. It is a comprehensive description of the steps considered necessary to efficiently handle a sensitive, personnel matter. Besides the recommendations for investigation and deposition of each case, it requires a final report on each instance to prevent recurrence.

Exhibit A-2 is a similar manual from another company. The first manual (A-1) defines the acts which it covers as "an intentional act which results in the diversion of money or property and which is admitted or can be proved." The second manual separates "violent illegal acts" from "nonviolent illegal acts" and provides for somewhat different treatment in each kind of offense.

Exhibit A-3 represents the coverage given in one company's *Employee Relations Guide* regarding "ethical principles and legal standards." This guide covers such offenses as kickbacks, billing customers at inflated prices, billing for merchandise not delivered, and concealing or misrepresenting facts to avoid criticism or punishment for errors of judgment.

It appears that an increasing number of companies are taking positive steps to make clear to their employees company policies on conflicts of interest and the offenses defined in part five of this study.

The internal auditor's position in fraud detection is being reinforced by such directives. This is another indication that the internal auditor's responsibility for the control of fraud is growing.

Exhibit A-1

PROCEDURE MANUAL		Subject	Manual No.
Issued 1/1/76	**Effective 1/1/76**	IRREGULARITIES	1234-0001
☐ Complete Revision	Supersedes	REPORTING	
☐ Partial Revision (see asterisk)		INVESTIGATING	
☐ No Change		RESTITUTION	Page No.
Distribution			

PURPOSE
To provide a uniform procedure for investigating, reporting, and resolving acts of dishonesty, fraud, or theft which involve employees or nonemployees of the company. Unless unusual circumstances surround a loss of $1,000 or less, local management will handle it and will not be required to submit a report to corporate headquarters.

REFERENCES
1234-0002, Insurance and Self-Insurance
1234-0003, Fidelity Bond — Irregularities
1234-0004, Audit Shortages

DEFINITIONS
Employee — The term "employee" as used herein is as appearing in fidelity bond. (**Note:** These are for bond purposes only and do not necessarily reflect actual, legal, "employee" status.) This includes regular or temporary employees, wholesale commission consignees, commission truck agents, commission truck consignees, retail contract managers, and all other similar agents or consignees who are covered by fidelity bond.

Nonemployees — This includes dealers and all others while acting on behalf of the company or while in possession of money or property belonging to the company or in which the company has an interest, whether or not a contract or bond exists.

Irregularity — This means any loss to company of money or property which results from an apparently fraudulent or dishonest act of an employee(s) or nonemployee(s) either acting alone or with others. The term "fraudulent or dishonest act" is to be interpreted as an intentional act which results in the diversion of money or property and which is admitted or can be proved.

EXCLUSIONS

A. Any loss occurring while products are in transit in commercial carriers' equipment unless an employee, insured agent, or insured consignee is involved. (Irregularities involving commercial carriers will be handled by accounting and regional traffic offices as determined in *Procedure Manuals 1001-0001, 0002,* and *0003.*)

B. Any loss of product, cash, or other shortage which is based solely on an inventory or audit computation and procedure deviations which do not involve dishonest acts and where there is no factual evidence of fraud which is admitted or can be proved. Such losses are defined as audit shortages with reporting requirements as outlined in *Procedure Manual 4321-0010.*

RESPONSIBILITIES

Local management — The unit manager/controller or his appointed representative is responsible for promptly preparing and distributing required initial notices and subsequent reports, undertaking investigation, requesting headquarters' assistance, if necessary, and arranging for restitution and/or filing for payment under fidelity bond coverage.

Local Office of General Counsel — When a suspected irregularity exists, the nearest representative of the Office of General Counsel should be consulted before embarking upon any contact with the employee(s), distributing the initial or final written notification, and preparing the *CO-0012 — Proof of Loss Claim* or any other written communication relating to irregularities which implicate specific individuals. If any attempted contact with local management is made by a legal representative of the employee(s), he should be referred directly to the local representative of the Office of General Counsel.

North American Division:	Controller's — Coordinate headquarters' reporting and undertake any investigation this department deems necessary under the circumstances.
	Respective functional management — Review reports submitted to headquarters and assist field management as requested.
Corporate Department:	Undertake any investigation and other required action as deemed necessary under the circumstances.

PROCEDURE

1. **Notification of Irregularity** (whether covered by fidelity bond or not)
   A. All employees are responsible for bringing irregularities or suspected irregularities to the immediate attention of their supervisor or manager.
   B. Local managers or their designated representatives should undertake an immediate investigation of the situation reported as an irregularity and determine the need for immediate telephone notification to the Corporate Security and Safety Department.

C. *Initial report* — Depending on the circumstances and in the judgment of local management, immediate telephone notification may be required. This will depend upon the value of the property involved, the number or level of employees, the method used to commit the irregularity, or possible exposure which may prove detrimental to the company. Headquarters' management, upon receipt of the telephone report, will contact the other departments as deemed necessary. *Whether or not a telephone notification is made, a confidential letter must be mailed within ten days after the discovery describing the irregularity.* All subsequent correspondence relating to the irregularity is also to be marked "confidential." *Distribution of a report is limited, and a recipient should not prepare nor distribute additional copies.*

The initial report should cover the following points:
1. Name(s) and address(es) of the individual(s) involved, if known, and any allegations or implications of dishonesty relating to such individual(s) should be documented with incriminating information or admissions from them
2. Location of the office, plant, site, terminal, etc., where the irregularity occurred
3. Type of operation
4. Actual or estimated amount involved
5. Explanation of the circumstances of the irregularity
6. Action taken, including method of investigation, facts uncovered, present status of employee, and steps taken to protect company assets from further loss
7. Indications whether the most recent audit of the location uncovered any circumstances which might have indicated that an irregularity was in progress

D. *Interim reports* — It is anticipated that final reports will be issued within ninety (90) days of the initial report. Where this is not possible, an interim report is to be issued and then each six months thereafter, indicating the current status and the forecast of progress.

E. *Final report* — After the investigation and all the actions within the control of local management are completed, a final report (identified as such) is to be submitted as soon as possible.

The final report should cover the following points:

1. Amount involved exclusive of insurance or other recoveries
2. Name and position of employee(s) and nonemployee(s) involved
3. Methods used to effect the irregularity
4. Time period over which the irregularity occurred
5. Means of disclosure
6. Statement as to whether there was:
   a. An absence of internal control
   b. A circumvention of internal control through collusion
   c. Effective internal control

7. Steps taken to prevent recurrence in instance 6a and 6b above
8. The names of the insurance companies and other persons from whom recoveries were made and amounts recovered

F. Local management's responsibility for reporting irregularities under the provisions of the subject manual is in no way relieved by the fact that reports and other correspondence are or will be issued on the same subject either by local management or others. *Irregularity reports must be distributed in accordance with paragraph 1G of this manual and must satisfy all requirements listed in paragraphs C and E with respect to the initial or the final reports as the case may be.* Local management must submit a report which in all cases provides management with comments on all the items above and other items as applicable.

G. Distribution of *Initial Report* and *Final Report:*
Original: Manager, Corporate Security and Safety Department
Copies:
Corporate Insurance Department
General auditor
Manager, North American Division Operations Audit
Respective North American Division Functional Management
North American Division Controller, attention of respective functional accounting department's manager
Local Office of General Counsel
Local management as determined by the unit manager/controller responsible for reporting
File

2. Investigation

Investigation must be conducted discreetly to protect innocent individuals and to preclude, insofar as possible, any basis for claims of defamation.

A. Provided the employee(s) does (do) not resign, the individual(s) suspected of being involved in an irregularity may be transferred to another position, continue on present position under strict surveillance, or be suspended until an investigation of the irregularity is completed. Termination of the employee is not recommended during the initial investigative stages. Action taken will depend on attendant circumstances. Appropriate final action will be taken during or after the investigation.

B. Pending results of the investigation, the employee's(s') salary or wages should be continued provided he did not resign. Depending on attendant circumstances and with the Office of General Counsel's approval, an employee(s) may be suspended without pay.

C. The fidelity bond coverage ceases to cover an employee(s) immediately subsequent to the discovery of the irregularity. Should management retain the employee(s), any further losses incurred as a result of an additional irregularity by this same employee(s), if not reinstated by the bonding company under the company's blanket policy, will be charged against the affected North American Division or field unit.

D. Written reports containing any implication of dishonesty on the part of the employee(s) should be prepared and released only after consultation with the Local Office of General Counsel.

3. Restitution

A. Cases involving possible restitution should be pursued by local management with direction from the local Office of General Counsel familiar with the relevant laws of the particular area.

B. It is most important that no expressed or implied assurance be given that the company, its agents, or employees will not testify, initiate, nor assist in legal action where restitution is sought from an employee(s) or from someone on his behalf. Before restitution is accepted, a written disclaimer should be prepared by the company supporting this position and signed by the respective employee(s).

The recommended format of this disclaimer is as follows:

Dear _____ :

In accepting restitution due this company by reason of handling of certain property of the company, it is understood that neither the company nor any of its agents or employees has given or is giving any promise or assurance to conceal any facts or not to institute or to assist in penal proceedings. We wish you to confirm this understanding by your endorsement below.

C. Although not essential, a handwritten confession in the employee's(s') own language should, if possible, be obtained. Where practical, General Counsel should be present when a confession is obtained.

4. Insurance Claims

A. Notify the Corporate Insurance Department (see paragraph 1G) as soon as an irregularity is suspected.

B. Local management should file form *CO-0012—Proof of Loss Claim* in quadruplicate with support documentation when the amount of loss exceeds the $1,000 deductible and when there appears to be no reasonable chance of recovery. It is expected that bond claims will normally be filed within 90 days after detecting an irregularity.

Distribution:
    2 copies: Corporate Insurance Department
    1 copy: (as applicable)
      Manager, Marketing Accounting
      Manager, Manufacturing Accounting
    1 copy: File

C. After a claim is filed, any further settlement with the defaulting employee(s) must be coordinated with the Corporate Insurance Department for routing to the insurance carrier.

CORPORATE ADMINISTRATIVE PROCEDURE
ILLEGAL ACTS

1. **PURPOSE**
   To establish the standard procedure for handling and reporting any known or suspected illegal acts perpetrated or committed against the company or its employees in the performance of their duties.

2. **ORGANIZATIONS AFFECTED**
   Corporation, worldwide

3. **DEFINITIONS**
   A. *Violent illegal acts* are defined as, but not limited to, thefts, burglaries, robberies, arson, assaults, riots, and civil disorders.
   B. *Nonviolent illegal acts* are defined as, but not limited to, defalcations, misappropriations, or fraudulent misuse or disposal of company assets.

4. **RESPONSIBILITIES**
   A. The respective divisional presidents, subsidiary presidents, and general operating managers are responsible for the administration of this procedure and for ensuring that each of the following individuals is notified, as appropriate and as the circumstances and immediacy of each individual illegal act committed against their respective organizations dictate:
   • President
   • Executive/group vice president
   • Corporate controller
   • Vice president, employee relations
   • Director of the Law Division
   • Director of audits
   • Director of public relations
   • Director of safety
   • Manager of insurance

   B. The Law Division is responsible for:
   • Initiating legal action, as appropriate
   • Advising and assisting the director of audits

   C. The corporate controller, group controllers, and divisional controllers are responsible for:
   • Instituting adequate controls that will minimize the possibility of nonviolent illegal acts and, at the same time, provide a means of discovery of their occurrence
   • Advising and assisting the director of audits

   D. The director of audits is responsible for investigating all reports of illegal acts perpetrated or committed against the company or its employees in the performance of their duties and for:

- Obtaining all the facts, determining the extent of loss, identifying responsible parties, gathering evidence, and conducting the interrogation of responsible parties with the advice and assistance of the Law Division
- Coordinating the necessary legal action on substantiated illegal acts as directed by the Law Division
- Establishing the mechanism to recover losses wherever possible
- Recommending to the appropriate management, with the advice and assistance of the corporate controller and/or the appropriate group or divisional controller, changes which will minimize the possibility of recurrence
- In the case of nonviolent illegal acts committed by an employee of the company, notifying the vice president, employee relations, of such act and consulting with him concerning appropriate action

E. The director of safety is responsible for advising and assisting the appropriate management with respect to minimizing the possibility of recurrence of violent illegal acts.

F. The manager of insurance is responsible for handling all insurance claims resulting from illegal acts committed against the company.

G. The director of public relations is responsible for handling all press inquiries concerning illegal acts committed against the company after clearing the information to be released through the appropriate management and the Law Division.

H. All employees are responsible for reporting illegal acts committed against the company or its employees in the performance of their duties in accordance with this procedure.

5. **PROCEDURE**

Companies in the United States, Canada, Mexico, and the Orient
Handling and Reporting of Violent Illegal Acts

Any known or suspected violent illegal act perpetrated or committed against the company or its employees in the performance of their duties shall be reported:

1. Immediately to the appropriate federal, state, and/or local law enforcement agencies after it is reasonably determined that no clear or present further danger to people or property exists and after all injured parties are assisted and medical authorities contacted

2. To the appropriate management as the circumstances and immediacy of each act dictate and in accordance with *Corporate Administrative Procedure 1.5,* "Accident Reporting," and *Corporate Administrative Procedure 1.22,* "Threats and Harassing Telephone Calls."

Handling and Reporting of Nonviolent Illegal Acts

Any known or suspected nonviolent illegal act perpetrated or committed against the company or its employees in the performance of their duties shall be reported in the most expeditious manner as circumstances dictate and in accordance with the following:

1. To the supervisor in charge of the particular function affected, who will notify his district manager or appropriate superior

2. The district manager or the appropriate superior shall notify the divisional president, subsidiary president, or general operating manager as appropriate and concurrently notify the director of audits

3. If the act involves individuals to whom the employee normally reports, the act should be reported directly to the director of audits.

Exhibit A-3

EMPLOYEE RELATIONS GUIDE
SUBJECT: OBSERVANCE OF ETHICAL PRINCIPLES AND LEGAL STANDARDS

SECTION 000

COVERAGE — 000.

The policies set forth in this section shall apply to all employees.

BREACHES — 001.

This policy is an extension of those principles set forth in the manual on *Principles and Objectives* in the paragraph entitled "Observance of Laws." It covers breaches of employee fidelity falling within the following three general categories:

1. Employee theft and employee fraud (theft with attempt to conceal) include all forms of misappropriation or conversion of company assets for personal gain or the gain of a third party, or parties, which result in a potential loss to the company.

2. While acting in the role of an employee of the company (alone or with others) so as to defraud a customer, supplier, or other third party for the personal gain of the employee or anyone else at the expense of such third party. Examples of such acts would include kickbacks, billing a customer at an inflated price or for merchandise which he did not in fact receive, or any other act of a similarly unethical or illegal nature.

3. Any other dishonest or unethical act or manipulation of the company's records to conceal or to misrepresent acts or decisions for the purpose of (a) avoiding criticism or punishment for errors of judgment or failure to follow a supervisor's orders or instructions;

(b) showing a better performance record than actually earned; or (c) otherwise misrepresenting employee performance, activities, or transactions being documented.

FIDELITY BOND COVERAGE — 002.

All employees must be eligible for coverage under the company's blanket fidelity bond as a condition of initial employment and continued employment. This bond covers the company against loss due to dishonest, fraudulent, or criminal acts committed by employees, whether acting alone or in collusion with others.

VIOLATION OF BOND CONTRACT — 003.

The commission by any employee of any of the acts described in Section 001.1 and 001.2 of this policy is a violation of the fidelity bond contract and is cause for immediate dismissal of that employee.

DISCIPLINARY — 004.

The commission by any employee of any of the acts described in Section 001.3 of this policy will subject the employee to appropriate discipline, including possible dismissal.

DISPOSITION OF POLICY VIOLATIONS — 005.

All instances of employee irregularities or dishonesty in violation of this policy are to be referred to the office of the general auditor for appropriate investigation and recommendation for disposition. Upon completion of his investigation, the general auditor will submit his findings and recommendations to the division head concerned. If his findings include any acts which may be in violation of the fidelity bond, he will advise the manager, Corporate Insurance Department, and the Office of the General Counsel at the same time.

1. Appropriate disposition of each case will be made by the division concerned, except that if an alleged violation of the fidelity bond has occurred and the division intends to take any action short of dismissal, the matter should be referred to the vice president of personnel and organization. It will be his responsibility to discuss the case with those concerned and to determine an appropriate disposition of the case.

Date Issued   Supersedes Issue Date   Issued By

chapter twenty-one

communication channels

messages

The Federal Trade Commission made a comprehensive investigation of the public utility industry between 1928 and 1935. It found that companies had misstated earned surplus; failed to distinguish earned surplus from capital surplus; paid dividends from capital surplus; and practiced deceptive or illusory methods of dividing earnings and accounting for assets, liabilities, costs, operating results, and earnings.

To correct these abuses, the FTC recommended to Congress the creation of an appropriate federal agency with power to set and to enforce uniform accounting standards and procedures. Subsequently, the U.S. Federal Power Act and the U.S. Federal Power Commission came into being. In 1964 a U.S. court of appeals decided against a company which claimed a right to nonuniform accounting and finally subjected that company and that entire industry to governmental accounting direction. It took about 30 years to make that one-way communication effective.

Since the inception of the U.S. Securities & Exchange Commission, there have been many attempts to impose a degree of uniformity in financial statements. However, the subject material is so vast and complicated that true uniformity is probably decades away.

The subject of fraudulent activities is an equally large and complex problem, and easy solutions to all aspects of this question are not going to come soon. However, the SEC has a positional advantage in combating corporate fraud. It has mandated power to force corporate disclosure of material facts that would affect an investor's valuation of a company.

If corporations were forced to disclose material frauds they committed such as illegal payoffs or bribes to obtain business, favors, tax concessions, etc., such disclosure could act as a strong restraint against the commission of those acts because concealment, as well as the act itself, becomes illegal. Disclosure also may make directors and management, as well as the corporation, subject to criminal penalties. Shareholders may sue for punitive as well as actual damages. How strong the SEC's message may become is for the future to tell.

Some corporations with numerous locations, branches, divisions, and subsidiaries find it worthwhile to instruct all units to report to corporate headquarters once a year on all employee thefts and frauds where the corporation was victimized. These reports are signed by an appropriate official in each unit and sent to a designated individual at headquarters, usually the general auditor. He reviews the cases, summarizes them, and issues a report on the worldwide corporate experiences. The report is widely distributed to management people and to departments concerned with security matters.

A summary of this type keeps top management informed on the aggregate crime problem of the company from year to year and ensures that appropriate personnel, such as the Insurance Department, are completely informed of all cases in which they may have a legitimate interest. It also informs unit management of problems that have developed elsewhere. This encourages activation of preventative measures.

The Institute of Internal Auditors, Inc., by a resolution of its Board of Directors, adopted a *Code of Ethics*. Article II states: "Members, in holding the trust of their employers, shall exhibit loyalty in all matters pertaining to the affairs of the employer or to whomever they may be rendering a service. However, members shall not knowingly be a part to any illegal or improper activity."

The employer in the business world is the equivalent of the combined interest of the corporation's shareholders. Directors and management are the agents and employees of the shareholders. Management hires internal auditors and can establish their organizational responsibilities and authority. The internal auditor obtains independence primarily through organizational status, reporting level, and objectivity. The public should recognize that internal auditors may not equate loyalty to the real employer—often tens of thousands of unorganized individuals unacquainted with the details of the business and primarily interested in dividends—with loyalty to a management whose interests may or may not coincide in all respects with those of the shareholders.

That an internal auditor should "not knowingly be a part to any illegal or improper activity" is an important statement and places an obligation on the auditor to disassociate himself from any such activity. It can be assumed that this does not mean merely to look the other way but to take positive steps to stop illegal acts. He has an obligation to conduct himself so that his "integrity should not be open to question" and to "exercise honesty, objectivity, and diligence in the performance of his duties and responsibilities."

opinions of internal auditors

One measure of the internal auditor's effectiveness in dealing with fraudulent activities of top-echelon people is what action he would take upon discovering such improprieties. Here is how a selected group of internal auditors answered the question "If the internal auditor learns that top management in his organization is committing massive fraud, should he consult with":

	Yes	No	No Answer
immediate supervision	81	13	8
outside directors of the company and/or Audit Committee of the Board	55	32	15
public accountants	53	29	20

Less than 25% said that they would consult with public authorities such as the SEC, state attorney general and/or a regulatory body, and the district attorney. None would disclose such wrongdoing to the public press.

The fact that only a bare majority would choose to consult with (or possibly the words should have been *confided in*) public accountants is a matter which might be a worthwhile subject for further research.

Another question was "Should he proceed until rebuffed by higher supervision and then drop his investigation and say nothing further about it?" The answers were:

	Yes	No	Non-Committal
He should drop the matter	8	88	6

This was a strong affirmation of the proposition that auditors are tenacious in pursuing their objectives. They were less certain about how to achieve a desirable conclusion. Thirty said the auditor should resign, whereas 65 said he should not.

Another item on the questionnaire pertained to the reaction of the internal auditor if he were discharged. The question read: "If the auditor is discharged because of the accusations he made against management-level people, should he seek justice by a civil suit against his former employer, assuming he felt he could prove his case?"

The answers were: 78, *yes*; 12, *no*; and 12, *neutral.* By an even greater margin of 82-8, the respondents considered this an ethical step.

Other questions were posed as follows:

In the following cases, try to indicate how you feel about the internal auditor's detecting fraud and reporting it. Assume that the internal auditor did not uncover the fraud under the following conditions. Assume adequate time was available for a comprehensive audit.

Indicate your opinion of the statement *the auditor should have been expected to have detected the fraud* in the following examples.

A total of 102 replies was received, but two did not answer this section. Replies were received from several foreign countries as well as the United States. The questions are rearranged to place the least number of *agree-strongly* replies first and proceeding to the largest number of those replies in the 12th case.

The auditor should have been expected to have detected the fraud.

CASE	AGREE STRONGLY	AGREE	NEUTRAL	DISAGREE	DISAGREE STRONGLY
1. A manufacturer spent $400,000 a year for advertising through one agency. Collusion between the advertising manager and the agency owner enabled the latter to defraud the manufacturer by billing in advance of insertion and again when the advertisement appeared. They split the $75,000 excess billing equally.	18	46	24	9	3

2. There were ten men who traveled regularly for the company. The auditor did not notice that one man regularly paid for his hotel bills with a credit card provided by a supplier and was brazen enough to leave the telltale voucher attached.

25	40	24	9	2

3. Invoices from suppliers were concealed from the auditor after the goods were received. Thus, booked payables on the cost of sales and expense items were reduced from a correct total of $250,000 to $100,000 to improve a poor-earnings record and serious cash-flow problems.

28	47	16	8	1

4. Traffic claims against common carriers were not booked as filed. The traffic manager arranged for carriers to send such refunds directly to him. He opened a bank account in the company's name with him as sole signatory and deposited these refunds there and later withdrew them. The loss in a year was $35,000.

31	41	15	12	1

5. The book inventory increased from $100,000 to $500,000 with little change in sales. The auditor checked only 10% of the dollar value and 1% of the physical inventory. The actual shortage of $125,000 escaped those tests.

44	41	11	3	1

6. In the previous three years, 575 doubtful receivables totaling $150,000 were written off to a reserve. In that time, not a dollar of recoveries was recorded on the books. The auditor did not investigate the cause for this lack of recoveries. The cashier diverted a total of $10,000 to his own pocket.

45	40	10	4	1

7. There was widespread overreporting of production by employees on incentive pay. This was so serious that the company was paying for 20% more production than was actually completed. The company suffered increasing operating losses which totaled $500,000 on sales of $15,000,000 in the most recent year against a forecasted profit of $1,500,000.

47	43	8	1	1

8. Payrolls were disbursed from a bank account set up expressly for that purpose. The actual gross pay records totaling $825,000 for a previous year were not reconciled to the grand total of the gross pay shown on the W-2

forms, which totaled only $750,000 or $75,000 less than the gross payroll per the books. The cashier wrote pay checks for nonexistent employees and cashed them.

53	37	9	1	0

9. Each quarter of the past year, the general ledger total of receivables was written down by a charge to sales because the total of the individual customers' accounts was less than the general ledger control. The differences by quarters were:
   1. General ledger $150,000
      Detail $145,000
   2. General ledger $135,000
      Detail $125,000
   3. General ledger $125,000
      Detail $112,000
   4. General ledger $115,000
      Detail $100,000.
   The auditor did not recognize that the total discrepancy was $43,000 and represented a breakdown in internal control.

59	34	6	1	0

10. The bank accounts had not been reconciled in several months. Although two bank accounts per the books showed substantial overdrafts, he did not investigate the cause.

62	28	7	3	0

11. Replies from one out of ten circularized accounts receivable contained disagreements with the company's balances. The replies were turned over to the Credit Department for follow-up. None were checked directly by the auditor. The fraud totaled $50,000 out of a total $1,000,000.

65	33	1	1	0

12. About one company check out of each 20 written was not supported by vouchers, was written to order of cash, and was charged to the cost of sales. Gross profits declined from a theoretical 40% to 30%.

80	18	1	1	0

coordination between internal and external auditors

It is common practice for internal auditors to coordinate their audit programs with those of external auditors. This avoids wasteful duplication of effort and expands total coverage. Because outside auditors usually have access to internal auditors' reports, they can better plan their own reviews of internal controls.

The Securities and Exchange Commission in Rule 17a 5(g) requires that independent auditors' reports on members of national securities exchanges, brokers, and dealers registered under Section 15 of the 1934 act contain a statement on internal controls. This statement must include a comment as to whether the auditors reviewed the procedures for safeguarding the securities of customers.

In some instances, certification statements issued by CPA firms carry comments on their reviews of internal controls. For example, in their certification of the 1973 nonbanking activities of the Morgan Guaranty Trust Company of New York, Price Waterhouse & Co. said in part . . .

> We reviewed and tested the system (including the procedures employed as they affect internal control, the extent of the segregation of duties within and among the various departments, and the scope of the internal audit programs) to the extent we considered necessary to evaluate the system as required by generally accepted auditing standards; our study included . . . review of the procedures followed by the Auditing Department . . .
>
> The objective of internal accounting control is to provide reasonable, but not absolute, assurance as to the safeguarding of assets against loss from unauthorized use or disposition and the reliability of financial records for preparing financial statements and maintaining accountability for assets. The concept of reasonable assurance recognizes that the cost of a system of internal accounting controls should not exceed the benefits derived and also recognizes that the evaluation of these factors necessarily requires estimates and judgments by management.

They added in their report the following:

> There are inherent limitations that should be recognized in considering the potential effectiveness of any system of internal accounting control. In the performance of most control procedures, errors can result from misunderstanding instructions, mistakes of judgment, carelessness, or other personal factors. Control procedures whose effectiveness depends upon segregation of duties can be circumvented by collusion. Similarly, control procedures can be circumvented intentionally by management with respect either to the execution and recording of transactions or with respect to the estimates and judgments required in the preparation of financial statements. Further, projection of any evaluation of internal accounting control to future periods is subject to the risk that the procedures may become inadequate because of changes in conditions and that the degree of compliance with the procedures may deteriorate.

There are two views on the desirability of the extension of the external auditor's certificate to include comment on internal controls. Those in favor claim that it adds to the reliance that may be placed on a certified statement. Those opposed believe that such a comment does not add creditability to certified statements. It is very unlikely that weaknesses could be properly explained within the framework of the space allotted to the auditor's certification and that such matters are properly directed to the attention of management and not shareholders of whom most would lack the expertise to understand the problems. As a result, only a trite comment that such reviews were made could be included.

The statement prescribed by The American Institute of Certified Public Accountants recognizes only the concept of *reasonable assurance* that assets are safeguarded and stresses the inherent limitations that should be recognized in considering the potential effectiveness of any system of internal accounting control.

It is difficult for any auditor to be assured that sufficient and effective internal controls are in operation for any specified time. Frequent personnel turnover, introduction of new systems, discontinuance of certain activities, and acquisition of new office equipment may be some of the causes of breakdowns in existing internal controls. If internal auditors have adequate and alert staffs to monitor changes in the organization, the work of public accountants is made easier provided there is good rapport between the two staffs.

The public accounting profession has trained thousands of certified public accountants for important positions in commerce, industry, and government. Public accounting staffs might be strengthened if there were a greater flow of talented, young internal auditors into the public accounting field.

One partner in a large public accounting firm thinks that worthwhile training would result if selected, younger employees of CPA firms were assigned to internal audit staffs of their clients for a period of time. Supervision would be by the chief internal auditor, and assignments would be set up to provide reasonable variety. Temporary transfers of personnel from other operating departments to internal audit is not unusual. Many managements recognize that their most promising people can benefit greatly from spending a semester or two with their Internal Audit Department. An extension of this practice may be a valuable adjunct to the training of future leaders of the public accounting profession and may benefit their clients.

the effective audit committee of the board

In 1940 the Securities and Exchange Commission suggested that corporations form Audit Committees of nonofficer directors. This recommendation came soon after the SEC had completed its examination of the McKesson and Robbins fiasco. A number of companies complied with this suggestion shortly thereafter. Since then, based on two separate surveys, it is estimated that less than 60% of public-owned companies have appointed Audit Committees of outside directors. Public accounting firms encourage the appointment of these committees.

In January 1977, the Board of the New York Stock Exchange approved a requirement that all U.S. based listed companies have audit committees of their Boards of Directors. The rule requires that members of an audit committee be outside directors free of any relationship that would interfere with the exercise of independent judgment. This requirement becomes effective June 30, 1978.

The value of Audit Committees, of course, depends on the ability and independence of those appointed to serve on them.

A competent Audit Committee inquires into the scope of both the external and internal audit programs, internal controls, and the staffing of audit departments. It suggests additional areas to be audited and asks auditors to explain the depth of their examinations in detail. It also undertakes other duties at the direction of the full Board of Directors.

Most companies which have an Audit Committee of the Board list in annual reports only the names of those who serve on the committee. Shareholders generally learn little or nothing of the activities of such committees.

The American Telephone and Telegraph Co., in its annual report for 1974, included a new and interesting section titled "Responsibilities for Financial Statements." It follows in its entirety:

The integrity and objectivity of financial data are the responsibility of management. To this end, management maintains a highly developed system of internal controls and supports an extensive program of internal audits. More fundamentally, the company seeks to assure the objectivity and integrity of its accounts by careful selection of its managers, by organizational arrangements that provide an appropriate division of responsibility, and by communications programs aimed at assuring that its policies and standards are understood throughout the organization.

The independent auditors observe generally accepted auditing standards in expressing an informed judgment as to whether management's financial statements, considered in their entirety, present fairly the company's financial condition and operating results. They must obtain an understanding of the company's systems and procedures and perform tests and other procedures sufficient to provide reasonable assurance that the financial statements neither are materially misleading nor contain material errors. While their procedures involve extensive testing of company procedures, it is neither practicable nor necessary for them to scrutinize every transaction.

The Audit Committee of the Board of Directors meets periodically with both management and the independent auditors to assure that each is carrying out its responsibilities. The independent auditors have full and free access to the Audit Committee and meet with it, with and without management being present, to discuss auditing and financial reporting matters.

The Columbia Gas System in its 1973 annual report acknowledged the activities of the Audit Committee of the Board of Directors. Columbia Gas continued to comment on this function in its 1974 annual report as follows:

The Audit Committee, composed of six outside directors, met in February, November, and December 1974 and in February 1975 with Columbia's independent auditors and held separate meetings with the System's internal auditor and accounting, tax, and financial personnel.

The committee has reported to the Board of Directors that, based upon such independent investigation, the accounting procedures of the System are proper and the income statements and balance sheets reflect fairly Columbia's results of operations and financial position.

Internal auditors of organizations with an active, competent, and independent Audit Committee are indeed fortunate. Such organizations will gain from the increased confidence internal auditors receive through encouragement and empathy of Audit Committees with broad business experience.

part six
conclusions

chapter twenty-two

conclusions for the internal auditor

Fraud in the marketplace, embezzlement in positions of trust, bribery in public life, theft of securities, check kiting, illegal political donations, mail frauds, overloaded expense accounts, manipulation of payrolls, issuance of false financial statements, credit-card swindles, illegal competition, kickbacks and payoffs, bankruptcy frauds, and arson are a few of today's challenges.

The outside criminal—the burglar or robber—usually visits his victim but once and leaves telltale evidence of his entry. But the *inside* criminal is a different story. How is he tracked down? The *inside* criminal may be the owner, the manager, or the lowest employee. All are in a position to steal on a continuing basis.

Here are four ways by which fraudulent activities are uncovered: (1) the reduction of the resource to a noticeable level of depletion; (2) the accidental discovery of the fraud; (3) the revelation by an informer; and (4) the diligence of an inquisitive "member of the accounting or internal audit staff who can concentrate on the problems of balances, of checks, and eliminations," as Brad Cadmus said.

It appears that the internal auditor can make the best contribution to the control of fraud when:

■ management clearly assigns the responsibility for handling cases.

■ the internal audit program is designed not only for operational audits but also provides for an imaginative approach to the possibilities of controlling fraudulent activity.

■ the internal auditor fully understands the legal implications of fraud.

- the auditor acquires the attitude that not every foozle is a fraud and has the keen perception of fraud when he comes in contact with it.

- the auditor gains training and experience in interrogation of suspects.

- the audit staff recognizes that recent disclosures of widespread payola have been made. Whether the payola was necessary or not, a serious loss of control over substantial funds occurs when such disbursements are made from *off-the-books* funds and from *laundered* money moved from country to country without records.

- the internal auditor is assured by public accountants and outside directors that his responsibility runs to them as well as to management when fraud by top management is suspected.

- the auditor does not place unlimited dependence on *internal control.* The internal control system that can't be penetrated has not yet been invented.

technical aids

The auditor does not need to become a criminologist to fulfill his obligations to his profession. However, it may be an advantage for him to learn more of what can be accomplished by modern technology. He needs an outline of practical applications.

Even amateurs use photography universally and effectively. Surveillance photography is a common tool in wide use by banks and merchants. Infrared film permits pictures to be taken in total darkness. It can detect erased writing. Special filters allow the photographer to go below the surface of paper to read what is covered.

A close-up picture on 35mm slide film may be projected on a screen several feet wide so that alterations in accounting records may be studied in great detail.

X-ray pictures are used to detect castings defects and fake art treasures.

Ultraviolet light may be used to reveal traces of a fluorescent powder on the hands of a suspect who handled an object dusted with it.

Effective closed-circuit television guards many major buildings. When surveillance is properly monitored, it is a deterrent to theft or vandalism.

using copiers for false documentation

Some embezzlers have used copiers to prepare false vouchers or other documentation to improperly support disbursements or to substantiate an asset. Here are several ways they have done this:

- Copy an original and use one or more copies for duplicate documentation.

- Copy an original, cutting to use only certain sections. Make a mock-up of these, adding new data such as dates, numbers, and amounts. Then copy the completed mock-up to get a revised clean copy.

- Cover certain features of an original to get an altered copy.

When modern copiers were first introduced, specially coated papers were used, and it was easy to distinguish a copy from an original. The next generation of copiers reproduced originals on plain paper making it more difficult to identify a copy. However, many original documents employ color to some extent, placing a limit on the potential risk of improper duplication.

In 1973, Xerox introduced a copier that produced very true color copies on plain paper. This development gave counterfeiting capacity to the amateur who for a few cents could make color duplicates which are difficult to distinguish from the original.

Here are some methods of detecting a color copy:

- If the surface of the paper is rubbed with white tissue, the smudge on the tissue will be a different color than on the copy. This occurs because the color on the copy is created by several layers of different colors. On original printed copies the color is solid and when rubbed the smudge will be the same color.

- Place a blank sheet of plain paper on top of a suspected item and apply a heated iron to a small area. If it is an original, the item will not stick to the plain paper. But, if the item is a color copy, the two will stick together because the toner will dissolve enough to cause adherence.

Here are some controls currently in use:

- Some organizations control the use of color copiers by allowing only designated individuals to operate them. Precautions are taken to restrict access to the area where the copier is installed. However, as more color copiers are installed in places freely available to the public, these controls will be bypassed.

- Printing companies can design and print with special inks important documents, such as negotiable instruments, so that they won't reproduce well.

case studies

The major difficulty in compiling a comprehensive study on frauds from an auditor's viewpoint is the scarcity of explicit descriptions of the means by which auditors have discovered frauds. A broad-based survey of actual cases with such detail would be of inestimable value in attempting to identify the most successful techniques. This study includes several significant contributions which are very much appreciated. However, many responses to the questionnaire sent to selected members of The Institute of Internal Auditors did not include any responses to the request for significant cases.

The Bank Administration Institute publishes and circulates to a restricted clientele well-written case studies of bank frauds. By controls over those who receive the case reports, BAI hopes to avoid preparation of a guidebook for *embryo embezzlers*. In a booklet titled *A Study of Internal Frauds in Banks*, BAI analyzed 1,932 fraud cases in several categories. This covered a three-year study (1968-1970). It quoted the *FBI Annual Report* for the fiscal year ending June 30, 1971, showing that in one year the FBI investigated 4,941 fraud cases occurring in insured commercial banks.

While it is recognized that a major case-study survey might very well serve as a guide for the wrong parties, it is important that auditors be made aware of the best techniques of fraud detection.

resolution of the internal auditor's role in crime detection

The purpose of this study is to make auditors aware of potential areas of fraud. The position has been taken that auditors should not be fiscally liable for failure to uncover fraud if they perform their work with professional care in accordance with contemporary standards. It is a logical corollary of that position that the profession must accept the responsibility for the improvement of skills in the detection of fraud.

About half of the internal auditors queried said they believed that management would support a more aggressive role by auditors in fraud detection and additional training for auditors in fraud detection. A majority of those who did not express an affirmative position said they didn't know if management would support them in either respect. Management apparently bears some responsibility for a better definition of the internal auditor's proper role in the detection of fraud and for communicating that definition to them.

Comments by some internal auditors were:

Rapid growth in complex nature of modern business makes this role and training necessary.

Our company gives auditors a free hand to detect fraud.

While I believe management would spend for better fraud training, I think that they would not support the audit staff's making discovery of fraud its major goal.

I believe fraud has become too easy in general because of a trend in top management to be inadequately concerned.

Our company management strongly supports our efforts now.

Management is becoming more aware and concerned.

Our management views fraud detection as a role played by public accountants.

Management can be rather fickle in these matters.

Can't imagine any company that would not support these programs.

It is difficult to convince top management that any white-collar worker could be dishonest.

Modern management too often has a glaring defect — *It has not learned the art of effective internal communication.*

the need for more surveys and studies

The literature on the subject of fraud, as it is encountered by auditors, is scarce. There is an understandable reticence on the part of victims to share their experiences with others, even under the proffered cloak of anonymity.

The need for a fuller understanding of the multiple facets of fraud and the obvious difficulties of achieving that goal could not be better expressed than in the following excerpts from the report by the President's Commission on Law Enforcement and Administration of Justice. It is titled *The Challenge of Crime in a Free Society.*

White-Collar Offenders and Business Crime — Inevitably, crimes reflect the opportunities people have to commit them. Whether a person has access to a criminal opportunity depends very much on who he is, what work he does, and where he lives. Most of the crimes discussed in this report, those that have most aroused the public, are the common crimes of violence or theft that threaten people in the streets and in their homes. They also are the crimes that make up the greatest part of the cases processed by the higher criminal courts.

However, there is another set of crimes that are related to the occupational positions people have. They are committed in the course of performing the activities of particular occupations and exist as opportunities only for people in those occupations. Within this great reservoir of actual and potential crimes, the rather vague term "white-collar crime" is now commonly used to designate those occupational crimes committed by persons of high status and social repute in the course of their work. It differentiates these offenders and their crimes from those committed by low-status or disreputable persons.

The white-collar criminal is the broker who distributes fraudulent securities, the builder who deliberately uses defective material, the corporation executive who conspires to fix prices, the legislator who peddles his influence and votes for private gain, or the banker who misappropriates funds in his keeping.

Arrest, court, or prison statistics furnish little information about the frequency and distribution of these offenses or about the characteristics of these offenders. The reason is that they are only rarely dealt with through the full force of criminal sanctions. This is an area of criminal activity where the standards of what is right and what is wrong are still evolving and where society is still testing the effectiveness of less drastic sanctions for controlling undesirable conduct on the part of individuals or corporations.

Reducing the scope of business crime is particularly difficult. The offenses are often extremely hard to detect, especially since there is often no victim but the general public. Sometimes victims do not even know that they were victimized. Merely determining whether an offense was committed frequently involves extremely complicated factual investigation and legal judgment.

Perhaps most important, the public tends to be indifferent to business crime or even to sympathize with the offenders when they are caught. As one executive convicted and sentenced to jail in the electrical equipment conspiracy said: "On the bright side for me personally have been the letters and calls from people all over the country, the community, the shops and offices here, expressing confidence in me and support. This demonstration has been a warm and humbling experience for me." It is unlikely that a convicted burglar would receive such letters and calls.

The commission has not been able to investigate the many different kinds of business crime and antisocial conduct in detail, so it cannot recommend specific measures for coping with them. This would require separate analysis of virtually every aspect of the American economy and its regulatory laws. However, it is clear that such studies are needed to improve enforcement of statutes governing many kinds of business practice. The studies should conduct research into the scope of illegal and immoral conduct; consider noncriminal sanctions to deal with it; propose methods for strengthening administrative agencies; explore the need for higher penalties, including both fines and jail sentences for serious violations; and discover whether new substantive law is needed to deal with harmful activity that is not, or may not, now be illegal.

Auditors should decide what role they can play to meet that challenge through their professional societies. It is hoped that this study may serve to direct attention to the problems caused by those who defraud and to encourage auditors in their efforts to control fraud.

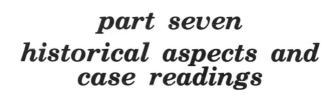

part seven
historical aspects and
case readings

chapter twenty-four

the lineage of deceit

Over· the past few decades, large conglomerate and multi-national corporations have become common. While opportunities for fraudulent activities are enhanced by the size and complexities of modern business, deceit and trickery are not of recent origin. Here are some examples:

Genesis

The book of Genesis describes the oldest recorded fraud. Isaac's older son Esau, took two Hittite women as his wives. The two wives made life difficult for Isaac and his wife Rebekah. When Isaac realized that he would die soon, he called Esau to his side and said, "I am old and blind, and I do not know the day of my death. Take your weapons and go hunt wild game for me and prepare a savory dish that I may eat, and I will give you my blessing."

Rebekah was listening when Isaac spoke to Esau. When Esau left to hunt for game, she told Jacob, her younger son, to fetch two good kids so that she might cook them for Isaac. Then she told Jacob to pretend that he was Esau and to go to Isaac with the meat and ask his blessing. Since Esau was a hairy man and Jacob was smooth, Rebekah covered Jacob's arms and neck with kid skin and dressed him in Esau's clothes. When Jacob appeared before Isaac, the old man asked how he had been able to return so quickly. Although he thought he recognized Jacob's voice, Isaac was convinced it was Esau when he felt the hairy arms. Thus, he blessed Jacob and ended by saying, "Be lord over your brothers, and may your mother's sons bow down to you. Cursed be everyone who curses you, and blessed be everyone who blesses you."

Shortly after Jacob had left, Esau returned from his hunt and prepared a dish for Isaac. Then he asked for the blessing his father had promised him. Isaac quickly realized that Jacob had received the blessing intended for Esau by guile. However, Isaac refused to bless Esau, saying, "I have made Jacob your lord, and all his brothers I have given to him for servants, and with wine and grain I have sustained him. What, then, can I do for you, my son?"

Two members of a family deceived an infirm father to defraud a son and brother.

Ancient Greece

Twenty-three centuries ago in Athens, Demosthenes was the greatest orator of his time. He used his talent to rally the Athenians against the conquering Philip II of Macedonia. Yet, as a youth, Demosthenes had been weak and inarticulate. He overcame these shortcomings by filling his mouth with pebbles and declaiming above the roar of the waves as they crashed upon the shore.

His father, a wealthy man, died while Demosthenes was a boy, but the three executors of the estate embezzled most of his inheritance. When Demosthenes became 20, he sued them to recover the small remainder. Later, after years of effort, Demosthenes became a very wealthy lawyer. One of his famous cases was the defense of Phormia, the banker, who, ironically, had been accused of embezzling money from the estates of minors.

After the Athenians were defeated by Philip, Demosthenes continued his lucrative law practice until he was exiled on charges of financial corruption. As Thucydides, one of the great Greek historians, said, "Men are more anxious to be called clever than honest and suspect honesty of simplicity."

Roman Era

The Roman Empire developed a system of concessions to accomplish many economic objectives. Syndicates were formed by groups of individuals who purchased shares called *partes*. The syndicates were owned by the most divergent classes of the public. These financial syndicates received a charter to collect taxes, to execute work, or to exploit the land. The agents of the syndicates were called *publicani* or *publicans*.

Their profits were large because they fleeced the subjected people without mercy. They used every means to exaggerate the tax that was lawfully levied. They increased revenues from the forests, the fields, and the mines by inhuman practices. Most of the profits went not to the government's treasury but into the pockets of the publicani and to the surpluses of the syndicates.

Since the Roman magistrates and military leaders recognized the political power of the directors of the syndicates, they were usually complacent when the publicani assessed interest at usurious rates when inhabitants of a province were even the least bit late with a payment.

Middle Ages

In the year 1271, Roger Bacon wrote: "The people, corrupted by the evil example of their betters, oppress and circumvent and defraud one another, as we see everywhere with our eyes. Of merchants and craftsmen, there is no question, since fraud and deceit and guile reign beyond all measure in their words and deeds."

in the footsteps of the explorers

When the nations of Europe emerged from the age of feudalism, they reached out to gather the riches of Asia and the newly discovered lands of the Americas. Some of them adopted the Roman system of private syndicates to accomplish their objectives.

Two of these chartered companies provide case materials for a study of the development of fraudulent activities.

The first is the story of John Law, a Scottish financier, who set up the Banque Generale in Paris in 1716.

When Louis XIV died on September 1, 1715, he left France a bankrupt government whose debts were more than 40 times the annual gross revenues. His successor, Louis XV, was his great grandson, a boy only five years old. Philippe, Duke of Orleans, became Regent of France. He tried to economize by reducing the size of the army and the number of office holders. In March 1716, he established a Chambre de Justice to investigate those suspected of defrauding the government. Harsh penalties, including death sentences, were applied to those found guilty.

However, 12 months later, the Chambre was dissolved by an edict that said: "Corruption was so widely spread that almost all classes were infected with it so that just punishments could not be laid upon so great a number of guilty persons without dangerously disturbing commerce, public order, and the State."

John Law, a 45-year-old native of Edinburgh, Scotland, had fled to France after killing a rival in a duel. The son of a banker, he had studied banking in many money centers of the continent and had become well-to-do from successful speculation in foreign exchange.

Law convinced the Regent that many of the French financial difficulties were due to the lack of a national bank. The Duke agreed to let Law establish the Banque Generale as a privately owned corporation. In addition to accepting deposits and making loans, the bank had the power to issue bank notes in the amounts of ten, a hundred, and a thousand francs. These notes quickly became popular since they were tied to a fixed weight of silver. They became the first French paper money and were acceptable for the payment of taxes.

In September 1717, Law secured a concession to form a company called Compagnie de l'Occident for the exploration of the entire Mississippi territory under French control. He sold 200,000 shares at 500 livres each — a high price. But three-quarters of the price was allowed to be paid in government notes at face value — three times their current worth.

With the funds secured from the sale of these securities and the resources of his bank, Law purchased the royal tobacco monopoly and all French companies engaged in foreign trade. On December 4, 1718, Law's bank was restructured as the Royal Bank, and its notes were declared legal tender. Law merged the Compagnie de l'Occident into a new company, Compagnie des Indies, and sold more stock at 550 livres per share.

Public speculation soon raised the price to 5,000 livres per share. The new bank took over the national mint, all tax collections, and the national debt by exchanging a share of stock in the Company of the Indies for 5,000 livres face value of the government bonds. By the end of 1719, shares in the Company of the Indies were selling for 12,000 livres each. Many investors were buying shares on a 10% margin. John Law was made comptroller general of France. Under his guidance, the French economy prospered. Industry expanded and foreign trade increased.

His company financed the production of coffee and tobacco in Louisiana. In 1718, the city of New Orleans was founded and named after the Regent. Law personally financed developments in the Arkansas River Basin. There were great problems and substantial losses. The speculative fever broke, and the price of the shares of stock dropped rapidly. As quotations for the shares dropped, commodity prices began to soar. Bank notes became worth less and less. In October 1720, it became public knowledge that the Regent, during the prosperity that Law had created by monetizing the national debt, had drawn 3,000,000 francs from the Royal Bank for gifts to friends and mistresses.

About the same time, a cashier of the Royal Bank absconded to Prussia with a large quantity of the bank's gold. The shares in the Mississippi Company fell to 200 livres each. On December 14,

1720, Law was discharged from his offices and left Paris with only 2,000 livres. He lived in Venice in poverty until his death nine years later.

An assessment of the blame would certainly show Louis XIV guilty of fraud in the extravagance which bankrupted the nation. And the Regent was guilty of embezzlement, as was the cashier of the Bank. John Law was guilty of two foozles. In his effort to bring France out of her economic troubles, Law monetized too much of the national debt and misjudged the profitability of his Mississippi scheme. He lost his personal fortune and ended his life as an exile from his adopted land.

The apparent success of John Law's economic system in France led to a similar development in England. The London stock exchange was organized in 1698, and the following years witnessed much speculation in shares of newly formed corporations.

In 1711, a group of financiers formed the South Seas Company, which obtained a monopoly of English trade with the Spanish colonies in the Americas and the Pacific. King George I became the governor of the South Seas Company, and the public was led to believe that large profits would be made within a short time.

In 1714, the English national debt was £52,000,000. The interest on it was £3,500,000 a year. These were huge amounts in those days. To relieve the government of this debt, a plan was designed to transfer £31,000,000 of the debt to the South Seas Company in return for shares in the company. The holders of government notes were invited to trade the notes for shares.

Within six days, two of every three noteholders did so. Many others purchased shares at prices that rose 60% in one month to a high in 1719 of £123 per share. Company directors bribed government officials and two mistresses of the King with gift shares. Having thus bought the government's cooperation, the company secured permission to put some new propositions into effect.

On April 12, 1720, the company offered stock at £300 per share. The stock was all sold immediately. With this new money and the government's payment of interest on the notes held by the company, the directors declared a 10% dividend. This drove the speculative fever even higher and on April 23, only 11 days after the previous issue, the South Seas Company floated another issue of stock at £400 per share. By June 2, the shares were selling for £890 each. In July, the directors sold another issue for £1,000 each. Soon after, word came from Paris of the collapse of John

Law's Mississippi scheme, and rumors that the Spaniards were restricting English trade with their colonies began to spread.

The directors and other insiders began to sell their shares, and the price of a share dropped to £135 by September 29. Parliament held a trial and sentenced government officials, including the chancellor of the exchequer and the directors, to prison and confiscated 90% of their estates. The Bank of England and the East India Company absorbed part of the shares of the South Seas Company. While the shareholders recovered a small part of their investment, many thousands lost their life's savings. The company's business decreased, but it continued in existence until 1853. It made profits in the slave trade until that source of revenue disappeared.

chapter twenty-five

the modern landmarks

Ward and Grant

The 19th Century saw the formation of many great corporations, especially the railroads. It also was an era of many infamous, fraudulent schemes. One of the most corrupt schemes involved the Erie Road. Daniel Drew, Jim Fisk, and Jay Gould fought Commodore Vanderbilt for control of the Erie. Both sides used all sorts of trickery, including bribery of judges and legislators. They flooded the marketplace with spurious Erie Railroad stock certificates, which they printed as fast as the presses would go. There were battles between market manipulators, and many small investors were hurt in the aftereffects.

A case with tragic consequences for a Civil War hero and later President of the United States, Ulysses S. Grant, occurred in the early 1880's. Grant's son Ulysses, Jr., called Buck, married the daughter of the former Senator Chaffee, a wealthy man.

Ferdinard Ward, a young man about the age of the junior Grant, had developed a reputation as a rising young Wall Street executive. The two young men formed the firm of Grant and Ward. Buck borrowed $100,000 from his father-in-law. After Grant left the White House, he also invested $100,000 and became a special partner. Ward ran the firm while the two Grants were largely figureheads.

Ward's scheme was simple. He used the Grant name to attract investors. Out of the funds invested, he paid large returns from their own capital. Ward not only used the Grants as bait for his *Ponzi-type** swindle but involved the president of the Marine National Bank in New York City. Ward and the president tapped

*See page 167.

the resources of that bank for speculation in the stock market until May 4, 1884, when the bank ran out of liquid funds. Ward prevailed upon ex-President Grant to request a loan from William H. Vanderbilt in order to save the bank. The latter responded with a $150,000 personal loan to Grant. But Grant turned the check over to Ward to deposit in the Marine Bank to tide it over.

Instead of depositing the check, Ward cashed it and then attempted unsuccessfully to escape to Canada. Three days later the bank failed. It was announced that the failure was due to overdrafts of $2,000,000 by Ward & Grant. Ward juggled the firm's books and, instead of showing the actual overdraft, Ward & Grant's books showed a balance on deposit of $600,000. Shortly after that, the firm of Grant & Ward was declared bankrupt with liabilities of more than $16,000,000 and assets of less than $70,000.

The failure of the firm resulted in poverty for the ex-President. It made him an embittered, sick man. A year later he died. Before his death, he said, "I have made it a rule to trust a man long after other people gave him up, but I don't see how I can trust any human being again." James Fish, the president of the Marine National Bank, went to prison for seven years, and Ward received a ten-year sentence.

On May 13, 1884, the 26-year-old president of the Second National Bank escaped to Canada with $4,000,000 in cash from that bank. The next day the Metropolitan Bank closed its doors. It was found that the head of that bank had used bank funds to speculate in railroad stocks. Several brokerage houses soon collapsed. A week after the Metropolitan Bank closed, it was learned that the cashier of the West Side Bank had gone to Canada with $95,000 in cash from that bank. These events led to the panic of 1884.

Charles Ponzi

Charles Ponzi gained a place on the list of master defrauders not by clever manipulation of a complicated business structure but by the very simplicity of his scheme. Today, more than 50 years after Ponzi worked his swindle, similar deals are described as *Ponzi-type* swindles.

In a classic Ponzi fraud, the investor's money is never invested. Early investors are paid gains or dividends from money paid in by later investors. Chain letters and pyramid sales proposals are Ponzi-type swindles in the simplest form.

Ponzi, after serving prison terms for bank fraud and swindles in Canada and the United States, moved to Boston, Massachusetts, in 1920. He had heard of the earlier swindles of a character who gathered in the money of investors by promising impossibly high rates of interest. A news article on the negotiability of postal reply coupons led him into an extensive study of the regulations of the Universal Postal Union. Nearly penniless, he formed a company to exploit his idea of gaining wealth.

He told potential investors that his company, Securities Exchange Co., had arranged to buy postal reply coupons in Europe at about one cent each and then redeem them in the United States for ten cents worth of postage stamps, which he claimed could be converted into cash. He promised a 50% profit in 45 days. Actually, he bought only a small quantity of these coupons, yet within eight months, he gathered $15,000,000 from thousands of people.

A Boston newspaperman learned that Europe had a total issue of less than $1,000,000 of postal reply coupons during the time Ponzi said he was investing $15,000,000. The investigation that followed brought Ponzi both federal and state jail sentences. He was deported to Italy, later migrated to South America, and died in Brazil as a pauper.

Ivar Kreuger

Ivar Kreuger was born in Sweden in 1880. He was the eldest son of the co-owner of two small match factories in Kalmar and Monsteras. After graduating from the Royal Technical University and working a year in hydraulic-power construction, he traveled in steerage to the United States in 1900. He did odd jobs in New York, Illinois, Colorado, and Louisiana. Then he left for Mexico, where he joined a party of 15 engineers working on a bridge in Vera Cruz. Within a few weeks, 13 members of the crew died of yellow fever. Kreuger also contracted the fever and returned to Kalmar.

In 1901, a year after his first trip to the United States, he returned to New York City. He got a job with a firm associated with the Fuller Construction Company and worked as an engineer on the construction of several major office buildings and hotels. At the same time Kreuger was getting a practical education, watching New York contractors handle political payoffs and kickbacks.

In the summer of 1903, he took a job preparing steel for construction jobs in a plant near Saarbrücken, Germany. After several months there, he went to Johannesburg, South Africa, to install German steel during the construction of the Carlton Hotel.

In 1906, he moved to Toronto, Canada, where he worked for a contracting firm, visiting company projects in Buffalo and Toledo. A few months later, he opened a restaurant in Philadelphia, but that enterprise soon failed.

When that happened, Kreuger obtained a position with the Consolidated Engineering Company in New York and, within a short time, became a manager and vice president. While in that position, he supervised the construction of Archbold Stadium and other buildings at Syracuse University. The Syracuse structures were of reinforced concrete, then a new type of building foundation requiring a special kind of iron, which was invented and patented by Julius Kahn. When Kreuger and Kahn met in Detroit, the latter suggested that Kreuger attempt to introduce the Kahn steel methods in Europe. The idea appealed to Kreuger, and he decided to return to Sweden.

On May 18, 1908, Kreuger, now 27 years old, and Paul Toll, a 25-year-old engineer, formed the partnership of Kreuger and Toll Company. Kreuger put up the equivalent of $2,500, which he had borrowed from his father. Toll put up nothing. The new building technique caught on quickly. By the end of 1908, the firm was hard at work building a six-story department store in the center of Stockholm. It was during this construction that Kreuger pulled his first big coup. He had promised to complete the work in four months with a daily penalty if the work took longer and a bonus if the work was completed before the target date.

Working in midwinter, Kreuger put up heavy tarpaulins, special heating facilities, and large searchlights to keep the construction going 24 hours a day. The steel and concrete skeleton was completed in a record two months, and Kreuger and Toll collected a bonus of more than $70,000. Within three or four years, Kreuger and Toll gained a reputation as the best building company in Sweden.

Three years later in 1911, Kreuger and Toll incorporated with capital of a million kronor—about a quarter of a million dollars. The charter of the corporation stated that it was to conduct operations in the erection of buildings and similar businesses but was not to carry on a regular trading business in securities. No change was ever made in the charter of Kreuger and Toll Aktiebolaget; nevertheless, within a few years, trading in securities ran into the hundreds of millions.

Meanwhile, during the last half of the 19th Century, several small match factories had been set up in Sweden employing a new process for making matches. By 1903, most of these small companies merged. Of the few that remained outside the combine, two were owned by Kreuger's father and his uncle Fredrik. Ivar's younger brother Torsten was managing the Kalmar branch and had purchased one of the two Swedish plants which manufactured match-making machinery.

One of the leading bankers of Sweden, Oscar Rydbeck of the Swedish Credit Bank, invited Torsten to try to form a new match combine with the bank's help and using the Kreuger family-owned match business as the core. When Torsten refused, the bank asked Ivar to try to put a combine together.

First, Kreuger formed the Kalmar Trust with a capital of four million kronor—about $1,000,000. This was less than a third the size of the existing combine—the Jankoping-Vulcan Trust. He next bought the only other match-making machinery company and also acquired more match factories. Then he set about lowering costs and improving the quality of the matches he produced. He also started producing his own potash and phosphorus and began building a competitive foreign sales organization.

In its third year of operation, the Kalmar Trust made a net profit of more than $500,000. By then, it was doing almost as much business as its larger competitor. By the end of 1917, Kreuger negotiated a merger of both trusts into the Swedish Match Company with himself as president. In the merger, Kreuger managed to overvalue the shares of Kalmar Trust so that the smaller trust absorbed the larger.

In the meantime, Kreuger and Toll Company continued to grow. It now had six subsidiaries. The company was earning about $200,000 a year. In January 1917, Kreuger split Kreuger and Toll into two companies. One was the Kreuger and Toll Building Company, a contracting business run by Paul Toll. The other became Kreuger and Toll, Inc., a financial-holding company for Kreuger's personal purposes. By 1918 and following new stock issues, the authorized shares of this company were 16 million kronor or about $5,000,000. Its reserves were $7,000,000. A short time later, more than a quarter of the Swedish Match Company's shares (120,000) were transferred to K&T, Inc., for $2,000,000.

During the postwar period, Kreuger managed to capture most of the markets in Asia, England, and Germany. With the assistance of several Swedish banks, he began to buy scattered European match factories from owners impoverished by the war. Eventually, he controlled most of the industry on the continent. He speculated successfully in foreign exchange and invested in a German chemical company that was merged with others to form the giant I.G. Farben Trust.

As early as 1917, Kreuger had manipulated the books of his companies to draw off money for his personal accounts and to overstate balance sheets and earnings statements of the match companies. In order to keep key assistants unaware of overall conditions in the company, he carefully compartmentalized their activities and kept the interrelated affairs of his various companies in his head.

In late 1919, Kreuger formed a holding company, American Kreuger & Toll, which he capitalized at $6,000,000. Through this company in the United States, he accumulated shares in the Diamond Match Company and several other companies. He was able to obtain more than $400,000,000 which he channelled to Europe and into a maze of real and imaginary banks and companies. He kept the dollars flowing to him by paying large dividends and making loans to the nearly bankrupt countries of Europe in exchange for monopolies in the sale of matches.

In the meantime, he had put out stock issues in Sweden totaling 45,000,000 kronor in Swedish Match and 28,000,000 in Kreuger and Toll, Inc. In addition, he borrowed heavily for both companies.

Kreuger arranged for Lee, Higginson & Company, a highly respected private banking firm, to represent his interests in the United States and for their affiliate Higginson & Company to represent him in London. In 1922, the English firm handled $4,000,000 of a $10,000,000 issue of common stock in Swedish Match, more than doubling the outstanding stock in that company.

Several new companies were formed to funnel American dollars into the Kreuger complex: Industrie A.G. in Liechtenstein; Finanz Gesellschaft in Zürich, Switzerland; and the Continental Investment Corporation in Liechtenstein, which was capitalized at 60,000,000 Swiss francs.

In November 1923, Kreuger, with the help of Lee, Higginson & Company, formed the International Match Company, a Delaware corporation with initial capital of nearly $30,000,000 and with later issues of gold debentures totaling $15,000,000. Kreuger siphoned off most of these funds to his companies in Liechtenstein. Within nine years, International Match Company sold $148,500,000 worth of securities to the American public; and all but $4,500,000 was transferred to Europe. From there it disappeared.

International Match Company was audited by Ernst & Ernst, but Kreuger never permitted those auditors to inspect any of the books or balance sheets of the foreign subsidiaries. These constituted most of the assets of International Match Company.

The way that Kreuger siphoned the funds from International Match Company in the United States can be illustrated by the so-called "Garanta" deal. On July 2, 1925, Kreuger reported that he had signed a secret agreement with the Polish government whereby a Dutch company, N.V. Financeaelle Maatschappij Garanta, was to have a monopoly for the sale of matches in Poland. The stock in Garanta was supposed to be held by Polish citizens. Actually, there was no agreement with the Polish government. However, Lee, Higginson & Company sold a new issue of 450,000 shares of International Match Company stock on the basis that there was an agreement for a match monopoly with Poland.

Of $20,000,000 received, $17,000,000 was sent to Swedish Match on the pretext that Swedish Match had advanced this much to Garanta. Swedish Match had actually sent nothing to Garanta, and the $17,000,000 it received from International Match Company was a diversion of funds from International Match Company to Swedish Match Company.

Karl Lange, a Swede who had been discharged from a bank in Stockholm for dishonesty, acted as the sole officer and employee of Garanta in Amsterdam. He kept a simple set of books which, in the end, showed that Garanta received more than $25,400,000 from International Match Company and Swedish Match and that the same amount was debited to Ivar Kreuger. No trace of those huge sums has ever been found. Kreuger had a motto which he followed to the letter: *silence, more silence, and still more silence.*

During the last half of the twenties, he claimed that he extended his real and imaginary monopolies to many other countries. He had a continuing need for funds to bribe officials and to make legitimate loans to governments which had agreed to his schemes. In 1930, after the 1929 stock-market crash, Lee, Higginson and Company underwrote a $50,000,000 issue of debentures for International Match Company.

In 1927, France was in desperate need of external loans to stabilize the French economy. When American financiers refused to loan more money to the Poincare government, Kreuger stepped in and loaned the French government $75,000,000 at five percent interest for 20 years. In return he received the right to import unlimited luxury matches into France. International Match Company took $50,000,000 and Swedish Match, the rest. For this, Kreuger was awarded the Grand Cross of the French Legion of Honor.

Kreuger repeated this type of loan in Estonia, Latvia, Yugoslavia, Rumania, and Ecuador after American sources of funds were closed to those countries. In other words, Americans trusted Kreuger with funds to loan to countries which neither the U.S. government nor American financiers would support directly.

He bought African and South American iron ore properties as well as the Swedish pulp industry, newspapers, and telephone companies. He also purchased a substantial interest in the U.S. Diamond Match Company and the Ohio Match Company.

Kreuger purchased legitimate stocks and bonds such as General Electric shares and I.G. Farben and French bonds but overstated the quantity he held in order to inflate his balance sheets and to keep selling the securities of his companies. At the start of 1929, Kreuger and Toll securities were the most widely distributed securities in the world and were selling at several times their par value.

The American stock market crashed on October 24, 1929. Two days later, Kreuger announced that he was going to lend the German government $125,000,000 at six percent in return for a monopoly on both the manufacture and distribution of matches over a long period. Actually, he was a supporter of Hitler and wanted to strengthen Germany against Russia. The Soviets had expanded their match business, and Kreuger had been unable to do business with them. Kreuger obtained $50,000,000 from American banks and the rest from the French, who redeemed part of their debt.

As the depression in the United States became more severe, Kreuger found it more difficult to borrow there. American investors, to a large extent, had purchased Kreguer and Toll and International Match Company issues on margins. And, as brokers collected their loans, the shareholders sold. As quotations for his issues dropped, he threw in more and more of his resources. He also continued to buy more stock in American match companies and in various European brokerage houses as well as Paris real estate. As he took funds out of legitimate banks, he made what appeared to be simply transfers to other banks. Actually, much of it was to dummy banks which he owned or nonexistent ones. In this way, he could continue to report large cash reserves.

His position was now critical, and he resorted to counterfeiting. He had lithographs made of phony Italian government bonds with a face value of 500,000 English pounds each and five promissory notes representing interest of a million and a half English pounds each. He then forged the names of Italian officials. A total of $142,000,000 of bonds and notes was created out of thin air!

One of the Italian officials whose names he forged was Giovanni Boselli, the Italian director of monopolies. On the 47 forged instruments, he spelled *Boselli* three different ways. Kreuger had always been a calm and careful man, but this mistake indicated that he had begun to crack. Nevertheless, when Kreuger showed the fake bonds to the auditor of Kreuger and Toll, he counted them and wrote them onto the Kreuger and Toll books.

When an English director of one of his companies suggested that it would be wise to submit the intercompany books to an independent audit, Kreuger asked, "Do you think I'm a crook?"

In May 1931, Kreuger visited President Hoover in Washington. He then went to New York City to negotiate with International Telephone & Telegraph Company a proposed merger of the L.M. Ericsson Telephone Company of Sweden, which Kreuger owned. In mid-June, IT&T and Kreuger signed an agreement whereby 600,000 shares of Ericsson were deposited by Kreuger in a Swedish bank in exchange for $11,000,000. It was agreed that IT&T would acquire another 410,000 shares of Ericsson within 12 months after Price Waterhouse & Company had audited the Ericsson accounts for 1931.

When some of Kreuger's enemies in France organized bear raids against his companies securities and drove prices down, Kreuger poured all the funds he and his friends and associates could raise into their defense. By late October, he was back in Stockholm, requesting the Riksbank, the government bank, to lend him $10,000,000. To collateralize this loan, Kreuger pledged his shares in the valuable Boliden gold mine in Northern Sweden.

In January 1932, Kreuger again visited the United States. He made an attempt through Lee, Higginson & Company to borrow from the Bank of America. He also attempted to acquire control of the Bank of America through Transamerica, a holding company of the bank's stock. Both attempts failed.

Kreuger had several major payments due in February. A $2,000,000 loan to the Swedish Match Company was due in New York; $4,000,000 was due by International Match. He needed $1,200,000 to meet scheduled K&T dividends. He owed $2,000,000 to Turkey and more than a million to Lithuania as installments on match loans.

IT&T controller Chinlund and the Price Waterhouse auditors arrived in Stockholm on January 28. Chinlund asked top Ericsson managers some pertinent and penetrating questions. Finally, the Kreuger men admitted that Kreuger's previous balance sheets were erroneous. Kreuger's balance sheet showed that Ericsson had a large balance in cash and on deposit. Chinlund discovered that about $6,000,000 was actually an intercompany balance with Kreuger and Toll. There were other discrepancies. Following Chinlund's return to New York, the IT&T directors decided to rescind the contract to purchase Ericsson. They demanded that IT&T be repaid the $11,000,000 paid to Kreuger. By now Kreuger didn't have anywhere near $11,000,000.

From then on, Kreuger went into deep depression. His doctor kept him isolated for a period of rest.

On February 22 Kreuger's assistant in Stockholm talked with Swedish Prime Minister Karl Ehman, who earlier had accepted a $12,000 campaign contribution from Kreuger. Ehman decided to have the Riksbank and two private banks furnish the $2,000,000 Kreuger needed to meet the February 23 obligation of the Swedish Match Company in New York. Shortly later, Ehman was forced from office for this action.

The $4,000,000 loan problem of the International Match Company was solved by convincing four American banks to renew the loan after it was reduced by 10% and Kreuger had put up 350,000 Diamond Match Company shares from his personal portfolio as collateral. The third problem was met by convincing the Riksbank to advance another $1,250,000 to meet the Kreuger and Toll dividend due March 1.

Among International Match Company's assets were $50,000,000 worth of German government bonds, supposedly being held in International Match's name at the Kreuger-owned Deutsche Union Bank in Berlin. But, before leaving for America, Kreuger had transferred them to Copenhagen and had pledged most of them as collateral for his large private debt to the Scandinaviska Bank in Stockholm.

On February 25, Kreuger realized that he would have to replace the bonds in International Match's portfolio before A. D. Berning, the inquisitive Ernst & Ernst auditor, found that they were missing. Kreuger cabled his Stockholm office and arranged a meeting of the International Match's Executive Committee, which authorized the substitution of Italian government bonds for the German bonds. The Italian bonds were, of course, complete forgeries. Later, when auditor Berning asked why the Italian bonds had been substituted for the German ones, Kreuger promised to reverse the transaction at once.

On the afternoon of March 4, Kreuger signed the recision of the IT&T deal with Lee, Higginson & Company vouching for the return of the $11,000,000 by Kreuger to IT&T. That night he sailed from New York City on the *Ile de France*. Two days later, Berning called Berlin and asked an auditor there to see if the German bonds were in International Match's account. When that auditor replied that they were not, Berning decided to go to Europe himself to get an explanation.

Kreuger arrived in France and went to his Paris apartment. Plans were made for Kreuger to meet with Berning and the bankers in Berlin to settle the question of the German bonds. Kreuger told his associates he would go from Berlin to Rome to get the Italian government to buy back its bonds. Since the bonds were counterfeit, this was a lie.

On March 11, more bad news came from New York. A number of brokerage firms had issued margin calls to Kreuger because the value of Kreuger and Toll debentures had declined. Kreuger, who had a number of mistresses, asked one, a young Finnish girl, to spend the night with him.

The Finnish girl left Kreuger at 8:30 in the morning of March 12. Not long after, Kreuger went into his bedroom, lay down on the bed, and shot himself just below the heart. When Kreuger did not keep an 11 o'clock appointment, his friends became alarmed. A little after 1:00 PM, Littorin, a director of Swedish Match, and Miss Bokman, his secretary, arrived and found Kreuger dead.

Don Durant, a Lee, Higginson & Company official, who had accompanied Kreuger to Paris telephoned his New York office and advised the partners of Kreuger's death. He recommended that they make no public announcement of the death until the news broke in Paris. March 12 was a Saturday, and, in those days, the New York markets were open until noon, or 5:00 PM Paris time. Lee, Higginson & Company, with knowledge of Kreuger's death, cancelled some buying orders for Kreuger and Toll shares. Later they said they had done no trading after having heard the news. However, 165,000 shares of Kreuger and Toll were traded on Wall Street between 10:00 AM and noon, and most of the selling orders came from France. American investors, still uninformed about Kreuger's death, were on the buying side at a price of about $5 per share.

There was a delay in notifying the police, so they did not arrive at Kreuger's apartment until 4:00 PM. At Littorin's request, the police did not report Kreuger's death to the press until 6:00 PM Paris time . . . an hour after the New York markets had closed!

Kreuger had many enemies in France who had tried to bankrupt him by selling short. Within a week, one of the French speculators was arrested and sentenced to five years in prison for illegal stock dealing. No comprehensive investigation was made, and it has never been determined who flooded Wall Street with Kreuger and Toll shares that Saturday morning.

The Swedish Parliament, meeting at 10:30 Saturday night, declared a moratorium on all debts to Kreuger and Toll. Sunday, March 13 was declared a day of national mourning with all flags flying at half-mast.

During the week of March 14, the Stockholm Stock Exchange was closed. But on March 14, alone, transactions in Kreuger and Toll certificates totaled more than 670,000 shares at prices under $5 per share. This amounted to a third of all the transactions on the New York Stock Exchange. As of that date, there was no public knowledge that Kreuger had defrauded the public. Since the stock had sold as high as $46 a share in 1929 and at $27 in early 1932, unsuspecting Americans saw it as a bargain at less than $5.

On March 15, the Swedish government appointed a six-man commission, which engaged Price Waterhouse & Company to examine all Kreuger enterprises.

On March 22, Kreuger's body was cremated in Stockholm. Three days later, the investigating commission announced that an appraisal indicated that Kreuger and Toll assets probably would not cover its liabilities.

On the morning of April 6, Price Waterhouse & Company published its first report stating Kreuger had grossly misrepresented the true financial position of Kreuger and Toll and affiliated concerns in his 1930 balance sheets and that he had been flagrantly doctoring his figures. In mid-April, when a Stockholm printer admitted printing the Italian bonds at Kreuger's request, it was disclosed that Kreuger had forged the bonds.

As the investigation proceeded, 20 of Kreuger's associates, including his brother Torsten, were tried, found guilty, and sentenced to prison for terms ranging from a few months to three years.

Price Waterhouse & Company delved into the affairs of the hundreds of companies around the world that Kreuger owned, operated, or had an interest in. The auditors found his bookkeeping "so childish that anybody with but a rudimentary knowledge of bookkeeping could see that the books were being falsified."

There were nearly $700,000,000 of entries under debits or credits in the books of Kreuger and Toll, the Garanta Company, Swedish Match Company, and the Continental Investment Company which appeared in one set of corporate books but were not listed where they should have been as corresponding entries in another set. Continental, for example, had 117 charges against Kreuger and Toll, but the latter showed only 16 in its books.

In a final report, Price Waterhouse & Company wrote:

> *The perpetration of frauds on so large a scale and over so long a period would have been impossible but for (1) the confidence which Kreuger succeeded in inspiring; (2) the acceptance of his claim that complete secrecy in relation to vitally important transactions was essential to the success of the projects; (3) the autocratic powers which were conferred upon him; and (4) the loyalty or unquestioning obedience of officials, who were evidently selected with great care (some for their ability and honesty, others for their weaknesses) having regard to the parts which Kreuger intended them to take in the execution of his plans.*

Many prominent legal firms spent years trying to track down Kreuger assets and unravel contracts and agreements. Both Kreuger and Toll and the International Match Company in New York were thrown into bankruptcy. The American investors in International Match Company were eventually paid about 20 cents on the dollar for the $150,000,000 they had invested.

There were no criminal prosecutions in the United States. But the partners of Lee, Higginson & Company lost an estimated $9,000,000 as a result of the Kreuger bankruptcy, and the firm was dissolved. Lee, Higginson & Company, it turned out, knew little or nothing of the Continental Investment Corporation, which owed its parent International Match $75,000,000. International Match was supposedly holding 13 match concessions, but three of the largest were found to be false.

The Swedish Match Company survived as a viable corporation because Kreuger had kept that company relatively free of fictitious entries. Eventually, Swedish Match purchased the concessions in matches that had been owned by International Match and Kreuger and Toll.

Resource includes material by Roy Shaplan in his book on Kreuger.

Philip Musica

In 1913, Philip Musica was sentenced to prison for having defrauded banks of several hundred thousands of dollars. Following his release, Musica changed his name to Frank Donald Coster, moved to Fairfield, Connecticut, and established a small chemical business acquired in New York State.

Musica had three brothers. Two of them, George and Robert, changed their last name to Dietrich, and the third, Arthur, changed his name to George Vernard.

In 1926, Coster learned that the hundred-year-old drug firm McKesson and Robbins was for sale at a relatively low price because it had been losing money for several years. With the help of Bridgeport bankers, Coster, falsely claiming doctorates from the University of Heidelberg, bought the large drug house for $1,000,000.

The following year Coster issued $36,000,000 of new stock. He also began to buy up many large, regional, wholesale drug houses and acquired several subsidiaries outside the United States. His two brothers, using the Dietrich name, were active in the management of the business, concentrating on the Crude Drug Department, which operated out of Fairfield.

This department reported profits for several years, but the records showed that the profits were plowed back into ever-increasing receivables and inventories. Much of the inventory was recorded as being on consignment to a sales agency, W. W. Smith & Company, with warehouses purported to be in Montreal. In accordance with auditing procedures at that time, McKesson and Robbins' public accountants did not actually inspect inventories on consignment but accepted confirmations allegedly prepared by W. W. Smith & Company.

Julian Thompson, McKesson and Robbins' treasurer, had not been permitted to learn much about the Crude Drug Department. But in March 1938, he began to question the size of inventories Coster told him were in Montreal. His investigations proved that there were *no* inventories of crude drugs with the Smith firm. In fact, W. W. Smith was nothing more than a mailing address set up by Coster to conceal the fact that he had invented the growth of receivables, inventories, and profits to inflate the market value of McKesson and Robbins shares.

During his investigation, Thompson learned that W. W. Smith & Company had a Brooklyn office. He visited it to learn more about the real activities of that company and found a two-room office occupied by George Vernard, Coster's brother. All mail sent to W. W. Smith & Company in Montreal was forwarded to the Brooklyn office where Vernard would prepare replies. These were sent back to Montreal. Canadian postage was added, and the replies were then mailed. The only employee in Montreal was a girl whose sole duties were to receive and forward unopened mail.

Thompson confronted Coster with the facts he had gathered and threatened to expose him. Realizing the end was near, Coster had his attorneys throw McKesson and Robbins into receivership on December 5, 1938, with the statement that about $9,000,000 of receivables and $10,000,000 of inventory were nonexistent and never had existed. This action brought many government agencies, including the Securities and Exchange Commission, into the investigation. On December 16, when a federal marshall drove to Coster's home to place him under arrest, Coster committed suicide.

The SEC conducted hearings on this case from January 5 through April 25, 1939, and issued a 501-page report of its findings. In a summary of that report, the commission said:

To accomplish the deception, purchases were pretended to have been made by the McKesson companies from five Canadian vendors, who thereafter purportedly retained the merchandise at their warehouses for the account of McKesson. Sales were pretended to have been made for McKesson's account by W. W. Smith & Company, Inc., and the goods shipped directly by the latter from the Canadian vendors to the customers. Payments for goods purchased and collections from customers for goods sold were pretended to have been made by the Montreal banking firm of Manning & Company also for the account of McKesson. W.W. Smith & Company, Inc., Manning & Company, and the five Canadian vendors are now known to have been either entirely fictitious or merely blinds used by Coster for the purpose of supporting the fictitious transactions.

Invoices, advices, and other documents prepared on printed forms in the names of these firms were used to give an appearance of reality to the fictitious transactions. In addition to this manufacture of documents, a series of contracts and guaranties with Smith and Manning and forged credit reports on Smith were also utilized. The foreign firms to whom the goods were supposed to have been sold were real but had done no business of the type indicated with McKesson.

The fictitious transactions originated early in the life of Girard & Company, Inc., Coster's predecessor concern incorporated on January 31, 1923, and increased until they reached the proportions mentioned above. The manner of handling the transactions described above was the one in vogue since the middle of 1935. Prior to that time, the fictitious goods were supposed to have been physically received at and reshipped from the Bridgeport plant of McKesson. And prior to 1931, McKesson made actual cash payments directly for the fictitious purchases, which at that time were supposed to have been made from a group of domestic vendors, but recovered a large part of this cash purportedly as collections on the fictitious sales. The change from using actual cash to the supposed clearance through Manning & Company was not effected abruptly; but for some time after 1931, both systems were used. The Canadian vendors, however, were used only in connection with the Manning clearance system. From the report of the accountant for the trustee in reorganization of McKesson & Robbins, Inc., it appears that, out of an actual cash outgo from the McKesson companies in connection with these fictitious transactions of $24,777,851.90, all but $2,869,482.95 came back to the McKesson companies in collection of fictitious receivables or as cash transfers from the pretended bank of Manning & Company.

While Coster possibly took two or three million dollars for his own purposes, most of his fictitious purchases of drugs were returned to the company as collections of receivables merely to make it appear more profitable than it was. The brothers admitted their true identity and were given prison sentences of up to three years on charges of conspiracy and fraud. John McGloon, the McKesson and Robbins' comptroller, was found guilty since he should have questioned Coster's accounting manipulations and informed the SEC. He served a year in jail and paid a $5,000 fine.

The public accountants reimbursed McKesson and Robbins for more than half a million dollars as a refund of the auditor's fee.

Coster left a suicide note that ended with the cryptic words:

As God is my judge, I am the victim of Wall Street plunders and blackmail in a struggle for an honest existence — O merciful God, bring the truth to light.

Resources include an SEC bulletin and Price Waterhouse & Co.

Richard Whitney

During the 1920's, the Federal Reserve Bank lowered its discount rate to 3½%, and the government lowered corporate income tax rates. These factors combined to make corporate securities attractive. A speculative boom in stocks was the result. More and more shares were purchased on thin margins, and prices soared.

As the demand for funds to finance loans rose, interest rates responded until, in 1929, they hit 20%. Corporations poured their surplus cash funds into the call-money market because the return for liquid assets was high. The public, hungry for tips on stocks likely to advance, eagerly read advice peddled by so-called *financial analysts* who often acquired long positions in certain stocks. They wrote glowing reports on the prospects of those companies, and, when the shares went up in price, unloaded them on an unsuspecting public. Finally, in October the boom collapsed.

Richard Whitney, a vice president of the New York Stock Exchange and the principal broker for the J. P. Morgan investment bankers, was the leader of a banking group which halted the panic on the floor of the exchange on Thursday, October 24, 1929. Whitney, in the absence of the exchange president, went to the floor and placed large orders for leading stocks, stopping the debacle of prices.

However, a week later, prices again collapsed. By the end of that year, the stock market had regained some measure of stability. Shares of several major companies sold for a higher price at the end of 1929 than at the beginning of that year.

As a result of his bold action in the crisis of the previous year, Whitney became president of the New York Stock Exchange in 1930. He served in that office for several years. In his public statements, he continued to defend the right of the securities exchanges to self-regulation and strongly opposed the efforts of the government to impose controls.

As the depression of the 1930's deepened, Whitney's personal financial condition grew worse. In 1938, it was learned that for years Whitney had been stealing securities from customers of his firm and had been embezzling funds from the New York Yacht Club which he served as treasurer.

On March 8, 1938, the New York Stock Exchange suspended him as president. Within a month, he had been tried, found guilty, and sentenced to prison for a term of up to ten years. He actually served three years and four months in Sing Sing Prison. Following his release, he lived in New Jersey until he died in 1974 at 86.

Whitney's conviction brought about a reorganization of the New York Stock Exchange, including the hiring of a paid, full-time president to head a professional staff. His fall from power increased the influence of the Securities & Exchange Commission. This had important effects on the marketing of securities.

Resource includes articles from *The New York Times.*

Anthony De Angelis

Anthony "Tino" De Angelis was the son of Italian immigrants, living in the Bronx, New York City. Early in life he apparently became quite successful in a hog-butchering business. Eventually, however, this company went into receivership. He moved into the salad oil business in 1955, setting up the Allied Crude Vegetable Oil Refining Corporation in a dilapidated, two-story building in Bayonne, New Jersey.

By offering high prices to producers and low sales prices to commodity exporting companies, Tino obtained a large volume of business which, in turn, enabled him to secure capital in the form of loans from customers. No one questioned how he was going to generate a profit by paying high prices and selling low. Many of his sales were to United States government-sponsored overseas food donation projects.

In the early 1960's, it was learned that De Angelis had shipped rancid oil in inferior containers to several countries. When the General Accounting Office reported this condition, Senator John J. Williams told the Senate: "Should anyone have been surprised that the government was again the loser on about $70,000,000 worth of rancid oil? Practically all of the oil purchased from this disreputable source is either lying in domestic warehouses or deteriorating at ports throughout the world."

In 1957, De Angelis converted an old petroleum tank farm into salad oil storage tanks. He convinced an American Express Field Warehousing subsidiary to take nominal charge of his storage tanks and to issue American Express warehouse receipts for the contents. With such receipts, De Angelis could secure cash advances from banks.

American Express Field Warehousing hired Allied men, handpicked by De Angelis, to run the tank farm.

In June 1960, AEFW received anonymous telephone warnings that certain tanks contained water, not oil. When American Express inspectors checked the tanks, they found some did, indeed, hold water. But there appeared to be enough oil in other tanks to cover all the receipts they had issued. The inspectors did not know that they had dropped their measuring devices into a metal compartment containing oil while the tank itself was filled with water. The inspectors learned nothing of the swindle because they permitted the Allied men to do the gauging. The telephone warnings continued, but American Express made no further efforts to check the contents of the tanks. A number of Allied men were aware of the swindle. However, since they all drew large wages, none was willing to talk.

By the end of 1963, warehouse receipts totaled more than $87,000,000 supposedly representing more than 900,000,000 pounds of oil or *nine times* the actual inventory. Tino was using the money from bank loans on the fictitious inventory to buy futures in an attempt to corner the commodity markets for salad oil.

In May 1963, De Angelis obtained an agreement with Ira Haupt & Company to handle some of Allied's brokerage business with the understanding that, in exchange for handling the purchase of futures, Haupt would accept warehouse receipts from Allied and use them as collateral to obtain bank loans. Haupt then would use those funds to loan to Allied.

In October 1963, Tino began to forge American Express Field Warehousing receipts on a pad of forms stolen from the Bayonne offices. He began to flood the country with phony oil receipts. One large midwest bank accepted more than $30,000,000 worth as collateral.

In addition, De Angelis was working a check-kiting scheme with one of his largest customers, the Bunge Corporation, an export company. All the cash he could collect was thrown into the battle to support the futures market in soybean and cottonseed oil.

On Friday, November 15, 1963, De Angelis, no longer in possession of cash reserves, could not support the futures market. It dropped badly. On the following Monday, that market again fell. Tino realized his impossible condition and filed for bankruptcy.

Allied's debt to Haupt had risen to more than $14,000,000, and Haupt was holding more than $18,000,000 of forged warehouse receipts. When commodity exchanges demanded payment for existing contracts, Haupt misappropriated bank day-loan money. To repay the day loans, the Haupt firm pledged customers' stocks they held. At the same time, the Bunge Corporation learned that it held more than $3,000,000 of bounced Allied checks.

The New York Stock Exchange was shaken on November 20, 1963, when the news came that two large brokerage houses had failed because of the Allied bankruptcy. For a time, the ticker tape ceased printing prices. The death of President John F. Kennedy days later caused another quick drop in the Dow Jones Industrial Average from 735 to 711. The Dow undoubtedly would have gone much lower, but trading was stopped at 2:10 PM. The new Johnson administration and the governors took prompt action to restore national confidence. By the end of the month, the market had rallied and the Dow was up to 750, near the year's high.

Friday, November 22, 1963 — the swindle began to unfold. However, President Kennedy's assassination pushed the De Angelis story to the back pages of newspapers. During the weekend, the New York Stock Exchange evolved a plan to liquidate Haupt & Company and to provide up to $7,500,000 in funds to reimburse their customers. Williston and Beame, another broker involved to a lesser extent, was absorbed by Walston & Company and Merrill Lynch. The shortage in inventories had a stated value of $175,000,000. More than 50 companies and banks held worthless receipts.

On December 30, American Express placed its warehousing subsidiary in bankruptcy. This action prevented legal action against the parent company for damages suffered from any negligence in issuing warehouse receipts for nonexistent oil. American Express offered 60% on claims expected to total about $100,000,000.

De Angelis was sentenced to ten years in a federal penitentiary. In 1972, he was released after having served seven years. Shortly after, it was reported that he had reentered the hog-butchering business as a plant manager.

Resource primarily releases by major news services at time events occurred.

Four Seasons Nursing Centers of America, Inc.

Four Seasons Nursing Centers of America, Inc., was formed on September 11, 1967, to engage in the development, contruction, and management of nursing centers throughout the United States. It began business by purchasing five existing nursing homes and two under construction from Jack L. Clark, Amos D. Bouse, and Tom J. Gray. In exchange for their interests, which originally cost them looo than $54,000, they received shares in FSNCA. A summary of the principal capitalizations of the common shares follows:

864,000	Shares to Clark, Bouse, and Gray (at book value then)	$ 500,000
36,000	Shares purchased by Walston & Company, Inc. (underwriters)	45,000
150,000	Shares purchased as preferred and converted to common by Montgomery & Company, a partnership of the officers of Walston	500,000
150,000	Shares purchased as preferred and converted to common shares in a private placement	500,000
1,200,000	Total by original shareholders	$ 1,545,000
300,000	First public offering at $11 per share	3,300,000
100,000	Second public offering at $58.50 per share	5,850,000
1,600,000	Total shares	$10,695,000
	Less commission on sales to public	614,000
		$10,081,000
1,600,000	Plus shares issued 2 for 1 as stock dividend	
3,200,000		

Concurrently, with the public offerings, the original shareholders disposed of 557,800 shares for a net total of $27,986,200 after commissions. Trading in the shares commenced on the American Stock Exchange on November 12, 1968. The stock reached a high of 90¾ on October 31, 1969, after the split. The market placed a value of $304,300,000 on the 3,353,115 FSNCA shares then outstanding.

Public financing enabled FSNCA to embark on an extensive construction program. Each home was usually incorporated separately. By the end of 1968, FSNCA was managing 14 completed centers; nine were under construction; and contracts had been placed for seven more. FSNCA had tried, with only limited success, to sell to local interests portions of the shares in each subsidiary operating a home. It was necessary for FSNCA to carry construction costs until permanent mortgage and equipment financing could be arranged. In addition, the company was obligated to advance substantial funds to cover deficits of the homes until they could become fully occupied and profitable.

On November 6, 1968, a new corporation, Four Seasons Equity Corporation, was organized as a Delaware Corporation with sales offices in Oklahoma City. Initial capital was 800,000 shares. Sales at $11 per share were made as follows: FSNCA took 50,000 shares; Clark, Bouse, Gray and four others bought 70,000. In February 1969, Equity sold 545,000 shares to the public and 135,000 shares along with $714,000 in 6½% junior-subordinated debentures to 14 institutional investors. After commissions, the net proceeds to Equity were $9,400,000. FSNCA and Equity engaged in joint projects. By the end of June 1970, the two companies had 25 joint-nursing centers completed and operating and more than 50 others under construction.

Another company, FSN Corporation, was also formed as a subsidiary of both FSNCA and Equity to provide additional financing. FSNC was not listed on the American Stock Exchange as were FSNCA and Equity.

The accounting system employed by all three companies broke down in 1969. There were large differences in intercompany balances. The accounts were further complicated by an inadequate system of handling interim and permanent mortgage financing, by large cost overruns, and by wholly inadequate systems for the control and management of the nursing centers. FSNCA had designed an elaborate, centralized computer system; but unit terminals did not function properly, and the central computer was found to be inadequate.

On April 3, 1969, another joint-venture company, Four Seasons Franchise Centers, Inc. (Franchise) was organized. FSNCA supplied $12,800,000 and Equity supplied $2,200,000 of the $15,000,000 in capital for Franchise. Most of these funds were raised by the sale of $14,000,000 of new stock in FSNCA and

Equity to 14 investors. Franchise was organized to grant franchises to construct Four Seasons facilities in states which were not yet penetrated. In less than a year, Franchise reported sales aggregating $4,500,000 in advance fees. On May 5, 1970, the Board of Directors of Franchise terminated almost all of the franchise agreements and refunded fees it had collected.

From June 1969 until a year later, the companies borrowed heavily from overseas markets through Four Seasons Overseas, N.V., a subsidiary organized in the Netherlands Antilles. During these months, expenditures were over $1,000,000 a week while operating revenues were negligible.

As of June 1970, unpaid liabilities for trade obligations were about $11,000,000. Another $4,000,000 borrowed from the State of Ohio without security in March 1970 had been spent in the same month.

On June 26, FSNCA filed a Chapter X petition* in bankruptcy. Equity followed suit on July 22. The subsidiaries took similar action within a short time.

The trustee employed Arthur Young & Company to examine the records. Among other things, they found that 75 bank accounts had not been reconciled for as long as 12 months and that computer facilities could not produce detailed schedules of accounts to agree with total balances. The auditors found intercompany accounts irreconcilable. This created severe legal consequences for the treatment of each corporation's security holders.

After suspension of trading in FSNCA and Equity shares, a number of actions, mostly class-action suits, were brought against the companies. The basic charges were:

- Filing false, misleading, and descriptive statements, prospectuses, and financial reports

- Conspiring to manipulate the market price of the shares

The trustee proposed a plan of reorganization which combined the companies into a new corporation, ANTA Corporation. This plan was approved by the Securities and Exchange Commission. About two-thirds of the stock in the new company went to creditors and the rest to claimants who asserted claims for alleged violations of federal securities laws and other alleged frauds.

---

*When granted, a Chapter X petition to the courts results in the appointment of a trustee to control the operations of the business in place of the former management.

In November 1974, the United States Supreme Court sustained a lower court ruling refusing to permit the State of Ohio to press its claim for full reimbursement of $4,000,000 in Four Seasons commercial paper.

Two Walston officials pleaded guilty to criminal charges of securities fraud and conspiracy and were fined $40,000 each. Another former Walston officer was disciplined by the American Stock Exchange as a result of his having acquired 20,000 FSNCA shares at discount and having borrowed $420,000 from FSNCA officials to finance the purchase.

Resources include SEC bulletins and coverage by news services.

the derailment of the Penn Central

The Pennsylvania Railroad had paid dividends on its common stock each year since 1848 and paid $2.40 per share in 1967. As of the end of 1967, PRR stock sold for 61¾. The New York Central paid $3.12 in 1967. At the end of that year, NYC shares sold at 75⅜. However, in the early 1960's, earnings of both railroads had not been good. NYC had shown losses in 1961 and 1962. PRR had earned less than a $1 per share in those years.

About that time, negotiations to merge the two railroads started. It was felt that the merger would result in operating efficiencies and that diversification into real estate development would produce sizeable profits. On February 1, 1968, the two railroads were combined into the Penn Central. By the summer of that year, the common stock was selling at 84. On October 1, 1969, the name was changed to the Penn Central Transportation Company with the formation of a parent-holding company. The Securities and Exchange Commission reported the Penn Central troubles as follows:

For some time prior to merger, management had engaged in efforts to inflate reported earnings and, as the earnings plummeted due to merger related problems, these efforts intensified. The devices utilized involved not only rail operations but, even more importantly, the company's real estate and investment activities. Accounting personnel were expected to select the accounting method that would provide a maximization of income in every possible instance. While it was recognized the benefit was generally only temporary and would have to be made up in the future, the hope was that, by then, the operational conditions would be improved. Reported income in these situations was a reflection of weakness, not strength.

Also relevant, considering the financial condition of the company, was the noncash-generating nature of many of the earnings being recorded. Much of the loss was caused by the deficits from rail

operations. The payment of approximately $100,000,000 in divi-
dends in the postmerger period at the rate of $2.40 per share per
year on 24,110,000 shares also contributed to the drain. The
borrowings needed to meet the cash drain required large interest
payments in this period of high interest rates. When the borrowings
reached their peak, the interest charges on the additional
borrowings were approaching $50,000,000 a year. Cash was even
needed to support Great Southwest, a real estate development
subsidiary which management claimed was helping to support the
railroad.

Great Southwest played a significant role in Penn Central's
affairs. Great Southwest's financial results contributed significantly
to Penn Central's reported earnings, and the Great Southwest stock
owned by Pennco was Pennco's major asset when valued at market
prices. Penn Central, through Pennco, had acquired control of Great
Southwest and Macco Corporation, which later became a subsidiary
of Great Southwest in the early to mid-1960's as a part of its
diversification program. Macco quickly became a major problem
because of its large cash drains which had to be met by cash
advances from the railroads.

At about the time of the merger of the railroads, Great Southwest
and Macco embarked on programs to drastically increase their
reported earnings. The principal vehicle used was the "sale" of
large properties for very large reported "profits" to syndicates of
investors who were motivated to participate because of tax benefits.
These transactions involved only small down payments and
principal payments deferred to future years. Typically, there was no
obligation that the investors continue making payments. These
were essentially paper transactions which should not have been
recorded as profit. Senior Macco officials were under employment
contracts which provided they would be paid a percentage of the
profits reported. Because of large profits being reported, Macco paid
the officers hundreds of thousands of dollars in 1968. Penn Central
management then renegotiated the contracts which resulted in the
officers' receiving a total of $7,000,000 to sign new contracts.

As the company's financial condition deteriorated, management
relied more heavily on the sale of commercial paper to finance
losses being incurred. The company was not using commercial
paper for short-term borrowing. Instead, the full amount of
commercial paper was rolled over as if it were long-term
financing. Goldman, Sachs & Company was the sole dealer in
Penn Central's commercial paper, which at its peak amounted to
more than $200,000,000 outstanding.

On February 5, 1970, the transportation company announced a
$56,000,000 operating loss for 1969. This indicated a loss of
$16,000,000 for the fourth quarter — contrary to the company's
recent assurances that the fourth quarter would be in the black. In
addition to this loss, the company wrote off $125,000,000 in
passenger equipment and facilities as an *extraordinary item.*

On June 21, 1970 — two-and-one-half years after the merger — the bankruptcy of the Penn Central Transportation Company was announced. The day after the announcement, the stock of the company dropped to 6½.

The troubles of this company are too numerous to list, and to explain them in detail would require volumes. Here are a few of the problems.

Personality clashes between the managements of the Pennsylvania and the Central made efficient operations difficult.

The SEC charged that the chairman of the Board and the other defendants *engaged in a scheme to improperly increase the reported earnings of Penn Central Company.* The chairman consented to a federal court injunction barring him from violations of antifraud provisions of federal securities laws. He agreed to the injunction without admitting or denying the charges. That consent settled the SEC charges against him.

In September 1974, a federal court jury indicted two former Penn Central officials, two Washington lawyers, and a German financier on charges of embezzling $4,200,000 of Penn Central funds five years earlier in September 1969.

There were lawsuits against a Wall Street firm for millions of dollars on the charge that it had fraudulently sold Penn Central commercial paper at a time when the investment and banking firm allegedly knew of Penn Central's financial troubles. That firm maintained that it was merely a dealer and did not have duties of disclosure.

Many communities which had levied real property taxes against the railroad experienced financial difficulties when those taxes were not paid. Some communities where rail repair or maintenance facilities were important local industries were hurt when these facilities were closed.

Probably the most significant of the SEC's charges were these:

- *The unfortunate practice of skimping on maintenance to save current expenses and cash.*

- *The suggestions for increasing revenues through the use of the suspense account and for reducing expenses through delays in the booking of per diem charges, inventory losses, increases in reserves for damages, personal injuries and the like.*

- *The plan to charge current costs against a reserve instead of against current operations.*

- Under railroad accounting, certain facilities are not depreciated, but their costs (less scrap value) are charged to ordinary income when abandoned. Plans were underway for a Master Abandonment Program whereby, at some point in the future, ICC authority would be sought to establish a reserve against which both past and future write-offs could be made. In the meantime, the abandonments would pile up.

- A detailed review was made of the transaction of 15 officers whose trading was deemed to raise the most serious questions as to whether it had been based on material inside information. The 15 officers who, prior to bankruptcy, had sold about 70% of the stock they owned at the time of the merger included officials of the finance and operating departments. These officers had apparent access to information concerning the state of Penn Central's affairs which was reaching the public only with a serious amount of distortion.

- As in other major companies, Penn Central had an elaborate option system for its key employees. Many of these officers exercised their options through the use of large bank loans. As this study shows, the presence of such loans can clearly distort the purposes of the option system by encouraging officers to sell when the market in the company's stock declines, even though material, undisclosed information may exist at the time.

- Beginning in 1962, David Bevan, Penn Central's chief financial officer, and Charles Hodge, an investment counselor to the Pennsylvania Railroad, formed a private investment club (Penphil Co.). Its members included several other Penn Central financial department officers. The club made investments with funds borrowed from Chemical Bank. The bank made these funds available because of Bevan's position and because the railroad had a substantial banking relationship with Chemical. The investment club made investments in companies with club relationships which made inside information accessible.

- On at least two occasions, directors deliberately avoided confrontations with management on issues critical to testing the integrity of management and providing adequate disclosure to shareholders. On one occasion, in the summer of 1969, a law suit which claimed improper and unlawful conduct by Bevan was brought to the directors' attention. As they were obligated to do, they authorized an investigation. However, when Bevan threatened to resign, they cancelled the investigation, even though the charges appeared to be well founded and later proved to be essentially correct.

- *Another consistently unprofitable railroad property was the Lehigh Valley Railroad Company, a 97.3%-owned subsidiary of Penn Central. Losses in 1968 and 1969 were $5,000,000 to $6,000,000 per year. However, despite the very high percentage of ownership, Lehigh Valley's results were not included in consolidated statements, thereby permitting the parent to report a higher net income. The justification claimed was a fiction that the Lehigh Valley was being held only on a temporary basis.*

The Penn Central reported a 1975 first-quarter loss of $127,900,000, double that for the same quarter in 1974. The road had more than 9,000 miles of track on which trains must run slowly because of unsafe conditions. More than 10% of the fleet of 148,600 freight cars was out of service and in need of extensive repairs.

The problems of this important railroad continue. To date, the infusion of massive, federal financial assistance has not brought about a profitable operation or a permanent structure. It is difficult to identify the causes as either frauds or foozles. It may be that many of the causes were a mixture of both.

Resources include SEC bulletins and coverage by news services.

Equity Funding Corporation of America

In 1959, Stanley Goldblum combined his small insurance agency with another small business, selling funding programs. The merged company became Tongor Corporation of America. Three other men — Michael Riordan, Raymond Platt, and Eugene Culbertson — joined Goldblum as equal co-owners. Goldblum became president and chairman of the executive committee, and Riordan was executive vice president and chairman of the Board. Platt and Culbertson eventually sold most of their stock to the other two and left the company. In 1960, the corporate name was changed to Equity Funding Corporation of America.

EFCA began as an independent sales company, marketing mutual fund shares and life insurance policies. It developed a package program, requiring a customer to purchase mutual fund shares for cash over a ten-year period and a life insurance policy. Equity Funding paid the life insurance premiums and recorded the payment as a loan to the participant. Equity retained the mutual fund shares as collateral to secure the loan.

Subsidiaries were set up in states where laws required insurance agencies to be domestic corporations. The largest of these subsidiaries was EFC-Cal, a California corporation.

In the early years, the principal mutual fund sold was Keystone Custodian Funds. Prior to 1963, EFCA financed the funded loans through demand on short-term commercial bank borrowings. The mutual fund shares were placed in escrow. The following table shows how the funding business grew at a rapid rate but how, in later years, it declined as a percentage of gross business.

Growth of Business Reported by EFCA
(*in thousands of dollars)

	Total Gross Income*	Commission and Interest*	Percent of Income from Funding	Programs Sold	Funded Loans Outstanding*
1961	$1,766	$1,453	82%	2,309	$1,490
1962	1,836	1,479	81	2,180	3,337
1963	1,325	740	56	371	4,912
1964	2,869	1,492	52	682	6,914
1965	5,363	2,693	50	1,525	10,373
1966	7,487	3,905	52	2,763	16,478
1967	11,179	5,344	48	3,912	25,095
1968	19,179	9,306	49	5,783	36,311
1969	45,572	15,239	33	9,354	51,188
1970	60,913	18,559	30	11,139	63,324
1971	130,951	22,281	17	13,813	88,616
1972	152,601	N.A.	N.A.	N.A.	117,715

These statistics on the growth of EFCA's funding business were fraudulent because they greatly overstated the volume and scope of the actual operations. More than $85,000,000 of bogus income was created by fraudulent entries.

In 1964, the company sold 100,000 shares of EFCA's stock to the public at $6 per share. From that time, company executives realized that a good earnings record would increase the stock value and enrich insiders who held most of the shares. Also, inflated earnings and assets would enable EFCA to acquire other companies on advantageous terms in exchange for its stock.

While Jerome Evans, the company's treasurer, was preparing the 1964 financial statements, Goldblum ordered him to increase EFCA's reported earnings over amounts then on the books because arrangements were being made to receive *reciprocal commissions* of several hundred thousands of dollars. Goldblum told Evans that they would have to be disguised in the financial statements because securities regulations prohibited a company such as EFCA from accepting such rebates. Evans made an entry on EFC-Cal books as of December 31, 1964, to accrue the rebated commissions. It showed a debit to the funded loans receivable account and a credit to commission income of $361,984.97. This was probably the first fraudulent entry on EFCA books.

Each quarter thereafter, Evans was given amounts to enter on the books as *reciprocal commission income*. At first Goldblum gave Evans a precise amount for these adjustments. Later, he told Evans the amount of earnings he wanted to show and gave instructions that the amount needed to inflate the earnings to the desired level should be entered as *reciprocal commissions*. Each such entry increased the gap between the general ledger control for funded loans receivable and the underlying detail. The work papers of outside auditors contained almost nothing to support the loans receivable total.

By 1969, the total of the fictitious reciprocal commissions had grown so large that Goldblum decided that something had to be done to reduce it to manageable levels. It was decided to borrow money and not record the receipt of cash as loans payable but to credit funded loans receivable as payments. As of the end of 1968, EFCA reported more than $36,000,000, or 46% of its reported assets, as funded loans and receivables. Auditors confirmed only about $11,000,000 of funded loans outstanding to program participants. The rest was neither verified nor satisfactorily explained. The auditors did not question these entries, although an incredible volume of securities transactions would be necessary to generate such large *give-ups*. Moreover, such rebates were not permitted under existing regulations. The borrowings not recorded properly were:

Date	Amount	Lender
1/9/69	$ 1,961,250	Nerwirth
1/14/69	113,668	Merban
1/18/69	96,000	Merban
1/24/69	222,529	Merban
1/27/69	1,988,334	First Jersey Bank
2/13/69	4,533,480	Loeb, Rhodes International, Inc.
2/17/69	4,535,195	Loeb, Rhodes International, Inc.
Total	$13,450,456	

By the late 1960's several of Goldblum's early associates were no longer with the company. Riordan had died and Evans had quit. Marvin Lichtig was hired from the staff of the outside auditors and became treasurer. Samuel Lowell was hired as controller, and Fred Levin became president of Equity Funding Life Insurance Company. Later, Lowell and Levin became EFCA executive vice presidents and directed the later stages of the fraud with Goldblum.

The conspirators added $17,500,000 of bogus income to the 1969 financial statements by entries to accrue $17,200,000 in commissions *expected* from ongoing mutual fund contractual plans and $300,000 from anticipated interest. Usually, these entries were made in round amounts quarterly without any supporting detail.

To show a level of agents' commission expense commensurate with the volume of the fictitious funding business, the conspirators reclassified a portion of the real administrative expenses as *agents' commission expense*. This served to give the company the appearance of an efficient marketing organization.

All of these false entries were manual bookkeeping entries, and no attempt was made to introduce bogus entries into the funding program computer system. The aggregate totals of the data on the computer system were less than the manually kept controls, and it was impossible to reconcile the detail to the control total.

The use of this device to increase reported earnings is illustrated in the chart on page 196.

In 1968, Goldblum began to establish foreign subsidiaries. In November EFCA directors authorized a multimillion dollar underwriting of convertible, subordinated, guaranteed debentures to be offered in Europe for funding three foreign operations. A $25,000,000 offering was successfully sold. On February 6, 1969, the net proceeds were credited to an account opened by EFCC-NV at the Franklin National Bank and were then transferred to EFCA accounts. Other funds were borrowed abroad on unsecured EFCA notes. Many of these borrowed funds were credited to funded loans receivable. The liability was, therefore, not recorded. The following chart shows EFCA's international structure in 1970.

Intercompany accounts between EFCA subsidiaries should have been in balance but were not because many bogus transactions were not entered properly on the books of each subsidiary involved.

The Bishops Bank was used at least twice to generate fictitious income for EFCA. The first instance involved a bogus note for $2,000,000 set up on the bank's books as a loan to a Dr. Heinrich Wangerhof, a name invented by Goldblum and Lowell. The second bogus note, dated December 4, 1970, and signed by EFCA's

SUMMARY OF ESTIMATED BOGUS INCOME
FROM FUNDING FRAUD
(1964-1972)

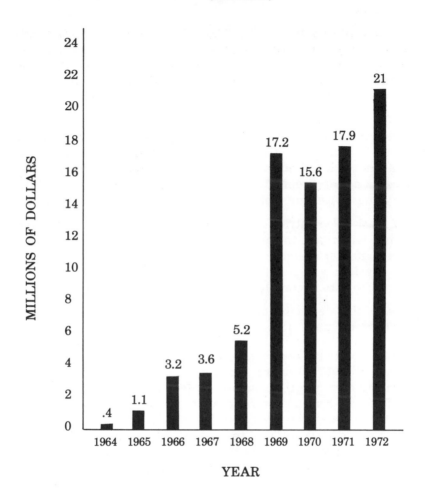

Italian subsidiary, was for $3,000,000. But the liability for this note was not picked up on EII's books. These two transactions, creating assets of $5,000,000 on the bank's books, were then passed on to EFCA. Bank auditors were furnished with a letter confirming both note balances by Joseph Golan, Goldblum's European Agent.

On April 1, 1969, EFCA acquired from Bernard Cornfield's Investors Overseas Services, Ltd., S.A., nearly all of the United States assets of Investors Planning Corporation of America. EFCA paid $6,300,000 in cash, $2,000,000 in notes, and 26,830 shares of EFCA stock with a market value at that time of $1,900,000. EFCA gained 2,000 sales representatives, 29 sales

EFCA FOREIGN STRUCTURE

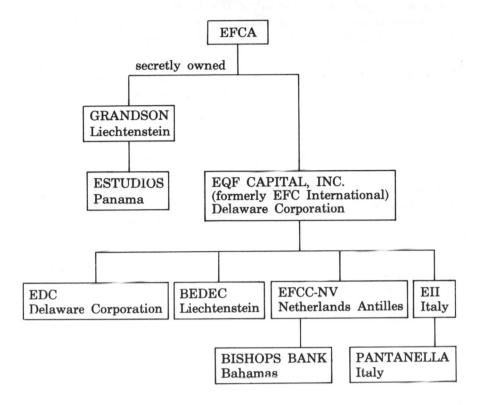

offices, and, supposedly, about 150,000 contractual plans for the accumulation of mutual fund shares. About 50% of the commissions charged clients were collectible over the last 137 monthly payments. These were called *trail commissions*.

The price paid for IPC was about $8,000,000 greater than tangible assets. This sum was set up on EFCA's books as an asset labeled *Excess of Cost over Net Book Value on Date of Acquisition of Subsidiaries*. On May 8, 1970, Goldblum instructed the company attorney, Rodney Loeb, to draft a contract of sale of the trail commissions to an unnamed European buyer. Goldblum and Lowell left for Europe on May 11 and made arrangements for Estudios, a secretly owned subsidiary of EFCA, to purchase most of the trail commissions for $13,500,000. The purchase agreement was signed by Goldblum for EFCA and by a fictitious Perez da Silva for Estudios.

Entries by EFCA included an addition of $18,000,000 to contractuals receivable and an accrual of $4,500,000 as commissions payable. In October, the commissions payable were eliminated by transferring the $4,500,000 to a reserve for bad debts. In November, the reserve for bad debts was transferred as a credit to funded loans receivable. When all entries related to the trail commissions were combined, the effect was an inflation of income amounting to $17,500,000 and a $500,000 decrease in funded loans receivable.

EFCA combined funded loans and contractual receivables on the balance sheet and in notes to the financial statements implied that, in the aggregate, they represented *the amount that clients owe as a result of the various Equity Funding Insurance Premium Funding programs offered by the company and net contracts receivable, together with loans and receivables, where Equity Funding programs have terminated and where the respective shares have not been liquidated.* The combination of true receivables with the inflated trail commission estimates was a deception perpetrated by obscure verbiage approved by the public accountants.

The Liechtenstein corporation, *Grandson,* was used to facilitate part of the major fraud. In 1970, Goldblum ordered an entry to record $9,000,000 in notes payable to Loeb Rhodes, Inc. The cash received in 1969 had been credited to income. To offset the payable in 1970, two bogus Swiss franc notes were prepared and purportedly bore the signature of the fictitious Dr. Heinrich Wangerhof, signed by Goldblum. Other activity in the Grandson accounts contributed to an overall addition of about $11,000,000 to the bogus assets of EFCA.

the insurance phase of the fraud

From 1960 through 1967, EFCA was only a marketing organization, selling funds and insurance issued by other companies.

In October 1967, EFCA began converting to a proprietary insurance operation by acquiring a small Illinois-based company, Presidential Life Insurance Company of America. This name was later changed to Equity Funding Life Insurance Company (EFLIC). In October 1971, EFCA acquired all of the stock of Bankers National Life Insurance Company, a New Jersey corporation. In June 1972, EFCA acquired Northern Life Insurance Company, a Washington corporation.

To utilize these insurance companies, EFCA modified its agreement with Pennsylvania Life Company and its subsidiary Pennsylvania Life Insurance Company, based in Santa Monica, California, whose policies EFCA sold from 1963 to 1968. To secure the modification, EFCA agreed to coinsure with PLC an agreed-upon amount of insurance underwritten by Presidential, later known as EFLIC.

Within a few months, Presidential entered into reinsurance agreements with other insurance companies, such as Connecticut General Life Insurance Company, Sierra Life Insurance Company, Phoenix Mutual Life Insurance Company, Great Southern Life Insurance Company, Kentucky Central Life, and Ranger National Life Insurance Company owned by Anderson, Clayton & Company. Under these treaties, a portion or all of the obligations of the policies were ceded to the reinsurer by the underwriter.

In the first year that a policy is reinsured, the reinsurer pays the ceding company a fee, generally from 100% to 190% of the premium for that year. In succeeding years, renewal premiums collected by the original underwriter are turned over to the reinsurer. Usually, 10% to 20% is returned to the original underwriter for administrative expenses.

EFLIC reported that, in 1969, 90% of the insurance it wrote was reinsured. This dropped to 60% in 1970 and to 50% in 1971.

The 1968 agreement with PLC required EFLIC to cede $250,000,000 in face amount to PLC over a three-year period, beginning with $125,000,000 in 1968. When the EFCA sales force was unable to produce the volume of insurance, meeting the commitment to PLC, EFCA decided to offer its agents and employees a special class of insurance with the first year premium forgiven. Since it cost them nothing for the first year, employees signed up for this insurance. It also cost EFCA nothing because it was reinsured. But it did help meet the commitment to PLC. When much of this insurance lapsed after the first year, new special-class insurance was written in 1969 and 1970.

When officers of EFCA realized during 1969 that they could not meet requirements to reinsure during the second year of the PLC agreement, Levin devised a scheme to record applications received but not paid for or approved by the underwriting department as if the policies had been issued and were in force and paid up. Entries were made in the premium-receivable and commissions-payable accounts on EFLIC books as though the policy were issued. This tactic was sufficient to meet the PLC volume requirements. EFCA, although it received no premiums from the insured, generated cash flow through the reinsurance considerations from the reinsurers.

By the end of 1969, the fallacies of these short-term solutions made new trickery imperative. Much of the special-class insurance had lapsed as employees and agents failed to carry the large policies they had acquired at no cost. Many of the pending applications that had been activated had not been consummated. If they had been purchased, a second-year premium was now payable to the reinsurer.

By mid-1970, the company faced disaster. It had moved to expensive new headquarters in Century City, Los Angeles. Many salesmen had left the organization, and the general slump in the economy and the stock market made it difficult to sell funding programs. EFCA common stock which sold as high as $81.63 in 1969 had dropped to $12.75. Goldblum and his close associates held large blocks of EFCA stock and had seen their paper fortunes shrink greatly. They decided to create and reinsure bogus insurance policies. This came to be known as *Y business* and was not a clever invention but merely an extension of the creation of policies from pending applications. The creation of bogus policies was thought to be merely a temporary solution to the overall problem, giving the conspirators time to seek the ultimate answer. In the interim, EFCA could report larger earnings which would generate cash flow.

The amount of bogus insurance premiums received from nonexistent policies was $5,500,000 in 1970, $10,000,000 in 1971, and more than $14,600,000 in 1972.

In addition to the reinsurance fraud, EFLIC obtained additional revenue from the reinsurers by filing death benefit claims on some of the bogus policies. In the summer of 1972, Goldblum and Levin discovered several EFLIC officers filing false death claims for their own benefit. The guilty persons were not discharged or prosecuted but were put to work on behalf of the company supervising an expanded false death-claim operation. False death claims exceeded $1,175,000 of which $1,031,000 went to the company and $144,000 went to the embezzlers.

Since second-year premiums had to be forwarded to the reinsurers, it was difficult to maintain the bogus policy fraud for very long. Therefore, by 1972, a negative cash flow began to appear on EFLIC books. It caused an imbalance in intercompany balances between EFCA, EFC-Cal, and EFLIC. By late 1972, the imbalance was approximately $16,000,000. Goldblum decided to have EFCA transfer $16,000,000 in cash to EFLIC. This sum had been secured by EFCA from the proceeds of a public debenture offering in December 1971. EFLIC recorded this cash receipt with a credit to the EFCA intercompany account.

EFCA recorded the cash transfer to EFLIC as a purchase of commercial paper and substituted fraudulent bank documents supporting purchases of commercial paper in place of the bank transfer to EFLIC. To prove to the auditors — Seidman and Seidman for EFCA and Haskins and Sells for EFLIC — that the fictitious purchase was real, EFLIC made it appear as if the paper had been redeemed in February 1972 and supported this ploy by moving about 90% of the cash back to EFCA. This transfer was booked by EFLIC as an advance to EFCA. Since the two auditing groups did not coordinate their work, they failed to detect this shell game.

To bolster the financial condition of EFCA during the 1972 audit, a bogus bond portfolio with a value of $24,000,000 was prepared. The conspirators leased office space in Chicago in the name of American National Trust. This name was similar to that of the American National Bank and Trust Company, also located in Chicago. To confirm the existence of the $24,000,000 in bonds, the auditors sent a request for confirmation to what they thought was a branch office of a real bank. A coconspirator received the request and confirmed it for the auditors. Apparently, the auditors did not realize that Illinois did not permit branch banking and that the office to which they directed their request was obviously unauthentic.

On March 6, 1973, Ronald Secrist, an assistant vice president, telephoned the New York State Insurance Department, asking for an appointment the next day. At the meeting Secrist told the story of the fictitious policies which had been reinsured with other companies. The New York Insurance Department informed the California Insurance Department, which, in turn, notified the Los Angeles office of the Securities and Exchange Commission. New York and California insurance officials decided to arrange for the Illinois Insurance Department to make a special examination under the guise of a regular triennial audit. Secrist had talked with Ray Dirks, analyst with Delafield Childs, Inc., in New York. Dirks went to Los Angeles on March 19 and talked with several Equity people, confirming what Secrist had told him. Dirks then advised his clients of what he had learned. As a result, rumors spread through the financial community, and the price of EFCA stock dropped from $28 per share on March 6 to $16 per share on March 26. On March 27, the New York Stock Exchange halted trading in this stock. On April 5, the company's petition for protection under Chapter X of the Bankruptcy Act was approved.

The following table compares the major sources of fictitious income with reported earnings. There were other minor bogus schemes and embezzlements, but only the important ones are shown.

COMPARISON OF ESTIMATED BOGUS FUNDING AND INSURANCE INCOME TO REPORTED NET EARNINGS
(1964-1972)

	Bogus Funding Income	Bogus Insurance Income	Minimum Gross Income From Fraud	Reported Consolidated Earnings
1964	$ 361,000	$ 0	$ 361,000	$ 389,467
1965	1,068,000	0	1,068,000	795,944
1966	3,155,000	0	3,155,000	1,177,355
1967	3,549,000	0	3,549,000	2,530,380
1968	5,152,000	0	5,152,000	7,825,857
1969	17,200,000	350,000	17,550,000	10,911,632
1970	15,600,000	4,000,000	19,600,000	11,715,625
1971	17,900,000	10,000,000	27,900,000	18,192,000
1972	21,000,000	14,667,000	35,667,000	22,617,000
Total	$84,985,000	$29,017,000	$114,002,000	$76,155,260

Over a ten-year period, there were many different facets to the fraud. Three public accounting firms and several regulatory bodies examined Equity records. Outside directors included a Harvard professor, a senior partner of a New York investment banking firm, and two experienced business executives. Apparently none was aware of the fraud. While scores of employees were aware of the frauds and the participants, none spoke up until one disgruntled participant sought revenge.

In November 1973, Goldblum and 18 other EPCA executives were indicted on felony charges, including conspiracy, bank fraud, mail fraud, securities fraud, interstate transportation of counterfeit securities, securities obtained by fraud, electronic eavesdropping, and filing falsified documents with the Securities and Exchange Commission. Before they went to trial, all pleaded guilty.

Judge Curtis set February 10, 1975, as the date when he would hand down sentences. However, on that date, he said he needed far more time to make his decisions because the materials in the case were so complex and massive. On March 17, he sentenced the defendants for violation of federal laws as follows: Stanley Goldblum, eight years in prison and a $20,000 fine; Fred Levin, seven years in prison; Arthur S. Lewis, three years in prison; Lloyd D. Edens, three years in prison; James H. Banks, two years in prison.

Goldblum could face additional charges in New Jersey and Illinois state courts. He is also a defendant in as many as 80 civil lawsuits.

Resource for certain background material and the charts are from the *Trustees in Bankruptcy Report*. Ray Dirks also provided his personal insight in the case.

Atlantic Acceptance Corporation

The Atlantic Acceptance Corporation was formed in Canada in 1961. By 1965, it had grown into one of that country's largest sales financing organizations. According to its reports, it had been an increasingly profitable company every year since its formation.

However, on June 14, 1965, an Atlantic check for $5,000,000 was found to have been written on insufficient funds. Shortly thereafter, when Atlantic defaulted on much larger obligations, it was learned that Atlantic had overstated profits because the firm had accepted high-risk business and had provided inadequate reserves to cover losses on loans. Atlantic had also taken into realized earnings an excess percentage of carrying charges on loans.

Subsidiaries incurred most of the bad-debt losses. But, rather than examine subsidiary accounts, auditors of the parent corporation depended on reports by other public accountants. Since these did not reveal the precarious state of receivables, auditors of the parent corporation made no inquiries.

The collapse of Atlantic caused losses exceeding $70,000,000 to it and to other companies depending upon it. A royal commission investigating the case concluded its report with the following:

Auditors expressing an opinion upon the consolidated financial statements should rely on the work of other auditors only to the extent that they take responsibility for it, as if the relationship between them were that of principal and agent.

National Student Marketing Corporation

During the 1960's, several organizations were formed to exploit the so-called *youth market*. Some of these hired campus representatives to sell items to college students or to distribute samples and advertising materials at universities.

In 1968, 32-year-old Cortes W. Randell conceived the idea of merging some of these companies into a national marketing organization. This national group would then contract with large companies to distribute products through representatives at thousands of schools. To accomplish his goal, Randell convinced a number of established student distributors to join him in the National Student Marketing Corporation, set up through exchanges of stock.

In order to sign up some large well-known companies, Randell resorted to devious tactics. For example, he attempted to negotiate a deal with the Pontiac Division of General Motors. When Pontiac rejected his proposal in writing, Randell altered the letter by changing the word *not* to *now*. He changed Pontiac's rejection to a commitment for $1,200,000 of business for the National Student Marketing Corporation. He then booked the false commitment as an asset. He also claimed an $820,000 commitment from Eastern Airlines and one of $534,000 from American Airlines. Later, both were found to be false.

Randell acquired financial support for the NSMC by selling large blocks of common stock to several large banks, college endowment funds, trust companies, and securities companies. He retained about 10% of the 11,800,000 shares outstanding.

In October 1969, NSMC acquired the Interstate National Corporation, a publicly owned insurance company based in Chicago. While it was only one of several acquisitions, Interstate proved to be Randell's undoing.

In acquiring Interstate, Randell used NSMC's nine-month, unaudited figures as a basis for the purchase agreements. Auditors from a prominent, well-respected firm supported the figures with a *comfort letter.*Such a letter normally would imply that the auditors had no reason to doubt NSMC's unaudited figures. This one, however, failed to bestow the expected blessing on the interim statement. In addition, NSMC financial statements showed the young company was growing rapidly. The price of its stock climbed from $6 per share in April 1968 to $144 a share by December of 1969.

While NSMC actually lost money during that nine-month period, Randell reported a $700,000 profit. He carried on the balance sheet an asset called *unbilled accounts receivable.* This represented revenue from fixed-fee contracts booked as soon as the company received word of client agreement with a sales or distributor program.

According to the Securities and Exchange Commission, NSMC included $1,700,000 in unbilled receivables for the year ended August 30, 1968, before any written client commitment had been received. Within a year, more than $1,000,000 of that had been written off as worthless. However, according to the government prosecutors, the proxy statement restated figures for 1968 concealed the write-off by understating 1968 sales of companies NSMC had acquired.

The auditors claimed they had to deal with the situation as it existed. Because NSMC was growing at such a rapid pace, proper records were practically forgotten. Also, Randell urged the auditors not to approach clients for written assurances that *commitments* existed. When the auditors insisted on making telephone confirmations, NSMC gave them a list of client names and telephone numbers. One of these numbers turned out to be that of NSMC's printer, not a client.

The SEC later argued that NSMC's law firms and the auditing firm should have withdrawn their services or should have notified the public of the true state of NSMC affairs to protect Interstate's shareholders and other investors.

On July 27, 1972, the SEC announced that the United States District Court for the District of Columbia had entered a permanent injunction against NSMC. The injunction enjoined the company from engaging in violations of the antifraud, reporting, and proxy provisions of federal securities laws. When NSMC was also ordered to file correct reports for 1968, 1969, and 1970, the market price of NSMC common shares dropped from $140 on December 22, 1969, to less than $10 by the following May.

In December 1974, Randell was sentenced to 18 months in prison and fined $40,000. He told the court that he had cleared only $1,000,000 but that it was all gone and that he was in debt.

Anthony Natelli, the partner-in-charge of the auditing firm that certified NSMC accounts, was given a one-year prison sentence and fined $10,000. Joseph Scansaroli, the audit supervisor, was sentenced to a year in prison and fined $2,500. Natelli's prison sentence, except for 60 days, and Scansaroli's sentence, except for ten days, were suspended. As of the end of 1976, this case was still in litigation.

Resource includes a compilation of data from numerous articles in periodicals, press, professional publications, etc.

Dairylea

Dairylea Cooperative, Inc., is an 8,800-member dairy products processor in northeast United States with headquarters at Pearl River, New York, and plants in New York and adjoining states.

On April 19, 1973, the New York State Department of Agriculture and Markets fined Dairylea $150,000 for adulteration of milk over, at least, a six-year period. The cooperative had lost $4,000,000 in 1971, another $9,000,000 in 1972 and had piled up an outstanding debt of $18,000,000 which creditors were pressing them to reduce.

Gerard Wegman, manager of Dairylea's Syracuse plant, complained to the cooperative directors that he had been ordered to adulterate milk. When he refused to comply, he was fired for reasons the directors claimed *were not substantially relevant*.

Wegman then informed New York state officials, who secured an admission from Dairylea management that Wegman's charges were true. When management also admitted that they had falsified and destroyed records, Dairylea paid $230,867 to the federal milk pool for filing false reports on its raw-milk usage. Later, management issued a statement placing the blame on *the ill-advised actions of a dozen persons among its 2,000 employees*. In fact, according to witnesses, adulteration had been practiced in several plants.

The most interesting facet of this case is the apportionment of penalties for a fraud upon milk consumers of a large area of the country over several years.

■ The manager of the plant who wouldn't *go along* with the scheme lost his position. He sued the six members of the executive council and five members of management for $300,000 in a civil suit for a breach of contract in his allegedly unlawful dismissal. He contended that those named had conspired to adulterate milk and, because he would not cooperate, caused him to lose his job. Upon a motion by the defense attorney, the case was dismissed without trial by the New York State Supreme Court.

■ The $150,000 fine by the New York State Department of Agriculture and Markets was, in effect, shared by all the members of the cooperative including those who neither participated in or knew of the unlawful acts. The state commissioner who acted as judge in the case was a former Diarylea county president. Despite calls to disqualify himself from rendering a decision, he did not excuse himself.

■ On November 15, 1974, a year after Dairylea admitted the widespread adulteration to the State Department of Agriculture and Markets, an Albany, New York, grand jury indicted the cooperative on 89 counts of possessing and 89 counts of filing false reports with the state. Both are felony counts. A second indictment charged Dairylea, four present employees, and seven former employees with conspiring to possess and to file false reports. These are misdemeanors.

Another employee was charged with perjury. All of these employees were at middle management or lower, according to a Dairylea statement.

Resource: The Gannett News Service.

Roswell Steffen

Roswell Steffen, an employee of the Union Dime Savings Bank for nine years, following experience at another bank, had been promoted to a supervisory position at a Park Avenue branch. He lived modestly on his $11,000 salary in a $275-a-month, New Jersey garden apartment.

When federal, state, and local authorities, investigating a large-scale bookmaking operation, confiscated a bookmaker's records, those records revealed that Steffen had been betting thousands of dollars a day on horse races and professional basketball games. Because of the size of the bets, detectives consulted bank officials in March 1973. Together they uncovered an alleged embezzlement of $1,500,000 by Steffen over three or four years. Steffen, a compulsive gambler, admitted he had gambled it all away.

When confronted, he said that he had taken $5,000 shortly after an audit. The next two nights he went to the race track. On the first night, he lost $3,000. On the second, $2,000. He said, "I've been trying to replace that $5,000 ever since the first night."

Steffen explained that he had access to the vault and that he supervised tellers, many of whom had only minimal experience. Due to this combination of circumstances, he was able to take cash from deposits and to manipulate input to the on-line computer, concealing the shortages.

The mechanics of the embezzlement were not complicated. For example, when a customer came in with a $20,000 deposit, Steffen would enter that amount in the customer's numbered passbook. He then entered the amount into the computer but recorded it as a deposit under the number of a blank, second passbook, which he later destroyed. The first passbook was returned to the customer who didn't realize that his deposit hadn't been recorded under his account number. As a supervisor, he had authority to use the system's override.

Over the years, he made hundreds of corrections to juggle accounts. Most of the time, he was juggling more than 50 accounts at once. Later, he found it more convenient to embezzle from two-year certificates of deposit because there would be 24 months before any juggling would be necessary.

When he was confronted by a customer who had discovered an error or omission of a deposit in his account, Steffen would blame the difficulty on either a data processing mistake or a new teller's posting. He made corrections readily and then altered another account to compensate.

This case is classified as a landmark in fraud because Steffen found that, with the authority and ability to control computer input, he could embezzle large sums of money without detection for several years. It showed for the first time that auditors must recognize the fact that they faced new problems of fraud on a large scale.

Steffen was convicted and served 18 months of a two-year prison sentence.

Resources: *New York Times* and *EDPACS*

Texas Gulf Sulphur Company

In November 1963, Texas Gulf geologists and engineers discovered a large mineral deposit in the province of Ontario, Canada. However, the discovery was not announced to the public until April 16, 1964, when the company described it in a press release. This release was worded very cautiously. It stated that further testing would be necessary to determine the extent of the find.

Before any public announcement was made, a company geologist was charged with advising certain people of test-drilling results and recommending Texas Gulf stock as a good buy. As a result of the geologist's tip, a Texas Gulf director, his broker, and the broker's customers purchased stock prior to April 16

Eventually, other officers, employees, and informed people bought Texas Gulf stock or made calls on the stock. Members of Texas Gulf top management who knew of the discovery accepted stock options, granted by the option committee while members of that committee were still unaware of the find.

The SEC brought charges against insiders who had purchased Texas Gulf stock before the news of the find had been made public. According to the SEC, these people had violated Rule 10-b-5, which prohibits purchases of stock by insiders before favorable news is released. The court found them guilty. In Mitchell vs Texas Gulf Sulphur, a private damage action, the court found that first press release deceptive and misleading.

Both of these actions were civil rather than criminal, but their impact could be a foretaste of a newer concept in dealing with illegal acts.

The decision of the Second Circuit Court of Appeals in SEC vs Texas Gulf Sulphur (CA 2 NY) stressed that material damage had been done because information that could be expected to affect the investment decisions of a reasonable investor, information that could be expected to significantly affect the market price of the stock, or information that causes insiders to alter their trading patterns in the stock was ruled as material.

During November 1963, Texas Gulf Sulphur common stock sold at about $18 per share or about 20 times earnings. In less than three years, the market price increased by 600%, and the price-earnings ratio doubled. The publication of the real value of the Canadian discovery obviously had a very material effect on the subsequent market value of the stock.

Resources: General news services

chapter twenty-six

cases that defined auditor liability

the Ultramares case

For many years, it was generally assumed that public accountants could be held liable for negligence only to those with whom they had a contractual relationship.

In 1929, when the plaintiff brought this case to court, the result was a major increase in the legal liability of public accountants.

The plaintiff, a creditor of the auditors' client, claimed that, relying on the certified financial statements, he had advanced substantial sums to the client. The balance sheet greatly overstated the financial condition, and the auditors did not detect false entries in the books. To recover losses, the creditor sued the auditors for negligence and fraud.

The jury found the defendants guilty. But the judge dismissed the fraud charge and ruled, as a matter of law, that the auditors were not liable for negligence to parties with whom no contractual obligation existed. The decision was eventually appealed to the highest court in New York State.

Judge Cardozo of the court of appeals said in his decision:

> *If liability for negligence exists, a thoughtless slip or blunder, the failure to detect a theft or forgery beneath the cover of deceptive entries may expose accountants to a liability in an indeterminate amount for an indeterminate time to an indeterminate class. The hazards of a business conducted on these terms are so extreme as to enkindle doubt whether a flaw may not exist in the implication of a duty that exposes to these consequences. Our holding does not emancipate accountants from the consequences of fraud. It does not*

relieve them if their audit has been so negligent as to justify a finding that they had no genuine belief in its adequacy, for this again is fraud.

The court of appeals, reversing the lower courts, ordered a new trial, but the parties settled out of court.

In effect, Judge Cardozo's decision established that fraud would create liability which could extend to anyone who relied on certified financial statements. This decision apparently made it unnecessary to prove intent to deceive in order to establish fraud, since gross negligence would indicate no genuine belief in the adequacy of the audit.

Ultramares Corporation vs Touche Niven and Company.

Continental Vending

Harold Roth was president of Continental Vending and owned about one quarter of Continental's stock. To finance his personal stock market operations, Roth had been borrowing large sums of money from Valley Commercial Corp., a Continental affiliate. Valley, in order to obtain money for the loans, borrowed from Continental.

During a 1962 audit, Roth informed Continental auditors that Valley was unable to repay a $3,500,000 loan because he was unable to repay Valley. Subsequently, when Roth offered to post collateral, made up mostly of Continental shares worth less than $3,000,000, the auditors certified the 1962 balance sheet, bearing a footnote that the receivable from Valley was fully collateralized.

Later, Roth pleaded guilty to filing false statements and using the mails to defraud and was sentenced to prison.

In November 1967, the auditing firm settled a civil suit against it for nearly $2,000,000. Two partners and a manager were found guilty of criminal offenses and were fined a total of $17,000. The appellate court stated it was not necessary to prove that the *defendants were wicked men with designs on anyone's purse which they obviously were not but, rather, that they had certified a statement knowing it to be false.* The decision established that auditors could be held responsible for a standard of fairness beyond generally accepted accounting principles.

United States Court of Appeals Judge Henry J. Friendly made the significant ruling in this case. It struck at a policy which auditors had long depended upon to justify their rationale. He said, "The first law for accountants is not compliance with generally accepted accounting principles but, rather, full and fair disclosure, fair presentation. And, if principles did not produce this brand of disclosure, accountants could not hide behind the principles."

In a word, *fair presentation* was a concept separate from *generally accepted accounting principles*. The latter did not necessarily result in the former.

This case is known in legal circles as the United States vs Simon.

Resources include the *Journal of Accountancy* February, May, and August, 1970.

the Bar Chris Construction Corporation

A December 31, 1960, certified financial statement was used to facilitate the sale of 5½% convertible subordinate fifteen-year debentures. When the purchasers found that the statements contained misleading information, they sued the officer directors, the controller, the company attorney, outside directors, the investment bankers who underwrote the issue, and the company's outside auditors.

The court decided that the reported earnings had been overstated by 14% but ruled that the overstatements were not material. The overstatement was achieved by: (1) an overstatement of the percentage of completion on some contracts; (2) a loan to Bar Chris recorded as a sale; (3) a sale-lease back to a factor booked as a sale; (4) subsidiary leased property leased by a subsidiary to an operator but treated as a sale.

The court also found that the current ratio was overstated 16%. It ruled that this overstatement *was* material and, therefore, ruled in favor of the plaintiffs.

Overstatements of the current ratio were achieved by: (1) including $150,000 due from a consolidated subsidiary in accounts receivable; (2) omitting a liability of $325,000 from the balance sheet; (3) treating reserves held by a factor as current assets, although some would not be released within a year; (4) understating reserves for doubtful debts by $50,000. In the footnotes to the balance sheet, contingent liabilities were understated by $375,000.

In the text of the prospectus, it was implied that there were no loans to officers, yet such loans actually totaled $386,515. No mention was made that serious problems on earlier construction existed with customers.

The court decided that no defendant had successfully established his *due-diligence* defense regarding all of the material errors. It went on to rule that the public accountants had spent too little time on the

S-1 review and that the in-charge auditor had been too readily satisfied with *glib* answers by Bar Chris personnel.

The in-charge auditor had asked the controller about uncompleted contracts and had been given a list of them. But he did not actually examine any of them. The court ruled this inquiry to be inadequate because the absence of prices from some contracts should have prompted further investigation.

The judicial summary was that there had been a material change for the worse in Bar Chris's financial position and failure to disclose this change made the 1960 figures misleading. The judge added that, as far as results were concerned, the auditor's S-1 review was useless.

The decisions did not expand upon the point that a 14% overstatement of profits was not material but that a 16% overstatement of the current ratio was material. The facts are that earnings after correction were nearly double the preceding year. On that basis, the exact degree of improvement in earnings was of minor importance. The circumstances made the current ratio a more critical factor.

This court decision extended the liability for misleading information in registration statements to directors, public accountants, and underwriters of the corporation's securities.

Ecott vs Bar Chris Construction Corp., 283 F. Supp. 643 (S. D. N. Y. 1968).

Yale Express

Yale Express was organized in 1938 to control motor carriers and freight forwarders. The principal, wholly owned subsidiary was Yale Transport Corporation, which operated on regular routes, serving 1,800 communities in New England and the Mid-Atlantic States. Yale's headquarters were in a rented building on 12th Avenue in New York City. Its main terminal was in Maspeth, New York.

Prior to 1960, Yale was owned by the Eskow family. On July 15, 1960, 300,000 shares of class-A stock were sold to the public. Half of the stock came from the Eskow family holdings and the rest from the corporation. In August 1963, Yale Express sold to the public an additional 400,000 shares of class-A stock and $6,500,000 of 4¼% convertible subordinated debentures due August 15, 1983.

Annual revenues in the five-year period from 1958 to 1962 had increased from about $11,500,000 to $29,000,000. However, inefficiencies crept in, and the operating profit dropped from 9.5% to 7.5%.

In May 1963, Yale Express purchased nearly all of the outstanding stock of the Republic Carloading and Distributing Co., Inc., for $13,208,000. Republic was nearly twice Yale's size with 1962 sales of $55,000,000 compared to Yale's $29,000,000. Profits for each company in 1962 were nearly equal at approximately $1,000,000.

However, costs began to increase; collections of receivables were neglected; and the corporation failed to charge customers for certain services. Then a computerized billing system and sophisticated terminal handling equipment were installed. These expensive frills contributed to a $1,500,000 loss in 1963 and a $4,500,000 loss in 1964. Finally, on May 24, 1965, Yale Express filed a Chapter X petition with substantial liabilities.

In the meantime, company bookkeeping had deteriorated. In 1963 and 1964, profits had been reported. But, in 1965 the auditors reported that the company had actually lost money during those years. As a result, shareholders filed class-action suits against the public accountants who had certified the original financial statements, the principal underwriters of the securities sold to the public, and some management. The complaints alleged violations of federal securities laws and of the Interstate Commerce Act as well as common law fraud.

The class-action suits were settled for slightly more than $1,000,000 with the public accountants paying about two-thirds of that amount.

Fortunately, the trustee was able to dispose of unprofitable lines, reduce expenses, raise rates, and eliminate the sophisticated freight handling and billing equipment. The return to profitability was rapid.

On December 31, 1972, Yale Express was discharged from bankruptcy with all creditors paid in full. The company had been reduced to a medium-size carrier with annual revenues of about $12,000,000. Management mistakes had caused its downfall, and a well-executed plan of contraction had rescued it. The auditors, who had absorbed most of the settlements of the shareholders' class-action suits, ended up with 12% of the ownership of Yale Express as their share of the bankruptcy settlements.

This landmark case is important because it laid the foundation for imposing on public accountants the liability for interim financial reports and not just the annual certification of financial statements.

the First Securities Company

Lester B. Nay was the owner and president of a small brokerage business in Chicago, Illinois. In 1968, Nay committed suicide, leaving a note disclosing that his company was bankrupt and that he had been defrauding some of his clients since 1942.

Nay had induced certain clients to invest more than $1,000,000 in spurious *escrow accounts* by promising high returns. He instructed these customers to make their checks payable to him. But, instead of setting up escrow accounts, he diverted the funds to his own use.

Since there was no record of customer payments on First Securities' books or in the firm's reports to the Securities and Exchange Commission and to the Midwest Stock Exchange, and since Nay enforced a rule that only he was permitted to open his mail, he was able to conceal his fraud for many years.

Ernst and Ernst, auditors of Nay's brokerage business, didn't learn of his fraudulent practices until after his death. When this happened, investors in the escrow accounts charged the auditors with aiding the fraud by failing to make a proper audit report on material inadequacies in First Securities' internal accounting controls and for failing to discover Nay's mail rule. The investors claimed that, if Ernst and Ernst had discovered that practice, it would have uncovered the fraud.

A federal district court made a summary judgment in favor of Ernst and Ernst, but in September 1974, a federal appeals court in Chicago reversed that decision. Chief Judge Luther M. Swygert wrote the opinion for the appeals court. He contended that the auditors could be judged as abetting a fraud of which they admittedly had no knowledge if their audit had missed something important because of lack of due care. The judge ordered a trial to determine whether, in fact, the accounting firm had met its responsibilities properly.

The case finally reached the United States Supreme Court.* On March 30, 1976, the court ruled in a 6-2 decision that investors can not collect damages from accounting firms unless the investors can prove that the accountants actively participated in the scheme. The decision, written by Justice Powell, said that mere negligence was not enough to hold the auditor liable.

The SEC was not among those who brought the case to the Supreme Court, but it had argued in a friend-of-the-court brief that private negligence suits should not be precluded altogether. The decision drew much attention to a refutation of SEC arguments.

This case is important because it reenforced the definition of fraud as an intentional act of deception and stayed the trend to extend liability to those who are unaware of a fraud or who did not discover fraud in the course of an audit examination.

---

*Ernst & Ernst vs Hochfelder, 74-1042

chapter twenty-seven

authors and activists

the Sutherland school

Edwin H. Sutherland (1883-1950) taught at the universities of Illinois, Minnesota, Chicago, and Indiana. Among his writings are *Principles of Criminology* (1939), *The Professional Thief* (1937), and *White-Collar Crime* (1949).

As a criminologist, he repudiated the theories of biologism and hereditary qualities and that crime is a function of distinct character types. Sutherland's theory insists criminal behavior is learned essentially the same way as is any other part of the surrounding culture. In other words, a person becomes criminal when, through association with others, primarily in intimate and personal groups, he encounters more definitions favoring violation of law than definitions unfavorable to violation of law.

In 1940, Sutherland published *White-Collar Criminality*, the paper that gave this distinct type of crime its name.

In 1949, Professor Sutherland made a study of 70 large nonfinancial corporations in the United States. He reported that these companies had 980 decisions rendered against them for violations of government regulations. That's an average of 14 per corporation. Of the 980 violations, 779 were crimes. Sutherland's theory of differential association advances the principle that criminal behavior is learned from those who look upon it favorably. Lawbreaking may be normative in certain organizations. Persons exposed to varying standards may learn values, rationalizations, and techniques that will enable them not only to violate the law but also to justify such violation. His studies led him to the conclusion that criminality is widespread in the business world.

Donald R. Cressey, Albert K. Cohen, and Lloyd E. Ohlin were Sutherland students who carried on his work with their own studies and bibliography.

As an example, Cressey, in 1953, analyzed embezzlement, a common form of white-collar crime, and classified it into three types:

- *Independent businessmen* is the name given to violators who convert *deposits* entrusted to them for specific purposes while maintaining their regular businesses at the same time.

- *Long-term violators* are employed individuals who convert funds belonging to their employer's clients by taking relatively small amounts over a long period of time.

- *Absconders* are persons who violate their trust by removing funds or goods entrusted to them and then severing connections with the trustor by leaving his employment or the vicinity.

The Sutherland school believes that businessmen in the first category are often admired by other businessmen for their cleverness and that the businessman who violates laws does not lose status among his business associates.

Gilbert Geis, in his book *White-Collar Crime*, compiled a collection of studies by Sutherland, Marshall Clinard, Richard Quinney, Robert Caldwell, and others. Included is an examination of the 1961 heavy electrical equipment antitrust cases, involving price-fixing. Fines totaling $1,787,000 were levied against corporations, $137,000 against individuals. Jail terms were imposed on seven defendants, four of whom were vice presidents. Under the treble-damage clause, the companies were subject to millions of dollars in claims from customers.

The guilty persons went to great lengths to conceal their activities. They minimized telephone calls, even used public telephones for most of their communication. They used fictitious names and conspiratorial codes. Their meetings were referred to as *choir practice*. They used plain envelopes for mailing material to each other. They were careful not to leave wastepaper with incriminating data lying around.

The federal government initiated grand jury action after receiving identical bids in sealed envelopes for complicated electrical equipment. About 200 persons testified before four grand juries. Some revealed information concerning the divisions of markets among various companies as well as price fixing. A Senate antitrust and monopoly subcommittee learned that, while some executives realized their activities were illegal, they did not consider them criminal. Instead, they felt they were correcting a demoralized, cutthroat market, unprofitable for all companies involved.

The defendants gained nothing for themselves. By stabilizing prices at a reasonable level, they might have enabled more plants, including weaker companies, to continue operating and helped people to remain working. Laws, however, are not designed to provide escape for those who can rationalize or justify their violations.

accounting literature

Most authors of standard accounting textbooks devote but a few pages to fraud, embezzlement, forgery, and similar subjects.

Other writers have given more than casual attention to such matters. They include:

Dr. George E. Bennett

Bennett was a professor of accounting at Syracuse University and a member of the New York State Board of CPA examiners. His book *Fraud: Its Control Through Accounts* was published in 1930 by Century Press under the auspices of the American Institute of Accountants. Dr. Bennett packed much valuable information on fraud into 130 pages. His text was one of the few guideposts available on this sensitive subject and was used by many auditors.

Bradford Cadmus and Arthur Childs

Under the auspices of The Institute of Internal Auditors, Inc., the first edition of *Internal Control Against Fraud and Waste* was printed in 1953 by Prentice Hall. Bradford Cadmus was the managing director of The Institute, and Arthur Childs was a past IIA president. This book was an important influence on internal auditing from the day it was published. While it stressed the importance of internal controls, it gave many case histories of the circumvention of such controls by employees and others.

In 1964, The Institute of Internal Auditors published Cadmus' *Operational Auditing Handbook.* Cadmus had recognized the great opportunities for internal auditors to contribute to better and more economical operations under effective controls. While he advocated operational auditing, he did not lose his perspective when he wrote on page 65: "Thus, a survey of the potential control risk by the internal auditor would comprise a weighing of pro's and con's and an appraisal of the possible chance of fraud."

Harvey Cardwell

Published in 1960, Cardwell's *Principles of Audit Surveillance* was "primarily concerned with laying the foundation for specialist's knowledge of the inside theft." Theft preventive measures and the general subject of internal control are excluded. It is probably the best book available on surveillance methods. Cardwell summarizes the weaknesses of internal controls in his advocacy of audit surveillance thus:

- *Internal controls are always a practical compromise between effectiveness and cost; hence, the protection afforded by it is never complete.*

- *Internal controls deteriorate easily; and small changes in procedure, apparently unimportant and innocuous, will often destroy or impair internal controls.*

- *Internal controls can usually be circumvented by collusion.*

The Chamber of Commerce of the United States

In 1974, the Chamber of Commerce published a handbook on *White-Collar Crime*. It is a 92-page booklet filled with practical ideas on ways to combat business crimes.

Lester A. Pratt

Pratt wrote *Bank Frauds: Their Detection and Prevention.* A second edition was published in 1965. Although written for those interested in the detection and prevention of bank frauds, it includes material of general interest to all auditors.

Allan E. Penfield

In a brief article in The Institute of Internal Auditors' journal, *The Internal Auditor* (spring 1963), Penfield reported on the "History of a Defalcation Involving a Trusted Company Employee." He concluded his article with:

> *It points out a danger that may be confronting many other auditors; namely, to regard operational auditing as the primary function to management, while the examination for fraud is a lower-grade and "less professional" function of auditing. The Institute itself may be guilty in this respect; the preponderance of articles in* The Internal Auditor *upon operational auditing might mislead some readers into thinking that the discovery of fraud is no longer an important responsibility of the internal auditor. The public accountants disclaimed this responsibility long ago. If the internal auditor also does so, who is left to discover fraud?*

Much more attention is given to fraud in legal literature than in accounting publications. Through case histories well documented with names, places, and dates, along with judicial decisions to buttress their interpretations, the auditor can learn more about fraud from that profession than from his own.

Charles R. Wagner, an assistant professor of accounting at Creighton University, in the November/December 1973 issue of *The Internal Auditor,* called attention to the lack of case material in accounting literature and called for corrective action. This deficiency will not be met until more auditors are willing to share case data under the cloak of anonymity, if necessary.

Recently, *The Internal Auditor* carried the following series of articles dealing with various aspects of fraud: "The Other Aspect of Fraud" and "Employee Theft and Fidelity Bonding" (November/December 1974), "Facing the Problem: Fraud" (July/August 1975), "Accountants and Auditors vs White-Collar Crime" (June 1976), "Are Internal Auditors Responsible for Fraud Detection?" (August 1976), "Lessons from Equity Funding" (October 1976).

the probers

Many disclosures of fraudulent activities appear in business magazines and newspapers. These exposures are the work of investigative reporters and financial analysts who, with journalistic skill, reduce intricate schemes to easy-to-read stories. Some examples are:

Barmash, Isidore—*Great Business Disasters*
Clarke, Thurston, and Tigue, John J., Jr.—*Dirty Money*
Daughen and Binzen—*The Wreck of The Penn Central*
Dirks and Gross—*The Great Wall Street Scandal*
Dunn, Donald H.—*Ponzi! The Boston Swindler*
Elias, Christopher—*Fleecing the Lambs*
Hutchison, Robert A.—*Vesco (This study covers the operations of the Investors Overseas Services under Cornfeld and the subsequent capture of its assets by Robert Vesco.)*
Kwitny, Jonathan—*The Fountain Pen Conspiracy*
Mackey, Charles—*Extraordinary Popular Delusions and the Madness of Crowds*
Miller, Norman C.—*The Great Salad-Oil Swindle*
Raw, Page, and Hodgson—*Do You Sincerely Want to Be Rich?*
Smith, Adam—*The Money Game and Supermoney*
Sobel, Robert—*Panic on Wall Street*
Tobias, Andrew—*The Funny Money Game*
Woodward, C. Vann—*Responses of the Presidents to Charges of Misconduct*

Private investigators, primarily concerned with pilferage, shoplifting, and theft of materials and supplies from the premises of their clients, have written about their work. While this type of investigation falls outside the normal activity of auditors, their writings give insight into their techniques of investigation and interrogation of suspects. Some of these are:

Jaspan, Norman—*The Thief in the White Collar*
Lipman, Mark—*Stealing*

There are also interesting books on the scientific aspects of fraud detection. Two of these are:

Hall, Jay Cameron—*Inside the Crime Lab*
McGrady, Mike—*Crime Scientists*

chapter twenty-eight

notes from audit experiences

the embezzler's defense: divert attention

A clever embezzler will adopt a plan of defense against discovery of his scheme as soon as he has perfected that scheme. But sometimes an investigation comes from an unexpected source.

A California branch had shown unexplained decreases in profitability for some time. Auditors had written several letters to the branch manager analyzing accounts and suggesting probable causes. Audits of the branch were made but were unsuccessful in determining the cause of the losses.

After one especially strong letter, the manager replied that he had solved the problem. He wrote that a stockroom employee had admitted stealing and had been discharged. Pay records showed that a low-paid employee had been separated, but the losses continued.

After another audit letter, the manager wrote that he had made a further investigation and had learned that another employee, a close associate of the first, was also involved and that the second employee had also been discharged. This was repeated yet a third and fourth time.

Another audit visit and confidential talks with a few senior employees finally brought out the fact that the manager was the guilty party. He had been covering his peculations by discharging innocent employees. His plan involved approving and paying phony invoices which he had prepared. Payments were going to a mistress and a bookmaker.

Several key employees had been aware that the manager was the culprit, but they were unwilling to talk until the situation grew so serious they could not conceal it any longer. Eventually, they banded together and informed the visiting auditor.

The fraud could have been discovered months earlier if the previous auditors had gained employee confidence and had shown that they were trustworthy and good listeners.

collusion—it can be vertical

There are many instances of collusion among equals in organizations. People working together at one level can readily learn their coworkers' moral standards and can plan and execute fraudulent acts more readily through their close daily contacts. The following instances illustrate that collusions can also occur between persons at more than one level.

A store manager in a large city purchased expensive clothing, foods, liquor, home furnishings, and similar items. He arranged to have the bills sent to the store, charged to inventory, and paid for by company funds. A *score sheet* was kept of the illicit purchases. Each month the total was added to the physical inventory, avoiding a reduction in earnings through the cost of the improper purchases.

The store manager had been sharing the items with his superior, the company vice president of sales located at corporate headquarters a thousand miles away. From time to time, the vice president would authorize policy credits for this store in amounts ranging up to $5,000. When the store manager received these credits, he would post them as a credit to his *score sheet* and would reduce the inventory account on the books.

When the Corporate Credit Department noticed that this store was having difficulty paying its bills because inventory appeared to be too high, an audit was requested. The auditor counted and priced inventory. The total was nearly $50,000 less than book value.

The store manager, carrying the burden of operating the fraud, had received only about 20% of the proceeds, while his *protector* had taken 80%. Both of these long-time employees were released without prosecution. They agreed to make restitution, part of which came from their pension funds. As a result of this case, all policy credits now must have controller approval also.

Another company wished to sell a marketing subsidiary. When the manager of the subsidiary asked if he could bid to buy it, the division general manager said that the company would sell the unit to him at a very favorable price if the manager met three conditions: that the general manager be cut in for one-third ownership;

that the manager put up the money for the general manager's share; that the general manager's share be registered in the name of a *friend*—his mistress.

The transaction went through as planned. However, a short time later the general manager died, and his estate was found to be a tangle of unfinished deals.

customers as coconspirators

A European manufacturer sold at lower prices in his export markets than in his home country. The difference between the two price levels presented a tempting target for anyone in a position to take advantage. The company's export sales manager recognized the opportunity and was in a position to profit from it.

During a trip to Latin America, he arranged for a dealer to receive invoices for goods that would never be shipped. The dealer would not be expected to send remittances to the company. For his cooperation, the dealer would receive *commissions* of 5% of the invoice totals. The dealer was told that, as soon as payments were received from the unidentified true consignees, he would be credited for the invoices sent him earlier. The sales manager explained that these arrangements were necessary to circumvent some difficulties in exporting to a third country. While the dealer was probably not naive enough to believe the story, a 5% commission for doing nothing appealed to his profit instincts.

Upon his return to Europe, the sales manager prepared fictitious orders from the Latin American dealer. He designated another dealer, about 1,000 kilometers from the plant, as consignee. Then he told the Billing Department to use export prices since the consignee was shipping the order to a customer of the Latin American dealer.

The sales manager had arranged for the consignee to purchase materials at 15% below the domestic wholesale prices for cash. The consignee was willing to buy at the discounted price as it allowed him to undersell his competitors. The sales manager thus came into possession of sizable cash funds. And since the terms of sale in the export market called for cash in 90 days, he could hold the cash for three months before the Latin American account would be due.

As the scheme progressed, the company's books showed sizable increases in foreign sales compared with domestic sales. Management did not realize that part of the domestic market was being supplied by sales classified as export sales.

The sales manager—after personally receiving payment for several shipments—possessed a large sum of money which he intended to turn over to the company when the Latin American account came due. Not only had he convinced management that he was a successful sales manager, but he also began to believe that he was both clever and lucky.

Therefore, he decided that, while he had possession of such a large sum, he would double or triple it at a nearby gambling casino. Unfortunately, he lost the entire amount. In an effort to recoup his losses, he increased his illegal sales but continued to lose at the gambling tables.

The Latin American account became more and more past due, and the Credit Department became more insistent that the dealer pay. Finally, the dealer realized that he was the victim of a fraud and told the company what the sales manager had arranged. The manager was discharged but could make little restitution because gambling losses had drained most of his funds, including personal assets.

false medical claims

A claim approver at a regional office processed fraudulent group medical payments totaling $53,000. Payments were made to the order of bona fide claimants by issuing drafts endorsed in the claimant's name and negotiated by another party, presumably friends of the claim approver.

The fraudulent drafts were issued as follows:

- No more than two fraudulent drafts were issued on the same policy holder.

- Often, the fraudulent draft bore a number either preceding or following that of a bona fide draft.

- All fraudulent drafts were issued on active claim cases involving frequent payments.

- In some cases, a fraudulent draft preceded the issuance of a valid payment. For example, fraudulent drafts were issued to the order of the claimant in amounts apparently supported by documentation. Then, a week later, the bona fide draft was issued to the order of the proper payee, usually a doctor or a hospital.

During a routine home office audit of group claims processed by the regional office, an auditor noted that the endorsement on a cancelled draft did not match the claimant's signature in the claim file. Furthermore, the draft bore a secondary endorsement, and a copy of the draft voucher was not in the claim file. Duties were rearranged to avoid repetition.

The bonding company contested payment on the grounds that the company was negligent. The fraud occurred during a period of high volume and high personnel turnover. The bonding company also claimed that individual cases were not carefully reviewed by the person signing the draft.

phony physiotherapists

A casualty claims representative, conspiring with a compensation-claim-payment clerk, posed as a physiotherapist to receive payments for alleged treatments through various workmen's compensation cases.

Payments to four pseudo physiotherapists amounted to $17,000. District attorney investigators uncovered a widespread fraud ring that had been in existence for 18 months before it was detected. Detection came from including compensation payments in a verification program.

A confirmation letter, returned by the post office as undeliverable, caused a copy of a draft to be sent to the claims manager. A further investigation revealed that the true claimant had received no such treatment.

inside adjuster

An inside adjuster was issuing second drafts on property losses. In some cases, these drafts were drawn for amounts equal to the legitimate losses. After the insured's endorsement was forged, local dishonest contractors cashed the drafts. Then all draft copies were destroyed.

A local supervisor, suspicious of the adjuster and a contractor, mentioned his suspicions to a visitor from the national claims office. Immediately, banks were alerted to watch for drafts presented by the contractor under suspicion. Seven drafts turned up on the first day. The contractor had tried to cash a $56,000 draft for alleged work done in another state.

In four instances, phony accounts were opened in out-of-state banks to facilitate cashing drafts. The adjuster drew one check in a Las Vegas gambling house. Subsequently, the case was turned over to postal inspectors for criminal action.

small-claims adjuster

An adjuster handling claims under $250 was making false accident reports against legitimate policies. After drafts were issued to fictitious claimants, the adjustor cashed them at a bank where he was known. Then both home office and branch office draft copies were destroyed. When the adjuster used a policy number with one digit missing, the home office caught the claim as not covered—no policy. Eventually, a field audit and review of original drafts under $250 disclosed many more similar cases.

The loss involved more than $40,000. Finally, the adjuster confessed and was sentenced. Restitution was sought from the bank that cashed the drafts.

employment-fee splitting

A personnel assistant in a branch office conspired with an employment agency employee to furnish the names of employees transferred from another office. The agency then billed the company for agency fees, amounting to 60% of the first month's salary. The agency then split the fees with the personnel assistant. An audit of payments made showed that the branch office was using agency help more than was customary. Inquiries turned up evidence that the fees were paid for transferees, not new hires.

The total loss was more than $20,000. Restitution, so far, by the owner of the agency has amounted to $10,000. The company later established an audit-confirmation letter, asking employees if they had used an employment agency.

the embezzler's ego

A manufacturer had an important, new product he wanted to introduce with impressive fanfare to obtain publicity and promote enthusiasm among marketing people. The importance of the new product justified the expenditure of hundreds of thousands of dollars to promote sales.

A young man—we will call him Buck—was assigned the task of organizing the big show. Buck called on a friend who ran a small agency in New York City for help. Let's call the friend Grabber. Grabber had some experience in staging extravaganzas. Together they planned the show.

Buck and Grabber hired an entire resort hotel with theater facilities. They engaged major acts, a company of actors, an orchestra, and stage effects.

Buck, as producer and director, actually handled most of the details and did the hiring for the show. Thus, he was able to arrange for an overload for his own benefit, on most of the services he purchased. The talent suppliers billed Grabber, who added a percentage for his overhead and profit. He had no reason to question bills with the overload that Buck had added since that meant money for him.

Grabber also saw a good opportunity to reduce his overhead by charging his secretary's time as a direct-labor cost. He gave her the title of assistant producer, even tripled her salary while she was working on the project.

Buck became so involved in the day-to-day operations of the project that he lost his identity as the client. He gave himself a fancy title in Grabber's organization and even had special letterheads printed. His ego prompted him to show the letterhead to some coworkers at his employer's headquarters. This proved to be his undoing since they took the letterhead to the company auditor.

When Buck traveled, he charged traveling expenses with a credit card issued to Grabber. However, he didn't stop there. He also turned in expense statements to his employer and was reimbursed. He invented hotel bills for his lengthy stays in New York, although he actually stayed at Grabber's secretary's apartment, presumably without cost. His employer had given him full and final authority to approve Grabber's invoices.

Finally, the months of planning paid off, and the pair staged a really impressive show. At nearly the same time, however, an auditor uncovered the padded, false, and duplicate bills which allegedly had supported Grabber's invoices. When Buck and Grabber admitted the entire scheme, the company decided to discharge Buck. But, as a condition of not prosecuting Grabber, the company made him hire Buck.

While planning for the spectacular had been underway, Buck had taken on several other small projects, and for a while, the conspirators worked together and completed them. Upon completion of these projects, they lost Buck's company business—three-quarters of their total volume.

After that, they made appearances at management seminars, lecturing on sales promotion. But financial pressure on them increased, and before long, the duo broke up. As a reason for the breakup, Grabber stated, "Buck doesn't realize that he is no longer the client but an employee, and I can't tolerate his high-handed methods any longer."

It was an unusual form of retribution or punishment yet very appropriate and effective.

a postmortem audit

An affable branch manager with an unusually close employee relationship and a weakness for the fairer sex, found his life-style expenses exceeding his income.

Since he was handy with tools, he designed some advertising novelties. They were clever, animated, colorful items, suitable for point-of-sale displays. He took the novelties to his company's advertising agency and said he had arranged for sources to supply hundreds of these items. He said his sources would bill the agency for the displays and would handle distribution. The agency could then add its 15% fee and send invoices to him for approval.

Since the agency could make a profit with no effort except rebilling, it did not question the arrangement. For months, the agency made its payments to three apartments in different sections of the city. In turn, the company paid the agency on authentic invoices. There was little evidence to cause an auditor to raise a question.

The manager kept a set of the novelties on display in his office. He pointed out to an auditor how effective they had been in his marketing plans and how many had been placed in various spots throughout his territory.

Several months after the auditor's visit, the police, answering a call in the middle of the night, found the manager in his bedroom shot to death. At first, police investigators charged the manager's wife with homocide, but, eventually, decided they did not have enough evidence to warrant a trial and dropped the charge. The police never determined whether the manager's death was murder or suicide.

An auditor later learned from employees that the manager had forced three of them to rent apartments in their names and had threatened them with the loss of their jobs if they talked. The manager paid the rents in cash and installed a different female friend in each apartment. It was from these apartments that he had sent invoices for the fictitious displays to the agency. He used invoice forms prepared in the name of dummy companies.

He had curtailed legitimate advertising efforts so that total advertising expenditures remained within the advertising budget. He had falsified the detailed analysis of expenditures against budget line by line in his reports to headquarters.

After the manager's death, the three employees talked freely. Another employee had refused to cooperate in the rental scheme but had been afraid to discuss the matter during previous audit visits.

The loss amounted to thousands of dollars, but, under the circumstances, the company did not attempt to gain restitution from the estate.

the manager's second role

A field sales office manager of a national firm felt he needed extra money. For two years, he contracted for substantial installation jobs and temporarily recorded them on contract forms which he had designed and printed. He represented himself in these contracts as a third-party contractor and had the customer make payment to his *firm*. Later he recorded some of these sales, charging accounts receivable and crediting sales, to maintain a good sales level and gross profit.

During that two-year period, there were two audits. On each visit, the auditor sent confirmation requests on accounts receivables. There were no replies from customers whose accounts did not include installation charges.

The fraud was detected when, at the close of the fiscal year, the manager tried to *catch up* on accounts receivable credits by depositing personal checks without sufficient funds to cover them. Up to that time, he had been able to disguise his personal checks on accounts receivable as customer checks. Later, the manager confessed that, during the audits, he had called certain customers, advised them that the auditor had made an error in account balances, and told them to disregard the confirmation request.

The manager admitted diverting $38,000 of company funds to his own use. Prosecution followed.

an officer's open account

Most companies allow officers and other key employees to have open accounts for ordinary business expenses and usually designate someone to supervise the collection of any outstanding balances. However, one company had been mailing statements without review to officers for several years.

In an examination of these accounts, an alert auditor noticed that the assistant treasurer's balance was as high as $40,000 most of the time. At the end of each fiscal year, a check payment brought his balance to zero. But the balance went right back at the beginning of each new year.

The assistant treasurer was found to be using his business expense-advance account as an interest-free loan to play the stock market.

To prevent a recurrence, monthly statements for all officers are now routed through the controller, and the controller's statement goes through the vice president of finance.

unneeded packaging supplies

A company operated a commissary at a foreign location where food and other staples could not be purchased from local merchants. The commissary operated in two divisions: wholesale and retail.

The wholesale division received all incoming commodities and then sold them to the company dining hall and to the company-sponsored social club. The wholesale division also packaged commodities from bulk quantities and transferred them to the retail division, operating as a supermarket for company employees.

In general, packaging materials were controlled in inventory accounts and charged to expense on the basis of issue requisitions. One of the few exceptions to this practice was cellophane, which was charged directly to expense. In the course of his regular audit program, an auditor examined certain purchases of cellophane—approximately 255 rolls amounting to $10,000—within the previous six months and noted that:

■ Purchases were made from local suppliers.

■ Payments were made in cash from a working fund.

■ Receiving reports for cellophane were signed by an employee who apparently also sold merchandise to the commissary.

■ There were marked fluctuations in unit prices of purchases.

When the auditor visited the commissary warehouse to make test counts of inventories, he did not see any evidence of the use of cellophane packaging. Instead, he found 90 rolls of cellophane stored in the retail division, even though it was charged to wholesale expense upon purchase. It was immediately apparent that the cellophane must have been on hand for an extended period as the cartons were covered with a good deal of dust. Furthermore, the cartons were of an international shipping type, bearing the markings of a United States manufacturer. This indicated the cellophane had not been purchased locally.

In reply to the auditor's inquiry, the assistant supervisor said that cellophane was not being used for packaging purposes but was being consumed gradually as retail shelving paper. He also said that the stock had been on hand for at least four years and that, at the rate of present consumption, it would last a long time. After the assistant had evidently mentioned the auditor's inquiry, the commissary supervisor informed the auditor that the cellophane had been acquired nine months earlier and confirmed that no other quantities were on hand. He also reported that it was not used for packaging purposes, and the present supply would last at least one year.

If 90 rolls represented a one-year supply, the auditor wondered what happened to the 255 rolls purchased within the previous six months. Adding up his information, he suspected that payments were being made for fictitious invoices listing goods never received. To avoid warning the commissary management of his suspicions, the auditor merely recommended that cellophane be controlled in an inventory account.

Then the auditor reported his observations to top accounting management and raised the question of spurious purchases of cellophane. Accounting management recognized the possibility of fraud, and assigned company personnel to investigate.

Invoices and purchase orders covering two years of local purchases were examined. It was found that:

- Invoices on hand implied that large quantities of cellophane had been purchased locally, even though cellophane was customarily purchased abroad.

- There was very little use for cellophane in the commissary.

- The alleged suppliers were unknown to local paper manufacturers, principal distributors, and customs authorities.

- On various occasions, purchase orders were made out in the name of an employee of the wholesale commissary.

The commissary supervisor was questioned, and all the points mentioned by the auditor and the company investigators were discussed. The supervisor could not assist in locating the local suppliers, claiming they were itinerant peddlers. He also claimed the word *cellophane* was used locally for all types of wrapping paper and bags and that some cellophane was given to a local supplier of chickens for sanitary reasons. He further claimed that bags had to be purchased locally because overseas suppliers could not meet the demand. In addition, he said it was occasionally necessary for an employee to purchase supplies in his own name and then sell them to the commissary in order to furnish ship captains with items out of stock.

A few days later, a local purchase order for cellophane came to the main accounting office. It was dated just prior to the interview. This substantiated continuing suspicions, so photostatic copies were made of a representative selection of invoices from alleged local suppliers. These invoices had been approved by various commissary employees, including the supervisor. The photocopies were then sent to a professional handwriting expert.

The expert stated that signatures of alleged suppliers had been signed so that they could not be identified with a person's habitual writing. Because of limited specimens, the person falsifying the signatures could not be identified.

About this time, the supervisor gave investigators a letter purportedly sent to him from the United States by one of the local suppliers. It stated that the supplier was discontinuing his business and moving to Europe. A few days later, it was proven that this letter had been typed on a commissary typewriter.

Faced with the additional evidence, the supervisor signed a confession. According to his statement, he drew money from the commissary cashier, giving a temporary receipt. Later, he signed a blank paper with a fictitious name—supposedly that of the supplier—to indicate payment had been received. This then went to the cashier along with a note on a separate piece of paper indicating what merchandise to include on the invoice.

He had instructed the cashier to fill in the quantities and to have a wholesale commissary clerk sign the invoice as having received the merchandise. The cashier also prepared a local purchase order and attached it to the invoice. At the end of the day, a cashier's disbursement receipt was prepared to cover all local purchase orders. The supervisor would sign the disbursement receipt and forward it to the cashier for approval and reimbursement.

The confession absolved any other commissary employees of criminal conspiracy. However, it was determined that two assistant supervisors and five commissary clerks knew of irregularities and had signed fictitious invoices as instructed by the supervisor. All were discharged.

Other avenues of fraud such as kickbacks from local suppliers, manipulation of cost prices to cover up shortages, manipulation of weights of meats and vegetables, mingling local produce with imported produce, switching regular brands to luxury brands, etc., were thoroughly investigated. Although many transactions could not be satisfactorily explained, no further accusations could be made because of insufficient evidence.

It is interesting to note that the supervisor actually began his fraud four years earlier to cover up large amounts of spoiled merchandise and to make the commissary operating report look good. This is one of the reasons why no one discovered the fraud earlier. When the supervisor received cash, he would ring up sales covering the value of the spoiled merchandise.

Unfortunately, his success at this deception and his attraction to a pretty nightclub cashier led to large-scale fraud for personal gain.

relating usage to base data

A marketing company, in a country where law required all documents such as invoices, receipts, payrolls, etc., to bear government fiscal stamps became involved in an unusual fraud case.

Each plant maintained its own stamp-imprest funds. These were reimbursed by delivery of the stamps purchased by the main office cashier. Requests for reimbursement were prepared on a standard company form and approved by plant superintendents. A main office group reconciled the total amount of stamps used, according to the daily plant sales reports, with the detachable portions of stamps attached to duplicate copies of invoices. However, these amounts were not reconciled with plant reimbursement requests.

The main office had been purchasing about $3,000 in stamps monthly. One-half of this amount was being reimbursed to one large bulk plant supposedly for use on plant documents. An auditor thought the amount of stamps being sent to this plant was excessive compared to its volume of business. So, he decided to reconcile reimbursement request totals with totals reported on the daily plant sales reports for a selected period of time.

He found monthly reimbursements were approximately $1,500, whereas the usage, according to sales reports, was about $900. After allowing $25 a month for stamps attached to payrolls, various miscellaneous receipts, and voided invoices, there was still a difference of about $600.

The office extended the reconciliation over the preceding 24 months when the superintendent and custodian had been transferred to this plant. This reconciliation indicated a total shortage of approximately $6,700. Reconciliations covering a reasonable period of time were also made for other plants. However, no other shortages were disclosed.

The auditor, along with the chief accountant, then visited the plant to count stamps and to reconcile the fund on the basis of stamps received from the main office with those actually used on invoices during the month. This turned up a shortage of $267.

When neither the custodian nor the plant superintendent could explain the shortage or the differences during the prior 24 months, both were discharged. However, no criminal action was taken against them. Steps were taken to prevent recurrences of this irregularity.

eligibility technicians' conspirary

Public welfare is big business. There are estimates—none of which can be verified—of the millions of dollars paid in fraudulent welfare claims. Welfare officers have attempted to reduce the fraud level in public assistance programs by employing *eligibility technicians* who conduct initial reviews of potential recipients.

In April 1974, a bank clerk in Minneapolis noticed an account deposit that included a welfare warrant dated six months earlier. Thinking it unusual that anyone would hold a warrant that long, she asked the Welfare Department if a warrant with *stale dating* was still valid. The department referred the matter to the Welfare Fraud Unit, which investigated.

The WFU questioned the eligibility technician assigned to the recipient named on the warrant and secured a confession. The first ET implicated two other ET's. It was then learned that the three had used similar methods and had encouraged each other in their fraudulent activities.

From mid-1972 to early 1974, they had conspired to steal $66,000 by taking 370 warrants out of 500,000 processed during that time. The three would either fail to remove the name of a recipient from the rolls until a month or two after eligibility terminated or request an emergency warrant payable on some false basis to a recipient for whom they were responsible.

It is often necessary for ET's to deliver warrants to recipients, as many recipients are mobile. These three ET's would forge the payee's endorsement and deposit the stolen warrants in their own bank accounts or in a bank account opened under a fictitious name. They also gave some of the warrants to friends and relatives who endorsed and deposited them in their bank accounts and then shared in the proceeds.

The Hennepin County Grand Jury investigated the case and, on November 4, 1974, indicted 13 persons, including the three welfare employees, who pleaded guilty. Since the three were paid at a level qualifying them for welfare assistance themselves, their desire for mor' money was their only motivation.

All warrants issued in 1973 and 1974 were reviewed for unusual endorsements. This led to the discovery that another employee, a man with 20 years of service in the Welfare Department, had engaged in similar activities. From mid-1961 to early 1974, he stole about 70 warrants totaling more than $12,000. He forged all of the endorsements and deposited the warrants in his personal bank account. He was indicted on December 11, 1974, and sentenced shortly thereafter.

Collusion may be a form of group therapy for bruised egos.

fraud by organized crime

An organized crime ring in real estate defrauded legitimate mortgage lenders by infiltrating two appraisal firms and inflating loan values on properties.

The ring would buy properties in depressed areas and then have them reappraised at inflated values. Next, they would transfer title, obtain a new inflated loan, and then abandon the property. The legitimate mortgage company would be forced to repossess the property for nonpayment, but the ring had already received the difference between the purchase price and. the inflated loan.

Lenders require a fire insurance policy protecting them from loss. To prevent detection of the inflated values, the ring placed representatives in an insurance company's field offices where they passed agency requirements, including credit report checks.

For three years, the agents wrote fire insurance policies. There was nothing to cause suspicion. In fact, one agent received special recognition for writing a large volume of fire business. All told, they issued several thousand policies. About 800 of these were issued on properties with fraudulent mortgages.

For the first three years, the insurance company had no way of knowing anything was wrong. Credit reports on the agents were good. Perhaps, the insurance company should have noticed an increase in cancelled policies due to repossessions; but the area had experienced a slight recession.

The ring hired a repair-and-maintenance manager to take care of purchased properties. Two of the agents and the maintenance man decided to make a little extra profit on the side from an idea that came to them while they were handling small windstorm losses. Five months later, after 300 payments totalling $70,000, the insurance company auditors caught up with them. Last reports showed a loss of $3,000,000 to the mortgage companies.

The insurance company's internal audit program finally detected the ring's activities. A part of that audit program required confirmations to be sent on a random basis. On the fifth month, five replies were received within a week. These started the investigation. Ironically, at the same time, a new clerk in the Claims Clerical Section *blew the whistle*—only because she couldn't understand some basic entries on one of the drafts.

Could the internal auditors have detected this loss sooner? They answered:

> *Even though five months is a fast turnaround, it doesn't give us much satisfaction. We could have detected the fraud in its second month—some $65,000 earlier. Our control system requires a printout of all claims drafts received with errors in the coded information, cancelled policies, or other odd sequences which present immediate matching problems.*
>
> *A few of the fraudulent drafts were issued on repossessed properties where the mortgage company had advised us to cancel the policy. The clerks assigned to check out support on the draft-error printouts were afraid they might be criticized for not finding all data possible; therefore, they did not refer these drafts to their supervisor.*
>
> *The problem really involved people and inadequate communications. Needless to say, we have changed our approach to auditing. Auditors now continually visit supervisors and employees. They discuss possible problems, suspect items, and answer questions involving possible frauds.*
>
> *Perhaps, the most important lesson an internal auditor can learn is this: No matter how small, a danger signal, such as errors or deviations from procedure, may be an indication of fraud far beyond the imagination of the auditor. The auditor has an obligation to determine the underlying cause and make certain it does not lead to an exposure to loss or to an actual loss.*

nonexistent transportation company

An internal audit of a manufacturing plant disclosed payments to a nonexistent transportation company.

The transportation company had been established—in name only—by the plant's warehouse and traffic manager strictly for the purpose of diverting company funds to his own personal use. Audit detection came from an investigation of unsupported disbursements for transportation.

Normally, freight bills were processed for payment only after an independent matching by the Accounts Payable Department of transportation company billing with applicable bills of lading. Billings from one company were being paid with the approval of only the traffic manager.

During the course of the audit, the traffic manager was interrogated by the internal auditor. The manager signed statements admitting that, while employed as warehouse and traffic manager, he had:

- sold management on a plan for renting a truck as opposed to using higher cost, commercial service to haul merchandise between company locations. A substantial savings was indicated by the plan, but an actual need for the service did not exist.

- purchased invoice forms printed with the name of a fictitious transportation company.

- prepared fictitious freight bills on the transportation company invoice forms, approved them, and processed them for payment to the Accounts Payable Department.

- personally rented a post office box which he used as the address of the fictitious transportation company. He also established and maintained a bank account, listing himself as sole owner of the transportation company.

- received checks payable to the transportation company at the post office box, applied a stamp endorsement *for deposit only* to the transportation company account, and deposited the checks in that account.

- withdrawn funds from the transportation company bank account by drawing checks payable to himself.

- deposited these checks to his own personal checking account.

Over several years, the traffic manager diverted $113,000 to his own personal use. In the case above, rental charges were built into the Warehouse and Traffic Department annual operating budgets. Although each succeeding year showed an increased budget for truck rental, the need was never questioned. In fact, the manager was considered for a *best-suggestion* award due to the purported savings involved.

double billings of TV advertising

An internal audit of a retail store operation disclosed double billings of TV advertising with kickbacks to the store manager via an advertising agent.

Over a period of one year, purchase orders were issued by a field location for one-minute, TV advertising, but the store actually had contracted for one-half-minute commercials. The TV station processed one-minute billings, which were approved by the field location and forwarded to the home office. The home office matched the store-approved invoice with the previously received purchase order and processed check payments for the full amount of the invoice.

The audit investigation included visits to the TV station accounting section. These disclosed a kickback of one-half of the check amounts to an advertising agent, servicing the retail store account. The advertising agent booked the amount received as income. He withheld an amount equal to the tax he would have to pay on this income and gave the net amount to the retail store manager.

Detection occurred during detailed investigations of other types of fraud at the same location and the expanded tests of all expenses. A clerk in the TV station accounting section provided details of payments to the advertising agent. Subsequent interrogation resulted in a signed confession from the store manager who had left the company prior to the investigation.

A recovery of $4,000 resulted from repayment of the overcharges by the former store manager.

an embezzlement the auditors overlooked

Should the auditor be held responsible for frauds not discovered during an audit with an adequate program and sufficient time allotted to carry it out? That question is not easy to answer.

Perhaps, the case of an embezzlement in a small branch store may help delineate this responsibility. The unit had a dozen employees, including a manager; an assistant manager, who also was head salesman; and an accountant, supervising all office employees except the purchasing agent. Accountingwise, it was a self-contained operation. Sales totalled approximately $1,000,000 a year.

At the end of December, auditors, on a schedule that called for a year-end audit every third year, visited this unit. The audit was programmed as a complete review, including disbursements and receipts, inventory tests, and circularization of receivables. The auditors reported no discrepancies but added qualifying remarks, stating that the small number of employees precluded effective means of internal control such as proper separation of duties.

On February 5, the assistant manager and the purchasing agent told the manager that they suspected dishonesty in the Accounting Department. They cited the following reasons:

■ Marvin Cone, the assistant manager, said that he had turned over to Andy Simonelli, the accountant, two cash payments from a customer, Albert Dow. One payment was for $226 on January 20, and the other was for $100 on January 21. No entries appeared on the daily cash-receipts record for these amounts. In the accounts receivable ledger, the Dow account showed a payment of $326 on January 21. However, no folio was entered.

■ Cone also said that Don McBee, another customer, paid $300 in six $50 bills on December 29. This payment was recorded on the cash-receipts records as $24.12 in cash and $170.20 and $105.68 in two checks.

■ It was evident that Cone had entertained his suspicions in silence for a long time because he claimed that a Lou Welk had paid $175.40 in cash on March 23 of the previous year. This payment was recorded on the cash-receipt record as $32.40 in cash and three checks in the amounts of $45, $20, and $78.

■ Arthur Doan, the purchasing agent, said he had received an unnumbered invoice, dated December 8, from the ABC Tire Company in the amount of $123.60 for four tires. And Simonelli, the accountant, told him the tires were for one of the company-owned cars. The purchasing agent approved the bill and turned it back to Simonelli, who prepared a check. The manager signed it on December 15 while the auditors were on the job. On December 10, Doan found a numbered invoice from ABC Tire in a wastebasket. The invoice, dated December 8, was for a $123.60 charge to Simonelli. Doan then looked at the $123.60 invoice he had approved for payment and realized that it was in the accountant's handwriting. He did not report these events to the manager or auditors at that time.

■ On February 15, the manager paid $53 in cash on his personal account. This did not appear on any cash-receipt record during that week.

After Cone and Doan reported their suspicions to the manager, he called the company's public accountants for advice on how to proceed. They reported the manager's conversation to their headquarters which, in turn, notified the client's corporate executive offices. The store manager had not informed his superiors of the problem, and corporate headquarters sent an internal auditor to the branch to investigate.

The internal auditor found additional discrepancies:

■ There was a ledger card among trade receivables with numerous debit and credit entries without folio references. But there was no heading on the card to show who owed the $1,269.01 balance at year end.

- A ledger card for Simonelli was also among trade receivables. It was an active account with a final credit balance of $324.17. Charges had been reduced by credit entries. There were no folio numbers for the credits, nor could any record of payments be found. It appeared that Simonelli was building a credit balance so that he could later make a large charge and avoid having a debit balance appear on any past-due list.

- The petty-cash fund was $24.67 over the $300 balance carried on the books. Simonelli later admitted that the overage was the result of temporarily adding cash from daily deposits— cash he had not had the opportunity to pocket.

- There were several instances where the cash discount on customer payments was considerably higher than the 2% allowable. For example, one customer paid $23.70 in cash but was credited with $96.85. The difference was charged to customer cash discount. Simonelli explained that the added $73.15 represented the amount of a duplicate shipment returned by the customer. If that were true, the sales account, not the customer's cash discount, should have been charged. A credit memo should have been issued to offset the duplicate charge.

Simonelli admitted the embezzlement of funds and was discharged without prosecution when he made restitution of $600— all he said he could afford.

He had an unusual explanation for his embezzlement. He claimed that a young woman who worked in the office needed an abortion. He wanted to help her but could not let his wife know that he had spent money for that purpose. He denied any responsibility for the young woman's predicament and strongly asserted that his interest was merely humanitarian.

The public accountants did not include the unheaded ledger card balance of $1,269.01 among those circularized. Of course, circularization would have been difficult without a name or address. They did not investigate or mention it in their report, and it did not fall within their statistical sample of accounts to be circularized.

An auditor would have had a difficult time discovering this embezzlement in the ordinary course of his examination based only on Cone and Doan's suspicions. However, if an auditor did not thoroughly investigate the additional discrepancies, he would be remiss in his obligation to use due professional care. Such discrepancies were quite obvious, and it would have required very little time to scan these records.

The manager and other employees had no prior exposure to embezzlement. They were a small group who thought they knew each other well and that none of them could commit such a crime. They put off, as long as possible, the disclosure they knew they would have to make one day.

negotiable instruments processed twice

A large regional bank processes customer deposits at its central headquarters.

A Central Processing Department supervisor stole checks that had already been deposited. She then gave those checks and the account number to an accomplice. The accomplice cashed the stolen checks at a branch bank, usually the same one that the original depositor had used. When identification was requested, the accomplice would explain that she had forgotten it, but would offer to supply the account number.

The supervisor then credited the depositor and routed the checks on their second trip through central processing to the makers' accounts.

Checks as large as $4,000 were cashed for nearly a year before the larceny plot was uncovered. Only the bank lost. Investigation was hampered because bank endorsements were not placed on the checks at tellers' windows. This made the Central Processing Department the weak link in the chain.

Auditors faced with shortages in cash accounts should follow the flow of funds, testing and evaluating every step in that flow. They should assume no area to be above close examination. It may be necessary to change existing procedures to close gaps.

part eight
wrap-up

chapter twenty-nine

a checklist

Some of the points stressed in this book are brought together in capsule form below.

1. *When something does not look right, be persistent in running it down.* In the Equity Funding case, financial analyst Ray Dirks uncovered fraud by following up information given him by Secrist, the disgruntled former Equity employee. Dirks, operating under a great handicap because he was without official credentials, nevertheless persisted with his questions.

2. *To obtain the best results, establish proper relationships with the people you audit.* People often become upset when they learn that an auditor is to begin an examination. Some become defensive about their work even if they have nothing to hide. Auditors who sense a half-hidden hostility may attempt to overcome it by *excessive* assurances that they are there to help not criticize. It is a foozle to assure auditees that an audit is nothing to worry about. Yet, a tough, arrogant approach is also objectionable and usually results in added resistance. It is important to be firm but friendly with those under suspicion.

Guilty individuals may be under a burden of mental distress that could erupt at any time into an emotional display. While it is important for an auditor to get all the facts, it is of greater importance that he remember he is working with human beings who are entitled to consideration and courtesy.

3. *Recognize improper actions, entries, and figures when you see them.* Several cases included in this study emphasize the need to be observant and to be able to notice aberrations. (See "An Officer's Open Account" page 230, "Nonexistent Transportation

Company" page 237, and "An Embezzlement the Auditors Overlooked" page 239 for illustrations of alertness.)

4. *Develop your ability to remember bits of information and, by association, place them in an overall pattern.* A new general manager of a small railroad suspected that information about the company was being withheld from him so he asked an auditor to examine the records.

He noticed an invoice for a sizeable amount charged to roadbed maintenance, but there were no details. Examination of records for two previous years disclosed similar payments also without details. Persistent questioning revealed that these payments were actually installment payments on a major construction project completed a few years earlier.

Here, the auditor found one piece of information, then looked for a second and third similar piece. When the outline was established, it was logical to complete the pattern of the deception by determining the extent of the offsetting credits.

In this case, the railroad had a substantial, unbooked liability that was being liquidated by annual payments of principal and interest. The insiders who controlled the company had decided to keep the true financial condition of the company from the general manager of operations.

5. *Dishonest people are poor liars. Listen for their double-talk.* Many people find it easier to steal than to tell a lie. When they operate alone, people often rationalize their embezzlements and other crimes. During unexpected questioning, they must improvise a lie. They have no time to evaluate the consequences of an untruthful answer. Few people want to be embarrassed by being caught in a lie, so they try double-talk. If the auditor retains some evidence from the suspect during questioning, he may be in a better position to recognize a lie and to understand the double-talk.

6. *Learn to ask open-ended questions — but only the right kind.* There is little disagreement with the desirability of asking questions that will elicit more than a *yes* or *no* answer. The auditor should avoid questions that might give the suspect the impression that the auditor does not understand how the system works.

It is a good idea to ask the suspect for his opinion of possible weaknesses. Sometimes it is advisable to ask compound questions. The tension of a guilty individual makes it difficult for him to handle compound questions deceptively. To be asked for an opinion is the purest form of flattery, and few people can resist an invitation to tell all they know. After the guilt is out in the open, the questions should deal with facts about the fraud.

7. *Don't trust an informer's allegations, but never ignore them.* Many frauds have been uncovered as a result of an informer's tip. Some informers are motivated to disclose what they have learned because of their own high moral standards. Others do so because they are unhappy with the way they have been treated. (Example: Secrist in the Equity Funding case.)

By a strange quirk of nature, an employee in a branch identified himself and furnished specific information indicating that the branch manager was an embezzler. An investigation proved that the informer was telling the truth. But it also proved that the informer too was a thief. It is difficult to understand why a guilty individual would invite an investigation of a superior when he too was involved in dirty work.

8. *Be alert to the possibility of false documentation.* Ivar Kreuger showed that it was possible to pass forged collateral for $140,000,000. The need to examine marketable securities for authenticity was given in Chapter Four. The risk of losses from the improper use of copiers was explained in Chapter 23.

9. *Don't rely on evidence that can not be fully supported.* When the records of a small state-operated off-track betting parlor were audited, a shortage of about $1,000 was found. The manager claimed that he had deposited the missing amount in the night deposit box at the bank. However, the bank reported it had not received any such deposit. Later, the manager was discharged and agreed to reimburse the parlor for the missing funds. He was not indicted or tried.

About eight months later the bank had to repair a malfunction in the night deposit box. When the repairmen dismantled the box, they found the missing OTB deposit. The president of the bank wrote a letter of apology to the ex-manager of the parlor.

The OTB agency returned the money to the ex-manager but refused to rehire him. Because he had no way to prove his innocence, the man suffered the loss of his job and unfavorable publicity. Remember, circumstantial evidence can not always be relied upon.

10. *Make sure that audit sampling is not only scientific but sensible.* The case of Minnie Mangrum was well publicized about 40 years ago. She had been a trusted employee for a savings and loan association for 27 years. However, during that time she embezzled nearly $3,000,000.

For 22 years government auditors examined her books and found few discrepancies. She was very adept at pulling certain depositors' ledger cards and replacing them whenever she needed them to balance her detail ledgers with the controls. She kept off-the-record accounts of customer deposits and withdrawals and added interest at appropriate dates.

The auditors should have exercised better control over the individual customer accounts when they made their tests. A similar case of inadequate sampling is given in Chapter 28, "An Embezzlement the Auditors Overlooked."

11. *Do not be misled by appearances.* Auditors who become overly suspicious of people who appear to be living beyond their means may create difficulty for innocent people. It is not uncommon for individuals with modest salaries to have substantial incomes from good investments, inheritances, or well-to-do spouses.

It's a mistake to assume that improper or illegal acts are involved simply because certain employees associate with or are entertained by a member of a supplier's staff. An overly strict interpretation of such a proposition may be counterproductive to the best interest of the organization. Likewise, a refusal of an individual to accept a promotion should not be interpreted as an attempt to conceal an ongoing fraud. There are many valid reasons why an individual may not want a promotion.

12. *Do not be satisfied with unreasonable answers to audit questions.* An unreasonable explanation could be one that is obviously inaccurate. But it could also be a *lazy* answer.

An auditor learned that a large, expensive piece of equipment was missing from inventory. There was no record that it had been sold. The supervisor of the stockroom said he couldn't remember the equipment, and he didn't offer to check further. He suggested that if the auditor rechecked sales records, he would probably find that it had been sold.

Instead of following that suggestion, the auditor asked the janitor if he could recall the equipment. The janitor replied that the stockroom supervisor had returned it to the manufacturer for credit. Checking further, the auditor learned that the stockroom staff had not prepared the proper papers to originate a charge-back, and, as a result, credit or cash for the equipment had not been received.

Another unreasonable answer could be *It is the fault of the computer.* People who do not understand EDP systems find them convenient scapegoats for all the difficulties they come up against.

Ignorance could be yet another cause for an unreasonable answer. A justifiable answer, under certain circumstances, should not be accepted from one who should be knowledgeable through training and experience. The case history given in Chapter 17 is a good example of employee ignorance.

13. Don't ignore unrecorded funds for which the organization has a legal or moral responsibility. The director of the Internal Revenue Service stated in December 1976 that of 900 large companies checked there was evidence of slush funds in 300. In some instances such funds are not shown on the books of the corporations. The secret funds are created through the diversion of revenues before booking and by payments from company funds on false or misleading vouchers.

Top management and directors frequently claim that they were unaware that such funds existed in their companies. In other companies, senior officers have been accused of such improprieties as laundering money through Swiss banks.

Many employee groups operate under company grants or by company-matched funds. While these are not company funds, there may be an intangible responsibility. One industrial organization had an employee bowling league with a large membership. The company and the employees jointly contributed funds. An audit of the league's treasurer disclosed a large shortage. He had drawn money on false vouchers. The company and the league's officers had agreed upon an audit program carried out by the company's internal audit staff.

A retail organization wrote off thousands of dollars in debts, doubtful of collection, over a three-year period. When an auditor noticed that there had been no recoveries, he checked the working papers for prior years. These carried notations that certain accounts had been turned over to an attorney for collection. Such accounts in bankruptcy were expected to pay a liquidating dividend. He even found letters from the attorney stating he had made some collections from specified debtors.

When the auditor phoned him, the attorney admitted that he had collected many thousands of dollars but *had not got around* to making an accounting to and settlement with his client.

Deposits made for one reason or another are often not returned promptly when the need for them no longer exists.

In many businesses, escrow accounts are active and carry large balances. Because they represent funds belonging to others, auditors may not devote as much attention to them as they should. The fact that cash or the special bank account are in agreement with the liability account is not sufficient evidence that the escrow account has not been abused.

14. Learn as much about the auditees as you possibly can. The auditor should not ordinarily become involved in the personal affairs of people being audited. But it often is worthwhile to investigate whether the official organization charts tell the real story or if circumstances have altered true rank and relationships. Personnel records of salary progression, length of service in present position, attendance records, and similar data may give some appreciation of job problems. If annual written performance reviews have been prepared, they may reveal job-related difficulties. Payroll records will provide data on payroll deductions such as wage garnishees and assignments.

15. Keep audit programs from becoming too limited or stereotyped. Very rarely does an individual cleverly conceive a fraud or design one with mathematical accuracy. Rather, he stumbles into the situation through a *foozle.* But if it produces loot for him, he may well repeat the *foozle.*

William Blandell of the *Wall Street Journal* described the Equity Funding case in these words: *It was neither brilliantly planned nor well executed, but a slapdash, helter-skelter scheme in which one fraud had to be frantically covered by a more blatant one.*

Auditors should constantly review their audit coverage. They should not ignore any potential area of waste and fraud. It is a good idea to watch for an emerging current of fraud and give prompt attention to any exposure that may exist in the organization. Many potential criminals become actual offenders when they try to copy well-publicized schemes.